The Gun Digest Book

METALLIC SILHOUETTE SHOOTING

2nd Edition

By Elgin Gates

DBI BOOKS, INC.

About the Cover

Since its introduction in 1983, the Dan Wesson 40V8S Super Mag, in both blue and stainless steel, along with the .357 Super Mag cartridge, has proven to be the most successful gun/cartridge combination ever introduced in the silhouette revolver category. This combination has won the IHMSA International revolver championship an unprecedented five years in a row, from 1983 through 1987, with perfect 80x80 scores. Photo by John Hanusin.

Publisher
Sheldon Factor

Editorial Director
Jack Lewis

Production Director
Sonya Kaiser

Art Director
Gary Duck

Associate Artists
Denise Comiskey
Paul Graff

Copy Editor
Shelby Harbison

Production Coordinator
Pepper Federici

Lithographic Service
Gallant Graphics

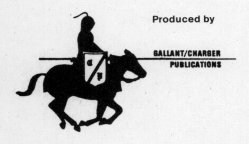

Produced by
GALLANT/CHARGER PUBLICATIONS

Copyright MCMLXXXVIII by DBI Books, 4092 Commercial Ave., Northbrook, IL 60062. All rights reserved. Printed in the United States of America. No part of this book may be reproduced, stored in a retrieval system or transmitted in any form or by any means, electronic, mechanical, photocopying, recording, or otherwise, without the prior written permission of the publisher.

Note: All load data and information in this book is the result of safe and careful testing by the author and other contributors submitting the material contained herein. Since neither the author, DBI Books, Inc., nor any of the contributors has any control over the components, equipment and techniques used with this published information, no liability or responsibility for any injury or damage that occurs is either implied or assumed.

The views and opinions expressed herein are not necessarily those of the publisher and no responsibility for such views will be assumed.

Arms and Armour Press, London, G.B., exclusive licensees and distributors in Britain and Europe, New Zealand, Nigeria, So. Africa and Zimbabwe, India and Pakistan; Singapore, Hong Kong and Japan. Capricorn Link (Aust.) Pty. Ltd. exclusive distributors in Australia.

ISBN-0-87349-021-5   Library of Congress Catalog Card Number 79-50059

CONTENTS

Acknowledgments 5

Chapter One: HANDGUN METALLIC SILHOUETTE: WHAT IT IS? 6
  The when, why, where and how of this exciting sport.

Chapter Two: LONG-GUN SILHOUETTING 22
  The sport began with rifles and there are hordes
  of shooters who prefer this facet.

Chapter Three: A VIEW OF THE PAST 44
  From a blood sport of Mexico to sophisticated handgunnery
  marks a long march of progress.

Chapter Four: SILHOUETTE CARTRIDGE DEVELOPMENT 56
  The author's experiments date back to his African safaris.

Chapter Five: TIPS & STRATEGIES FOR WINNING 70
  The basics are simple, but concentration is a must.

Chapter Six: FIRST MATCHES, EARLY HANDGUNS 76
  Thousands of rounds through a heavy-loaded handgun
  make it obvious which will last!

Chapter Seven: OUTSTANDING SILHOUETTE RECORDS 88
  With progress in the art of long-range handgunning,
  performance improved greatly.

Chapter Eight: GOODS FOR SILHOUETTE RELOADERS 96
  This sport eats up thousands of rounds and handloading is a must.

Chapter Nine: A MATTER OF PHILOSOPHY 106
  In silhouette shooting, a production gun must be just that!

Chapter Ten: SILHOUETTE LOADS FOR SINGLE-SHOTS 122
  A lot of experimentation went into this info; actually a search for safety.

Chapter Eleven: SILHOUETTE SIX-GUNS & LOADS 152
  A history of the revolver in the silhouette sport.

Chapter Twelve: THE UNLIMITED SILHOUETTE HANDGUN 172
  They're still seeking the ultimate for long-range handgunning

Chapter Thirteen: THE BRUTUS STORY 190
  Pertinent observations on loading the really big-bore silhouette guns.

Chapter Fourteen: CAST BULLETS FOR SILHOUETTE SHOOTING 202
   Other than personal satisfaction, this type bullet expands availability.

Chapter Fifteen: THE EXPANDED APPROACH 210
   Two new events — .22 silhouette and field pistol competition —
   are now being sanctioned.

Chapter Sixteen: ACCURACY & REVOLVERS 218
   Cylinder guns can lack accuracy and here's what to do about it.

Chapter Seventeen: THE SUPER MAG STORY 224
   How a cartridge was developed despite vast amounts of disinterest.

Chapter Eighteen: A MATTER OF PRICE 232
   Silhouette shooters rule against buying titles with tricked-up handguns.

Chapter Nineteen: PAST, PRESENT, FUTURE 240
   Handgun silhouetting has come far, but what about the next ten years?

Official IHMSA Rules 250

ACKNOWLEDGMENTS

The help and contributions of the following people are gratefully acknowledged:

Hugh Reed, of Federal Cartridge Company, was one of the few who really believed in the .357 Super Mag in the early days when few others did. Hugh had a special run of .357 Super Mag brass made up when no one else in the industry was interested.

Robert E. Fielitz, Remington's director of research, was gracious enough to give credit where credit was due by writing the letter of acknowledgment that appears in this book.

Ed Andrus of NRA was honest enough to acknowledge that the founders of IHMSA had conceived and established the rules for the handgun metallic silhouette game; and whose letter also is reproduced herein.

Warren Center was willing to listen to suggestions from myself and others; out of that came the heavy bull barrels in ten- and fourteen-inch configurations. Said barrels and many other improvements incorporated by Warren Center and Thompson/Center have made the Contender the winningest pistol in the history of the silhouette game.

Richard Beebe of Redding never was too busy to talk technical matters regarding the die designs needed for the various cartridges I developed for the silhouette game, and "came through" time after the time with the desired dies and other needed items.

Bob O'Connor was president of Dan Wesson during the difficult task I had in getting the long-cylinder concept across for .357 and .375 Super Mags when others refused to listen. Bob accepted my advice and specifications and even named the new silhouette model the Super Mag.

Sig Himmelman of United Sporting Arms also accepted the long-cylinder concept and built it into his Seville model. The ongoing succcess of these two revolvers in the silhouette game has been beyond our wildest expectations.

Duane Small, Dan Wesson's national sales manager, spark-plugged the generous support IHMSA has received from the company. His unflagging enthusiasm and appearances at the IHMSA Internationals year after year has given all of us a lift when most needed. One of my greatest moments in the silhouette game was when Duane presented me with a custom .357 Super Mag bearing the serial number E. Gates-1 at the 1984 Internationals, in recognition of the help I had given them.

"Pop" Gates started it all when he sent me down the road to hunting, fishing and the love of developing new and different cartridge/gun combinations at an early age. He was never willing to accept any gun or cartridge as automatically being the best or the last word, just because some big company manufactured and sold it.

Lee Jurras dreamed up the idea of the first handgun silhouette match and he rightfully deserves the credit for creating the sport.

Bob Hayden of Sierra, Dave Andrews of Speer/Omark, and Steve Hornady all have been staunch supporters of IHMSA and the silhouette game. They gave unstinting support in the early days by supplying the prototype bullets I suggested for the fledgling sport. I always saved a box of each prototype and there is one hell of a variety for the IHMSA museum collection.

David Bradshaw, of the IHMSA executive committee, supplied material and photographs used in this book. Virtually every new handgun that has been successful in the silhouette sport bears the imprint of his meticulous testing. Time after time, his suggestions and ideas have been incorporated in the final and successful designs of silhouette handguns.

Bill Bartram, chairman of IHMSA's technical committee, has offered meticulous testing and well written material that has helped the membership of IHMSA; some of his findings appear in this book. His one-man crusade in working with Browning engineers resulted in one of the finest .22 semi-auto silhouette-oriented pistols to appear on the market.

John Taffin compiled a goodly amount of the material, photos and load data that appears herein.

Joe Wright has written technical articles and compiled load data for the silhouette fraternity, some of which appears in this book.

To the officers, executive committee, regional directors, state and match directors and the 40,000-odd members of IHMSA who, by their all-out dedication over the years, have made IHMSA the outstanding handgun sport of all time, I also offer my thanks.

Finally, my gratitude to Dollie and Robert Gates, who held the fort down when I was building the IHMSA permanent range; for handling vital matters year after year, month after month, and day after day throughout the twelve years we have devoted to IHMSA and the handgun metallic silhouette sport.

If anyone has been overlooked, my apologies. I thank you, one and all.

Elgin T. Gates
Idaho Falls, Idaho

HANDGUN METALLIC SILHOUETTE: WHAT IS IT?

CHAPTER 1

The When, Why, Where And How Of This Exciting Sport Is Told By One Who Was There

Left: Author sets a target in place for a match. Targets are repainted after each round so that the contestant's hits can be verified properly. (Above) Author's career as a handgunner started in 1929, at age 6, at the Colorado Rifle Club near Denver. Young Gates, kneeling in front of the riflemen, who were conducting a schuetzen match.

WHAT IS handgun metallic silhouette shooting? What has made this relatively new handgun shooting sport so popular that over 45,000 members have joined IHMSA in the ten short years of its existence? What has made metallic silhouette the outstanding handgun sport of all time? Who and what is IHMSA, the International Handgun Metallic Silhouette Association?

Nothing has ever hit the handgun world with the dramatic impact of metallic silhouette shooting. How did it all come about?

As one of the founders of IHMSA and the handgun metallic silhouette sport, I know the answers. I've been a handgun aficionado all my life, starting at the age of 6 with an old .22 single-shot pistol handed down from my maternal grandfather. Under the watchful eye of my dad, whom I

The author took his first deer at age 9, but was proudest of this bison taken from Arizona herd when we was only 14. He shot the buffalo with his first cartridge creation, a 7mm/06, which has been the basis of silhouette cartridges.

Lee Jurras (left) promoted the first handgun metallic silhouette match ever held. Tim Zufle, with him, was one of those who competed in that first match. Bob Barnett (right), an early shooter, is IHMSA secretary-treasurer.

always fondly called Pop, I learned to plink at tin cans, sparrows and chipmunks. I didn't often connect, but it wasn't for lack of trying.

My next pistol was a Christmas present at the age of 9; a .22 Colt Woodsman. I still have that one.

Pop was a top competitor with rifles, shotguns and pistols and loved to experiment with different cartridges. One of his most successful, as I remember, was created by necking down the then-popular .30/06 to 6mm, using bullets pulled from old pre-World War I Lee Navy surplus ammunition which could be bought cheaply in those days. He rebarreled his Springfield with a 6mm Lee Navy barrel and chambered it for what he called the 6mm/06. For me, he rebarreled one of the then rather new Winchester .270 rifles with a 6.5mm Mannlicher-Schoenaur military barrel.

Bullets were from WWI surplus military ammo. It was a 6.5mm/.270.

Love of hunting, target shooting and ballistic experimenting ran in the family. I've never had cause to regret it. We lived in Denver, Colorado, during the 1920s and 1930s, and seldom a week passed that the family wasn't out at the old Colorado Rifle Club west of Denver, shooting rifles, pistols and anything else that had a trigger. Also on the weekends, we hunted on the plains east of the city and made some monumental inroads on the overpopulation of jackrabbits.

When I grew up a bit and could afford it — or convinced myself I could — I bought and owned just about every new handgun that came along, especially the newest of the big boomers. In 1935, I had one of the first S&W .357 magnum

Competitor in foreground is shooting a revolver in the freestyle category, while a friend spots his shots for him. Handgun metallic silhouette competition has come on as the biggest handgun shooting sport in history.

revolvers. In 1955, I bought one of the first .44 magnums, followed by the .41 magnum in 1964.

With a thirst for ever more handgun power, I was a pigeon who promptly plunked down $200 as a deposit for one of the first Auto Mags and just as promptly lost it, when the company went belly-up the first time. Eventually, by 1973, I had one each in .357 and .44 Auto Mag.

Throughout those years, the one frustration of my life was that there was no competition for the big magnums, other than paper punching with wadcutters in the .357 magnum. Firing at paper targets with one of the big magnums always gave me a sense of massive overkill. Even football-sized rocks on the side of a nearby hill seemed like flimsy targets for the smashing thunderbolts delivered from such boomers as the .41 and .44 magnums and the .357 and .44 Auto Mags.

Suddenly, in 1975, a brand-new handgun shooting sport was created, when Lee Jurras promoted what he called the first National Handgun Metallic Silhouette Championships, in Tucson, Arizona. I was there with my oldest son. I wouldn't have missed it for anything in the world!

This exciting new competitive handgun game provided worthy opponents for the big-bore magnum handguns, finally! It has proved to be the most exciting, interesting and exhilarating handgun game that has ever come down that proverbial pike!

Try it once and you will likely be hooked. Even minor success tends to bring instant gratification. On the other hand, you may feel a sense of frustration and near impotence, as you walk away from the firing line with the sud-

1.

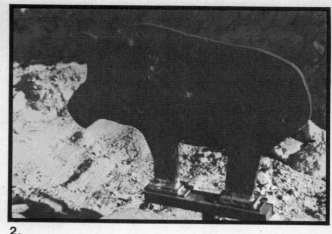
2.

3.

4.

5.

1. The chicken target shot at fifty meters is made from heavy steel and is life-size. **2.** The second target used in the silhouette sequence is a life-size javelina that is fired upon from a hundred meters. **3.** Life-size turkey target, like the rams, is cut from one-half-inch steel; fired at 150 meters; it is considered to be the most difficult among contestants. **4.** The life-size ram targets are the largest of the series and are set at two hundred meters; each weighs fifty-five pounds. The uneven terrain adds to the challenge. **5.** Though they are the largest targets, rams look small in open gun sights.

den realization that your big magnum handgun isn't really as potent as you had always thought it was. You may feel a bit ineffectual; at least thoughtful and subdued. And you can hardly wait to try it again!

Furthermore, shooting metallic silhouette targets with a handgun has opened up a whole new world of ballistics that has added more new pages to the loading manuals than any other branch of the firearms industry. During the past ten years, more progress had been made in long-range handgun shooting in regard to guns, equipment, loads and techniques than in all the years put together since the handgun was invented.

There is something about the game that appeals to whatever latent instinct there is inside a man who wants action whenever he pulls the trigger, and action is the name of handgun metallic silhouette shooting. As a spectator sport it has no apparent equal in the shooting world. Punching holes in paper targets at short distances has heretofore been the accepted technique of handgun competition, but silhouette shooting has added a new dimension.

As practice for actual hunting in the field, we've come to feel it is a country mile ahead of anything else on the horizon. For the man who doesn't hunt, for whatever the reason, but likes the machismo of shooting big-bore handguns, it provides a whole new set of challenges.

Level down on a half-inch-thick steel plate shaped like a

Competitor is shooting at turkey targets, the black specks just to the left and below the spotter's elbow. Shooter has knocked down the second and fifth targets; others are still standing. Unhit ram targets are in the background.

chicken, painted flat black, at fifty meters with your favorite big-bore handgun, whether it be a Thompson/Center Contender, Ruger .44 magnum, Dan Wesson .375 Super Mag, Smith & Wesson .357 magnum — or whatever. A low hit will take the leg out from under the steel bird with a gratifying clang. A hit high on the back can tumble it end over end. A fore or aft hit can send it spinning wildly. A miss will likely send up a spurt of dirt — and you will miss a lot of these targets in the beginning. We all have!

Next is the life-size javelina silhouette at one hundred meters, also cut out of half-inch steel plate. A bank of five of them is standing on the slope of a small hill. Your first shot is a miss. Then another miss and still another. Then there is a satisfying clang from a solid hit that topples the steel pig off its stand.

At the next firing point, you may be up on the side of a valley, shooting downhill at a row of five life-size turkeys that are 150 meters distant. You've had thirty seconds to load and two minutes to fire your five shots, one at each silhouette. More misses. Then you settle down, dig in and squeeze off a shot with tooth-gritting concentration. The chosen turkey, the fifth one, turns slowly to one side from a front hit, then topples over slowly as the metallic clash of the striking bullet comes back up the slope. How sweet it is!

Suddenly, it's your turn to shoot the rams. Oh, no! you

Although her handgun is hidden by the pistol box, lady in foreground is firing an unlimited gun. Standing shooter utilizes his Auto Mag for that competition. Both are firing at turkey targets set at 150 meters.

These shooters initiated the all-new silhouette range at Idaho Falls, Idaho, in 1978. Range holds a record 1608 international championship entries.

think, as you look at those tiny black silhouettes far over on the other side of the valley. They are life-size, but shooting them at two hundred meters with a handgun? Nobody can hit one at that distance!

But they do. Maybe you miss the first five — you get to shoot at a total of ten chickens, ten javelinas, ten turkeys and ten rams in banks of five for a total score of 40 — the first ten, or maybe you hit one on a leg. You get the satisfaction of a clanging sound, but the metal ram remains standing with regal contempt. Finally, with perseverance, skill, determination and luck, the moment comes when you tag a ram solidly and watch, unconsciously holding your breath, as the distant silhouette seems to hang there in suspended motion. Then slowly, almost majestically, it topples off the stand.

No one ever seems to forget the thrill of toppling that first steel ram, but you will not be satisfied with just one, because there are five in a bank and you get one shot at each, from left to right. As for spectator interest, let any shooter blow down the first nine silhouettes on any bank and you can bet that every eye on the range will be watching as he buckles down — probably with the two-minute shooting time coming to an end — to fire at the last silhouette. There will be groans of sympathy if he misses, applause if he cleans the rack.

Handgun metallic silhouette shooting admittedly isn't the only handgun game in town, but for sheer, spine-tingling exhilaration, most competitors feel it's way ahead of whatever is in second place. It is, in a simple phase, the epitome of long-range handgunning.

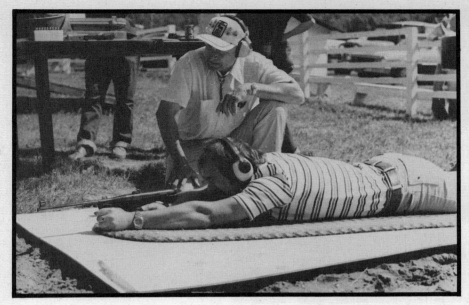

Author coaches shooter during the Canadian nationals in 1978. Gates has given up silhouette contesting to devote full time to the sport's development and continued promotion.

Author insists that one of the best things about silhouette shooting is that one doesn't need a flat range. Here shooters are resetting targets and spray-painting for next relay.

A year after that first handgun metallic silhouette championship in Tucson in 1975, the second handgun national silhouette championships were held in El Paso, Texas. During the tournament, twelve of us founded the International Handgun Metallic Silhouette Association. I proposed the name of the organization and, with experiences fresh in mind relative to other shooting organizations, I proposed the basic production-gun rule that would be the backbone of the organization and the unlimited rule that would lead to the greatest strides known in long-range handgunning, although none of us realized it at the time. The show was on the road!

The International Handgun Metallic Silhouette Association is now the sanctioning body for most of the handgun silhouette matches being held throughout America and the rest of the world.

Originally, the game was limited to big-bore handguns at the fifty- to two-hundred-meter distances. In 1979, the IHMSA .22 version was added, using the same rules, with two-fifths-size silhouette targets, and in 1986 the field pistol version was added for big-bore handgun shooters using the standing position. The field pistol targets are half-size. Both the IHMSA .22 silhouettes and the IHMSA field pistol silhouettes are shot at the same distances: twenty-five yards (or meters) for the chickens, fifty yards (or meters) for the javelinas, seventy-five yards (or meters) for the turkeys and one hundred yards (or meters) for the rams.

Association rules provide for four categories of competition for long-range big-bores. Production single-shots, production revolvers and unlimited guns all are shot free-

It doesn't require a great deal of expenditure to build a silhouette range. Dirt berms are pushed up in area behind targets so that spotters can see when the shooter has missed.

Silhouette game is popular through the entire year. Competitors shoot in snowstorm during this tournament.

style. The fourth category is for production guns fired in the standing position. Competition in the .22 division now includes five categories: single-shots, autos, revolvers and standing, all for production over-the-counter, out-of-the box pistols, plus the unlimited competition category. The field pistol event provides two categories of competition, both from the standing position. Production guns with open sights and production guns with scope sights both are allowed in their specified events.

The rules are specific. Production guns must be used as they come from the manufacturer. Only two exceptions are allowed: Sights may be painted to contrast against the usually black silhouettes and any catalog replacement grip or stock available to the general public may be used. Inside, only the engaging surfaces of the hammer and sear may be honed.

The unlimited category is just that: unlimited. The only restrictions are a weight limit of 4½ pounds and a barrel length not to exceed fifteen inches.

The initial reaction of the handgun industry to the new metallic silhouette game was one of near disbelief. How could anyone be crazy enough to shoot at heavy steel targets at those incredible distances when everyone knew handguns were short-range weapons?

The second reaction was one of chagrin when manufacturers learned silhouette shooters were using full-power loads — thousands of them — to shoot silhouettes. For well over a hundred years there had been no handgun use

New Hampshire match was held in snowfield. Note target size when viewed from the firing line. (Right) Resetting targets in snow is relatively easy with snowmobiles.

like this: sustained fire with heavy bullets and maximum powder charges. Sure, law enforcement personnel had fired multi-millions of wadcutters over the years in .38 Special and .357 magnum revolvers, but these were cream-puff loads that any pistol could handle with ease.

Likewise, the paper punchers and target shooters generally used wadcutters or other low-velocity ammunition with no detrimental effect on the handgun.

Handgun hunters used powerful loads, of course, but in small quantities, maybe twenty-five or fifty rounds to sight in and one or two more, if they were lucky enough to get a shot at a big-game trophy. That was about it — and once a year.

The average handgun lover who bought one of the big magnums might put a box of ammo through it in the course of a year, shooting at rocks or tin cans. There were a few exceptions, but not many.

Handguns for defense? Usually a few rounds to get the feel of it, then the gun went under the pillow or in the desk drawer.

In short, the industry had been building handguns for what might be called minimal service and none of them were designed or built for the rugged use they were going to get in this new silhouette shooting sport.

Right from the beginning, silhouette shooters were putting thousands of full-bore maximum loads through their handguns at the rate of several hundred a week — and that was just about every week in the year. Some handguns

This early handgun silhouette match was held at Lyman's Blue Trail Range in Connecticut. This was before most shooters began utilizing shooting mats, spotting scopes.

Author contends that silhouette shooting is a natural for wheelchair marksmen. Ron Campbell, Neodask, Kansas, shot in a match held in Oklahoma; did well in scores.

could handle it better than others, but long-needed improvements would be necessary, if manufacturers wanted their products to perform well in this new shooting sport.

In the early days of the silhouette game, I carefully assembled all the data and reports coming into IHMSA headquarters from silhouette matches all over the country and collated it. I had detailed statistics on what handguns were winning, by brand and model; which models were the most accurate; which were the least accurate; which were breaking down from the rigors of silhouette competition; what improvements needed to be made to other brands and models to turn them into top performers.

In short, hundreds of IHMSA silhouette ranges all over the country were acting as a gigantic outside testing laboratory and I had all the data and statistics that no manufacturer could duplicate on his own. It has long been said that once the engineers get through perfecting any product, all that remains to be done is to release said product to the public. If there are any faults, the public will find them.

I was naive enough to think this meticulously assembled

The late Steve Herrett, renowned for custom handgun stocks, set up this range in Jerome, Idaho, with a series of gong targets used for silhouette practice.

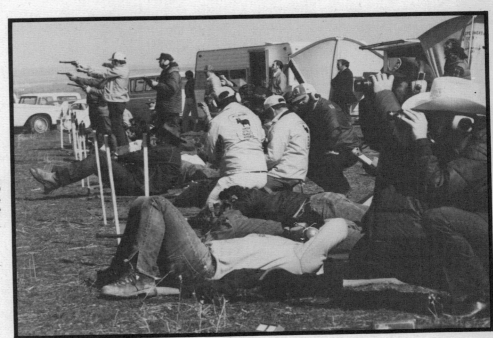

Within a year of its beginning, silhouette ranges had sprung up all over the country. This one was establihsed in 1978 in Salt Lake City by enthused shooters.

information would be welcomed with open arms. Like others before me, I quickly discovered that this valuable data would be the subject of derision, cynicism and outright disbelief by some. They were far more interested in reading the glowing accounts of some gun writers who always extol the virtues, not looking beyond. Test data showing the need for improvements didn't turn them on.

At that time, I was interested in the S&W Model 29 .44 magnum. It was a solid big-frame gun, but needed three small and inexpensive, but vital, improvements to make it into a top performing silhouette gun. I presented the needed improvements, first to a field rep, then to two top officials of the company along with an order for a five-hundred-gun IHMSA Limited Edition on the basis that said improvements would be included.

The order and the improvements were more or less spurned, including a request by David Bradshaw, who was with me on one factory trip, for a 10½-inch barrel Model 29 with improved sights. Bradshaw was one of IHMSA's top competitors and extremely knowledgeable about the needs of the silhouette game.

A classic case of the NIH syndrome, Not Invented

Bert Stringfellow (left) presents author with trophy for a regional championship early in the development of the International Handgun Metallic Silhouette Association. Stringfellow has been association vice president since 1977.

Here, killed the deal. They said they saw no need to build stronger, more rugged handguns for a new sport they felt was a flash-in-the-pan that would fade faster than it had come in.

About two years later, Smith & Wesson brought out what they called a Model 29 Silhouette that incorporated Bradshaw's 10½-inch barrel and improved sights idea, but they had discarded other suggested improvements. This model never did catch on. Of the 1142 entries in the 1987 IHMSA Internationals, only three were using S&W handguns.

Ruger had a strong, ruggedly built handgun and the price was right. This model become an instant success in the silhouette sport and apparently it was felt there was no need for the two vital improvements suggested, said suggestions coming from the crucible of silhouette competition.

Ruger stayed at the top of the heap for nearly four years. Then the revolver category came to be dominated by two manufacturers who did listen: Dan Wesson Arms and United Sporting Arms.

When the silhouette game was new, Dan Wesson revolvers were looked down upon as being inferior, and only an occasional one was noted in match results reaching IHMSA headquarters.

The old .357 magnum, which had been around since 1935, was fading rapidly out of the silhouette game as being too weak and inadequate to consistently knock down fifty-five-pound steel rams at two hundred meters. At that time, the .357 magnum was Dan Wesson's biggest caliber, but there were bigger and better things to come, as I soon learned.

The late Dan Wesson was one of the first to listen seriously. It was at the 1977 National Sporting Goods

With his revolver in full recoil, shooter raises a cloud of dust behind the javelina target he has just missed. The production gun rule makes it possible for all of the competitors to compete on equal terms with factory guns.

Show in Chicago. I received a cordial welcome from Dan Wesson and, when I started showing him the compiled silhouette data, he invited me to his room for a discussion in uninterrupted privacy.

That's when he told me about the .44 magnum he had in the works and listened with a keen ear to what I could pass on from the silhouette fraternity. Likewise, he accepted copies of all the silhouette data with obvious and sincere appreciation. I knew when I left his room that the silhouette game had found a kindred soul whose revolver would someday be a force to reckon with.

Later, after Dan's untimely passing, Bob O'Connor, president of Dan Wesson, and Paul Brothers, his chief engineer, who was working on the soon-to-come .44 magnum, also were keen listeners to some of our top IHMSA competitors of the time, like David Bradshaw who would successfuly push through our suggestions to make the DW .44 mag a top performer: sights, minimum groove barrels, tight exit holes in the cylinders, tight chambers, consistent cylinder alignment with the barrel, heavy shrouds, no muzzle venting on the silhouette models, a shallow forcing cone and so on.

The net result was that by 1983, the big-frame Dan Wesson .44 magnum and especially in .357 Super Mag would begin to dominate the silhouette revolver category in a manner unparalleled in any other type of handgun competition. (Development of the .357 and .375 Super Mags is detailed in another chapter.)

It took two years of hard campaigning just to get Colt to offer a .357 Python with the needed eight-inch barrel for silhouette competition.

They sent a field rep to the 1978 IHMSA Internationals at Salina, Kansas. There I presented him with a firm 1000-gun order for an IHMSA Limited Edition Python on the

From the early beginnings in 1976, IHMSA has developed two permanent ranges. One is located in Idaho Falls, Idaho, the other in Oakridge, Tennessee. Target setters set and paint the 20 sets of targets used in 1986 rifle shoot.

basis of an eight-inch barrel, with a few more simple improvements needed for metallic silhouettes.

After some lengthy dillying and an equal amount of dallying, covering a period of five months, I learned that Colt had chosen not to make the changes requested and the order was never filled.

The same was the situation with our pleas for a beefed-up big-frame version of the Python in .44 mag. The one thing that did come out of all the suggestions was a Python with an eight-inch barrel.

Three years later, Walt Gleason, then in charge of the custom shop, contacted me at the 1981 NRA convention to renew negotiations on the 1000-gun order of Pythons, agreeing to part of the original improvements, but not all. By that time, however, the once powerful .357 magnum had come to an ignominious end in silhouette shooting.

For the silhouette game, handgun hunters and the general public, I still feel a big-frame Python for the .44 mag cartridge, as well as a long-cylinder version for the .357 Super Mag, would be a winner. No one had a better quality revolver than the Colt Python. However, Colt's loss was Dan Wesson's gain...and Samuel Colt probably turned over in his grave.

United Sporting Arms was a one-man army in the form of Sig Himmelman, another small manufacturer who listened. He finally wanted the business the silhouette game could provide and came out with a precision stainless steel silhouette model in .44 mag. More important, he accepted our cylinder specifications for the .357 Super Mag, as had Dan Wesson, and went on to produce a high-quality single-action called the Seville that is superior to any other single-action on the market for our purposes.

It really didn't matter that the Seville was a near copy of the Ruger single-action, which in turn was based on the old Colt single-action. Himmelman listened and made the requested improvements in sights, barrel bore and groove dimensions, precision cylinder-to-barrel alignment, the long cylinder for the .357 Super Mag, precision fit of cylinder to frame and so on.

Warren Center of Thompson/Center Arms was really the first to listen and react to the needs of silhouette shooters. The first letter I wrote to him was in October, 1975 — just after the first handgun silhouette match ever held — asking him to provide fifteen-inch barrels for his Contender. Followed up with more correspondence and calls, the Super 14 barrel became a production item in early 1977.

The permanent range in Idaho Falls, completed in 1984, has a firing line 1000 feet in length with 80 shooting positions. Range was completed in time for international championships in 1984. This is the west half of the line.

Why fourteen inches instead of the requested fifteen-inch barrel? Simple, the way Warren explained it. Their barrel cut-off machine at the factory was limited to fourteen inches.

When the silhouette game first came into being, the T/C Contender was thought of — sometimes derisively — as an inexpensive single-shot pistol with no redeeming features; one which would never amount to anything alongside the seemingly Cadillac guns.

Be that as it may, Warren Center listened to silhouette shooters, then made yearly improvements in sights, lockup and preferred calibers, improving the grips and so on, to the point where the Contender now occupies the position of a precision shooting machine, the "winningest" handgun in silhouette history.

The same thing happened in the reloading components business. Manufacturers who listened, then created and supplied the bullets, other components and accessories needed for the demanding silhouette game have been rewarded by the finanical success of the extra business.

All in all, the handgun metallic silhouette sport has made a tremendous impact throughout the industry, as well as on the recreational activity of thousands of shooters and their families.

The founding principles of IHMSA are directed toward the legitimate sporting and recreational use of handguns for all Americans. Metallic silhouette competition, as administered by IHMSA, is meant to be an enjoyable, family-oriented shooting sport. All the resources of IHMSA and its members are dedicated to these principles.

Membership in IHMSA is $20 per year, which includes an attractive membership and classification card, a rule book, a handsome patch with the official emblem, scale or full-size templates for making silhouette targets and a subscription to *The Silhouette* which contains a schedule of all match dates across the country, plus match results, technical articles, field tests, loading data and so on.

Applications can be mailed to IHMSA, Inc., Box 1609, Idaho Falls, Idaho 83403.

LONG-GUN SILHOUETTING

CHAPTER 2

The Sport Began With Rifles And There Are Hordes Of Shooters Who Still Prefer This Facet!

Rifle silhouette shooters Tom Gatewood (right) and Al Jenson ponder scope setting on former's rifle at shoot.

THE SPORT of *siluetas metalicas* — or metallic silhouette shooting, as we know it today — came across the border from Mexico in the 1960s, first being tried by gringo shooters in Arizona.

The game had been around since the days of Pancho Villa, when live animals were used. However, sometime in the Fifties — and the exact time, place and circumstances are lost in time — the metal cut-out targets of animals were substituted. In Mexico, it had served the same purpose of

Rifle silhouette shooter practices dry-firing during NRA national silhouette shoot in Arizona held in 1978.

sport and entertainment that the more familiar turkey shoot served in the pioneer terms of this country, coming down to the modern day.

The Mexican beginning, if legend can be relied upon, had the participants using saddle carbines and military rifles. It was when it crossed the border from the south that the high-power rifle event evolved.

Before U.S. shooters were introduced to the game, the Mexicans had developed a set of rules that allowed the same type of match to be shot at various ranges. The sizes of the various silhouette metal targets, the types and sizes of the stands on which they were to be installed, the various ranges for each type of target, as well as the shooting equipment that would qualify all were determined by Mexican competitors before the first U.S. citizen dented his first

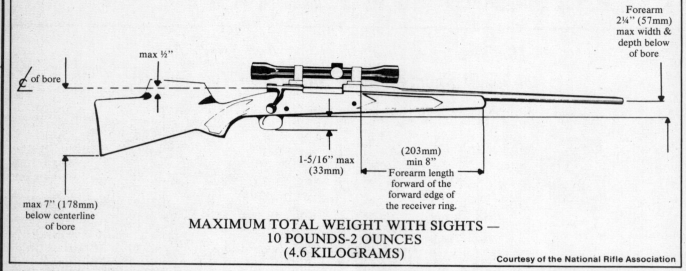

ALLOWABLE DIMENSIONS
HIGH POWER AND SMALLBORE RIFLE

CENTER OF COMB (IN VERTICAL PLANE THROUGH CENTER OF BORE) MUST BE BELOW CENTER OF BORE. MONTE CARLO OR ROLLOVER MAY NOT EXCEED ½" or 12.7MM ABOVE CENTER LINE ON THE OFF SIDE.

MAXIMUM TOTAL WEIGHT WITH SIGHTS —
10 POUNDS-2 OUNCES
(4.6 KILOGRAMS)

Courtesy of the National Rifle Association

primer in this type of match.

Although it goes largely ignored in this country, the Mexicans also introduced the *paloma* target — the life-size silhouette of a dove — that was used in smallbore competition. With a rifle, the established range for this event was 150 meters; if the pistol was the firearm designated, the dove target was set out at a hundred meters.

When the game came across the border, initially the Mexican rules were adopted largely intact. Research shows that the Mexicans had used the silhouette of a domestic sheep. Perhaps in a moment of wishful thinking, one of the early shooters — possibly Roy Dunlap — redesigned this particular target to include horns that made the silhouette more closely resemble a Rocky Mountain sheep than a barnyard pet.

In 1975, the International Handgun Metallic Silhouette Association was formed and an effort was made at that time to interest the National Rifle Association. The NRA, however, did not become involved in the handgun segment of the game until 1978, concentrating in the beginning on the rifle event. An NRA committee found that the Mexican smallbore version of the game did not have any particular appeal to U.S. shooters and went about reworking the basic concept, making it a miniature version of the high-power rifle game. The result was that smallbore competition was conducted on targets one-fifth the size of the standard big bore design and at distances one-fifth the range. The theory was that this provided the same challenge to smallbore fanciers as the big standard targets and longer ranges did for the high-power rifle enthusiasts. In more recent years, the NRA has developed an air gun course as well. The NRA also developed rules to define the rifles and pistols that are allowed in their versions of the game.

"Big game rifles as well as varmint rifles have proved to be quite satisfactory for this type of competition and a number of rifles have been specially built," an NRA spokesperson explains. "The use of a specially built rifle does not automatically guarantee a winning score.

"While there is no limitation on the magnification allowed in scopes, a high-powered target scope generally is considered to be more of a handicap than an advantage, because it magnifies any unsteadiness in a person's holding ability. Shooters now tend to use a ten- or twelve-power scope, although many still use a lower power, but not less than six-power.

"While 6mm is the smallest caliber allowed in high-

Shooters in foreground are dry firing at Black Canyon Range in Arizona. Those under the canopy fire for their score during an early silhouette shoot held by the NRA.

Mexican champion Alvaros Frescas takes aim at a distant ram at rifle silhouette competition in El Paso, Texas. Under the NRA rules, the shooter is allowed to rest elbow against body to improve shooting platform in standing.

First NRA rule book for silhouette shooting was drawn from the rules listed in the pamphlets on left that were generated by Mexican shooters who originated contest.

power silhouette competition, it is well known that a 6mm bullet will not knock the sheep target off its stand reliably. For that reason, most silhouette shooters use larger calibers. The most popular seems to be the .308 Winchester.

Although magnum calibers are not prohibited under the NRA rules, the majority of clubs ban them on their ranges, because of the increased damage to the targets, which becomes a major item of expense.

For smallbore silhouette competition, the rifle may be chambered only for the unmodified .22 rimfire short, long or long rifle cartridge. No special hot loads are allowed. Except for caliber restriction, all other equipment requirements are the same as for the big bore competition.

In the air gun configuration, any target air rifle can be used in the rifle class. The sporter air rifle classification limits the choice to any unaltered factory air rifle weighing less than ten pounds, two ounces. In air pistol competition, any .177 or .22 caliber air pistol is allowed.

Wes Blair has been a serious NRA rifle silhouette competitor for a number of years and has written extensively on the sport. We asked him to provide his knowledge and expertise for this chapter:

"The ram target is thirty-two inches long from nose tip to tail," he reminds. "The body, at its widest point, measures twelve inches. Rifle silhouette shooters fire at a bank of five of these heavy metal silhouettes at five-hundred meters — nearly 550 yards — and they shoot standing, without any of the usual target gadgets. Triple-A shooters, the highest classification, regularly take down two or three of these silhouettes out of five shots and sometimes will clean out a bank of five."

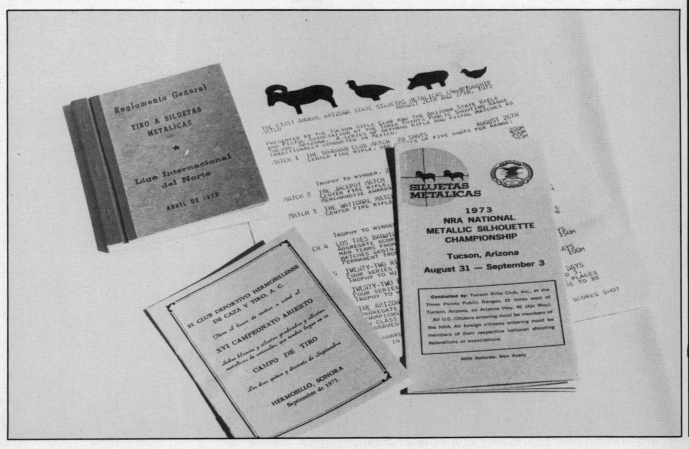

METALLIC SILHOUETTE SHOOTING

Although the silhouette game was designed for the hunter to sharpen his off-season shooting skills, the average sportsman would be hard-pressed to hit one ram out of five off the bench at five hundred meters.

"The fun part of silhouette shooting is easily seen," Blair adds. "Remember when you were a kid shooting at cans, bottles and boxes with your BB gun? You get the same exhilarating feeling when you send the small chicken silhouette spinning off the stand with your .22; even more of a thrill when you hear the metallic *whang* of a bullet hitting a pig at three hundred meters and watching it flop off the stand. The visual and auditory stimulus of cleaning out a bank of silhouettes can only be equal to that first kill on an elk.

"Silhouette shooting is a clean sport, and this well may be the reason so many women and seniors enjoy it. One does not have to fall down in the dirt or gravel to shoot. Most ranges have covered firing points with benchrests for sighting in. All shooting, once you are sighted in, is done from the standing position."

Rifles are relatively light, ranging from 7½ pounds for the sporting or light rifle classification in smallbore to the ten-pound two-ounce maximum for the heavy rifle. Many shooters are finding they do not need the maximum weight to shoot outstanding scores.

Until recently, a score of fifty-percent — twenty out of forty silhouettes — hits on the high-power course of fire was match-winning shooting. Thirty out of forty on the .22 course of fire would take the gold. But in hot-spot silhouette areas, this kind of a score won't take third place.

Conrad Bernhardt of Olympia, Washington, has top scores in the smallbore course of fire. He shot thirty-seven out of forty on the first match, thirty-seven out of forty on

Roy Dunlap (left) and Fred Weiland look over Dunlap's custom Remington Model 700 silhouette rifle. Dunlap is considered the father of rifle silhouette in the U.S.

Lones Wigger, former Olympic shooting champion, is an ardent silhouette shooter. He won the NRA title in the event in 1976 and continues to post high scorings.

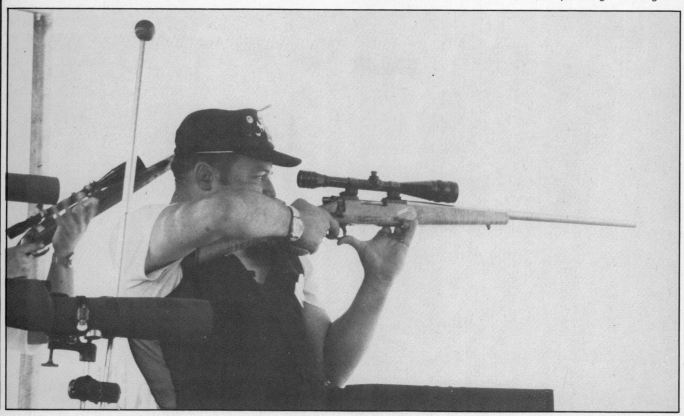

**Scale
1/2"=1"**

HIGH POWER RIFLE AND LONG RANGE PISTOL

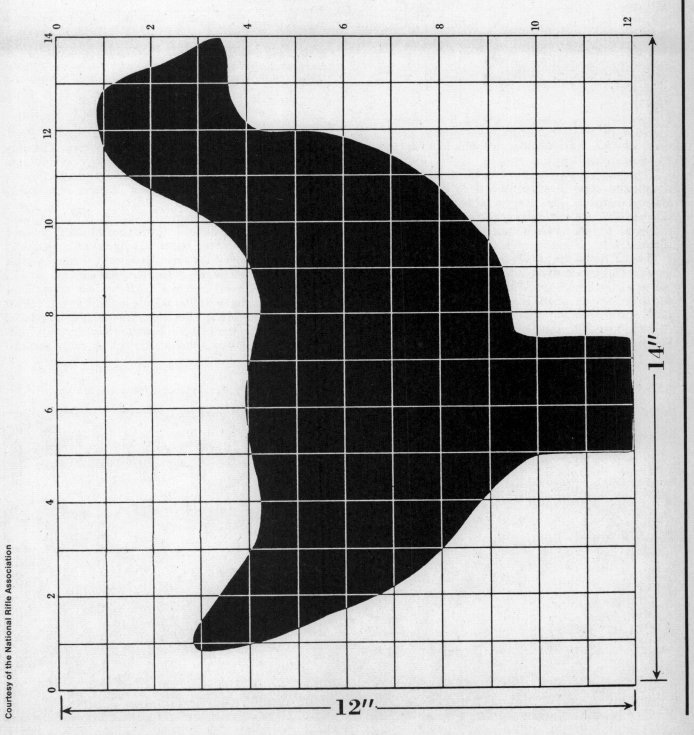

Courtesy of the National Rifle Association

METALLIC SILHOUETTE SHOOTING

Noted stockmaker Reinhart Fajen climbed on silhouette's bandwagon, designing this laminated maple stock for the event's rifles. He also has silhouette handgun stocks.

One of the first manufacturers to see the potential of the steel target sport was Savage with the Model 110-S. It was chambered for .308 and 7mm/08 for silhouetters.

the second match and another incredible identical score on the third match.

High-power silhouette shooters also have been racking up fantastic scores. Twenty-five to thirty out of forty scores are commonplace. This is terrific shooting when one considers that the silhouette shooter is firing at small targets at ranges up to five hundred meters, often in severe wind conditions.

"The .308 and the .30/06 were the most popular calibers for the chicken shooters and offered the best choice of bullets for the handloader. The recoil of these calibers tended to become uncomfortable in a 120-shot match, as the silhouette shooter is not allowed to use heavily padded shooting coats, slings, palm rests and other target gadgets. Many top shooters felt that on the unconscious level, they were anticipating recoil. This apparently creates anxiety and a tightening of muscles, affecting trigger control and contributing to fatigue. This is especially true of shooters who do not have the advantage of shooting on a weekly basis," Blair reports.

Six-millimeter chamberings, 6.5mm, .270 and practically every other caliber were tried out. Most did not have inherent accuracy, the bullet was adversely affected by wind or there just wasn't enough power to knock over the forty-pound ram targets at five hundred meters.

The 7mm/08 was used by a handful of Southwest silhouette shooters. In 1980, Remington introduced this caliber in their Model 788 and 700 lines. Savage also introduced the 7mm/08 in the 110-S silhouette rifle.

"With handloads, the 7mm/08 is a superbly accurate

A lineup of rifle stocks, actions and accessories at an exhibitors bench during shoot shows variety available.

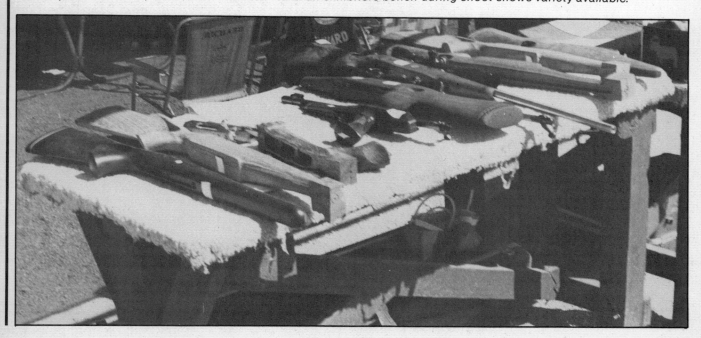

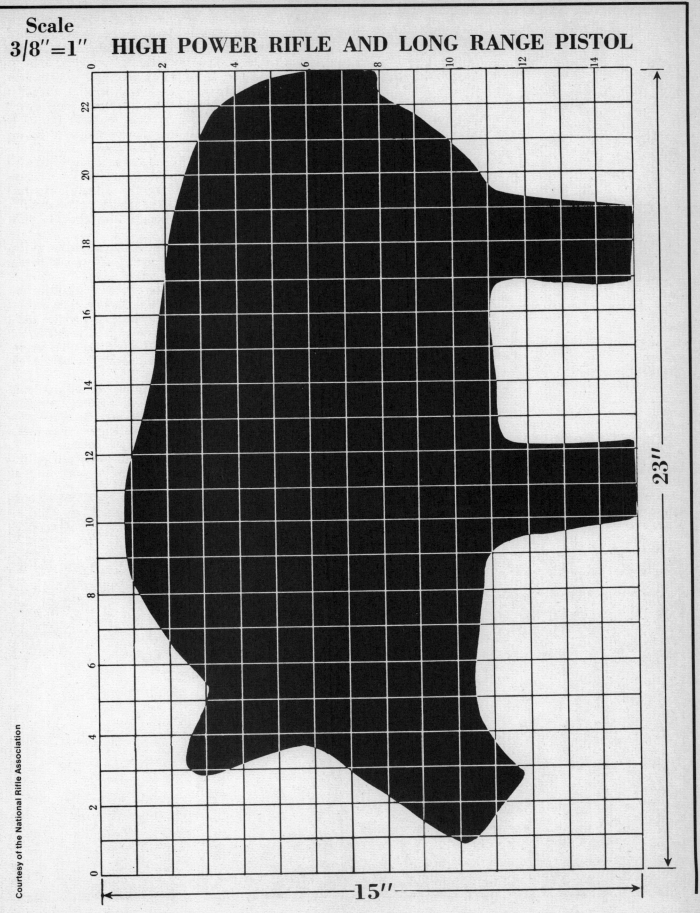

Bill Wolf, one of the early pioneers of rifle silhouette, shot matches in Mexico before it crossed border in '60s.

Among the pioneers of rifle silhouette are (from left) Jesse Rogers, NRA referee for the 1978 championships; Roy Dunlap, often credited with bringing the sport over the border from Mexico; Ben Avery, an early NRA referee; Mike Opsitnik, who was NRA referee in NRA title shoots.

cartridge with a wide variety of bullets available. For the short ranges of two-hundred and three-hundred meters, a load of 40.0 grains of 4320 powder with the Nornady 139-grain bullets is exceptionally accurate," according to Blair.

"This load gives an estimated velocity of 2750 feet per second (fps) out of a twenty-eight-inch barrel. The recoil is extremely mild. This light bullet is affected badly by the wind and, if wind conditions are poor, one should switch to the 162-grain bullet. Test firing, however, showed that the 139-grain bullet will take the sheep down.

"For longer ranges of 385 and 500 meters, or when wind conditions pick up, a 162-grain Hornady boat tail hollow point (BTHP), pushed by 38.0 grains of 4320, is extremely accurate with mild recoil. At 385 meters, I've shot five three-shot groups with one group at 2⅝ inches to a maximum of four inches."

(CAUTION — This load is over the maximum as recommended in the Hornady manual and should be approached with a great deal of care.)

"There are several production rifles — new and used — that are excellent for silhouette shooting. The Savage 110-S in .308 or 7mm/08 is an inexpensive choice and a good rifle for the beginning shooter. You probably will need some trigger work and a glass-bedding job is recommended. With these two added touches, you have a reliable chicken silhouette gun.

The Remington 700 Varmint Special in .308 and 7mm/08 is an excellent choice of many serious silhouette enthusiasts for a chicken gun, primarily because of the wide selection of custom triggers available. Ruger's varmint gun in their Model 77 .308 is also a frequent choice.

"Sitting in my gun cabinet was a little-used caliber .280 Remington in the 700 model. Silhouette gunsmith Ivan

**Scale
1/4"=1"**

HIGH POWER RIFLE AND LONG RANGE PISTOL

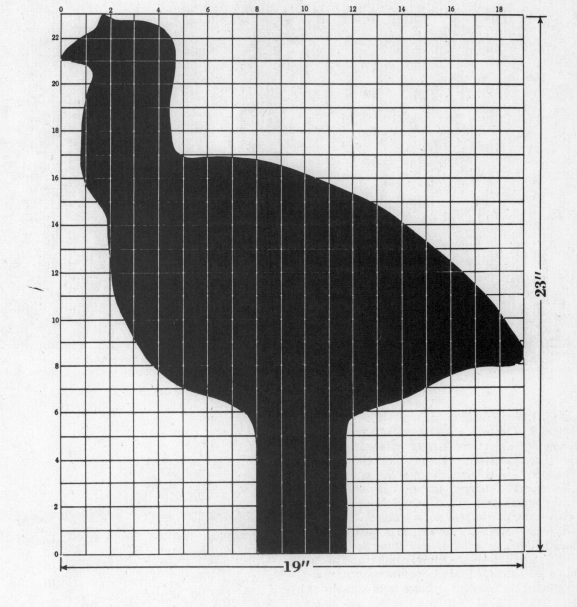

Courtesy of the National Rifle Association

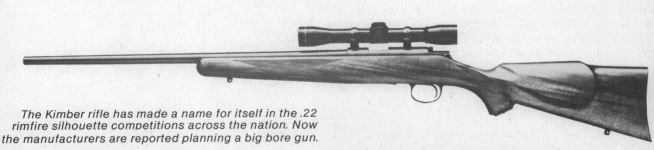

The Kimber rifle has made a name for itself in the .22 rimfire silhouette competitions across the nation. Now the manufacturers are reported planning a big bore gun.

METALLIC SILHOUETTE SHOOTING

Riflemen in Yuma, Arizona, were among those who brought the sport across the border from Mexico in early 1960s. The matches were held in other border towns as well and the sport caught on with enough verve to interest the NRA.

Lindgren of Olympia, Washington, screwed on a Shilen barrel in 7mm/08. This was a #4 barrel, kept to twenty-eight inches. A Green electronic trigger replaced the Remington trigger. The stock is one of Fajen's silhouette models, fiberglass bedded. The rifle weighs in at 9¼ pounds, including a Weaver T-16 scope. Accuracy is outstanding and even in the Washington State Championship, a grueling 160-shot match, fatigue was not a problem."

Buggy whip-thin barrels are growing in popularity with many silhouette buffs, especially those in the Southwest. Basically, this barrel is contoured from a bull barrel at the receiver, tapered to standard barrel dimensions in the middle, then expanded back to the bull barrel configuration at the muzzle.

The barrel is long, usually twenty-six to twenty-eight inches and is counterbored several inches.

"The philosophy behind the design of this weird-looking barrel is to give weight at the end of the barel for stability in the standing position. The taper is to keep the barrel light enough to make the ten-pound, two-ounce weight limitation," according to Blair.

Bill Fetterhoff is a well known silhouette and gallery shooting champion on the West Coast. Shooting with the Army Reserve rifle team, he nearly made 1984 Olympics.

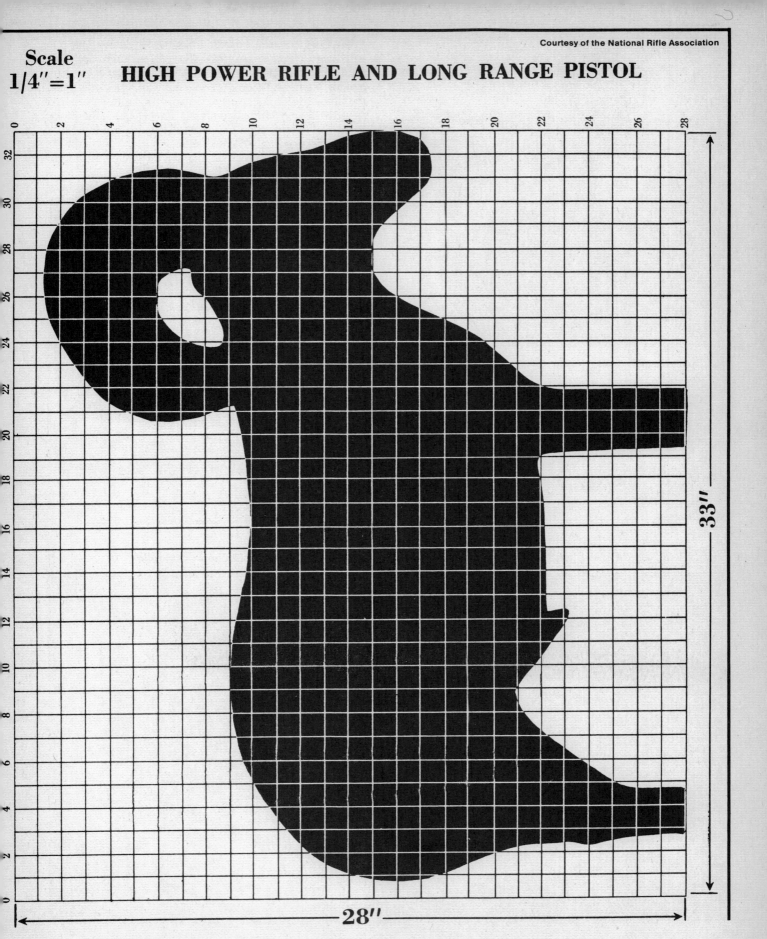

Weight becomes a problem when using heavy barrels and dictates lightweight stocks. Several manufacturers are producing fiberglass stocks that weigh in at about one pounds. Reinhart Fajen has come out with a stock designed for silhouette shooters. Lightweight wood can be ordered as well as heavy laminated maple. The design of this stock looks like it came right out of Buck Rogers, but it is functional and extremely comfortable.

Anschutz has dominated the .22 silhouette rifle field with the M64 MS rifle. The top of the line for silhouette shooters is the Anschutz 54 MS. This rifle is capable of cutting a one-hole group at one-hundred meters with match ammunition — in the hands of the right shooter, of course!

Two classes of rifles fired are in the .22 silhouette shoots. The light or sporting rifle has a weight limitation of 7½ pounds; the heavy rifle category is ten pounds, two ounces. Three rifles have seemed to dominate the light rifle cate-

Left: Silhouette shooters know their rifles well, but don't leave everything to memory. This shooter has note on ranges taped to stock. (Below) Although no longer made, the Weaver T-10 scope is prized among silhouetters.

The official Sports Afield perpetual trophy is awarded each year to the nation's rifle silhouette champion.

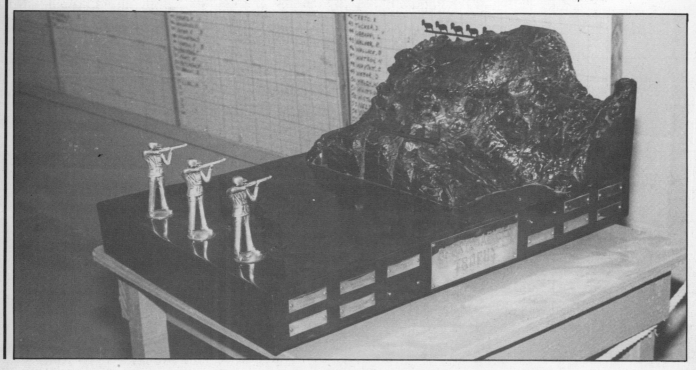

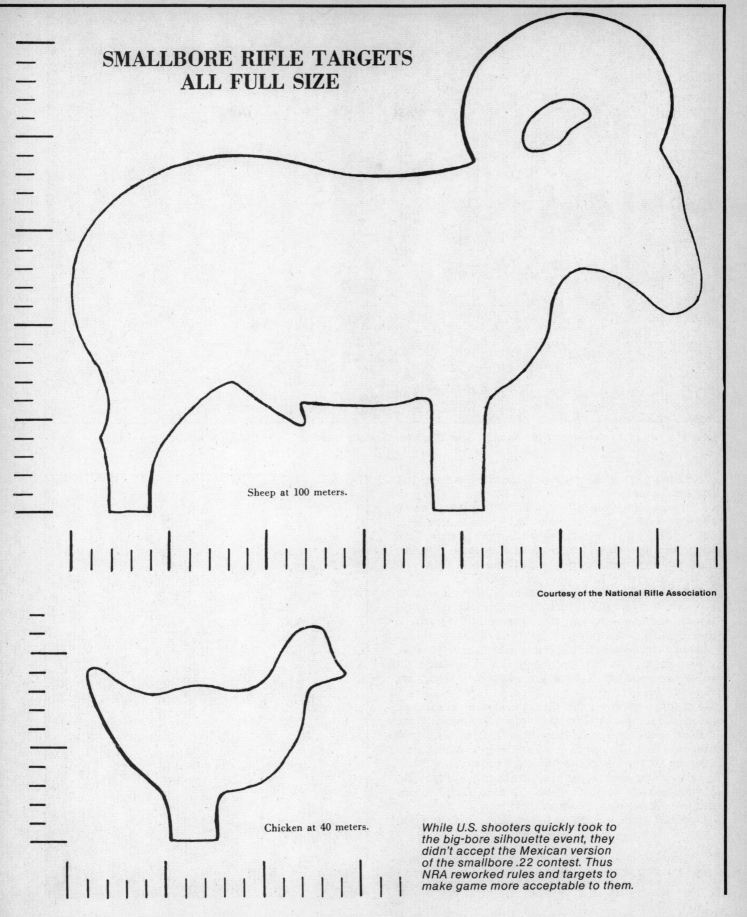

SMALLBORE RIFLE TARGETS ALL FULL SIZE

Sheep at 100 meters.

Courtesy of the National Rifle Association

Chicken at 40 meters.

While U.S. shooters quickly took to the big-bore silhouette event, they didn't accept the Mexican version of the smallbore .22 contest. Thus NRA reworked rules and targets to make game more acceptable to them.

A rifle silhouette competitor from Kansas, Stan Bigman, carefully cleans his rifle before firing for his score.

gory: They are the Remington 541S, the Anschutz 164 and the Kimber.

"Of equal importance to a quality silhouette rifle is a scope that allows one to make fast and accurate sight adjustments with one-hundred percent repeatability; the scope returns to its exact zero time after time. It is also important that these scopes be available in a variety of powers from 10 to 30x," Blair contends.

For the high-power shooter, one of the most reliable scopes is the Weaver T-model. No longer made, this model is treasured among the steel target fraternity. This scope is rugged and appears to handle the recoil of heavy calibers without mechanical failure in repeatabilty. The large target knobs are easy to read, extremely fast in making sight adjustments and tops in maintaining accuracy. Optics are clear and bright.

Leupold scopes have excellent optics and appear to rank among the sharpest and brightest. Many shooters who are building up a sporting class silhouette rifle choose a Leupold because of its fine optics and light weight. Blair uses a Leupold 16x on his sporting weight rimfire rifle.

Lyman silhouette scopes have long been one of the most popular models with silhouette shooters. These scopes feature superior optics, competitors claim.

Redfield silhouette scopes have been manufactured in

Bob Franklin of Hamilton, Montana, is a former three-state metallic silhouette champion and has held the AAA national crown. He fires match with left-hand action.

SMALLBORE SILHOUETTE TARGETS—FULL SIZE

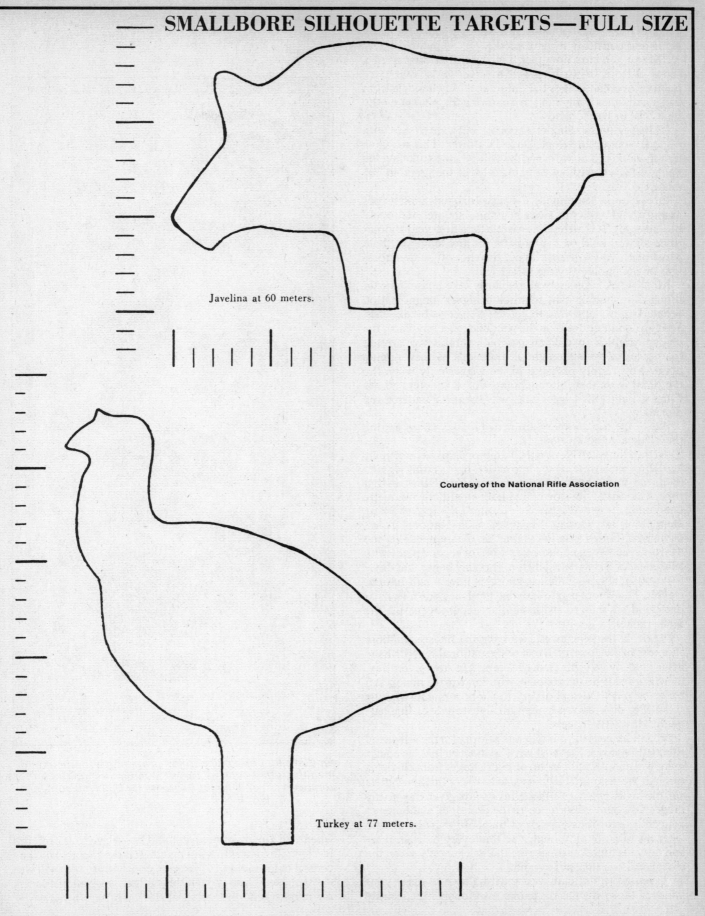

Javelina at 60 meters.

Courtesy of the National Rifle Association

Turkey at 77 meters.

METALLIC SILHOUETTE SHOOTING

10 and 12x. Wes Blair has used a Redfield scope for many years and considers it quite good.

"Many shooters now feel, however, that they need a scope of from 16- to 35-power to squeeze out that extra point or two that makes the difference. New models from these and other companies are entering the market all the time." Blair had found.

"The beginning silhouette shooter will want to start with a scope of not more than 10- to 12-power. This will give him a wide field of view and he will be able to locate his bank of targets without utilizing a lot of the precious 2½ minutes of time."

Of even more importance, the higher magnification scopes amplify holding errors. For a beginning shooter, this could be damaging. It is all but impossible for a first-year shooter to be able to hold on a silhouette for any length of time. Most often you will have to get the shot off as the crosshair or dot bobbles by the target."

Most AAA shooters who regularly take home the gold utilize a technique that requires a higher magnification scope: Instead of trying to get the trigger to break when your crosshair or dot is on the silhouette just anyplace, the champions pick out a blemish or bullet crater in or around the center of the silhouette and use this as their aiming point. They apply pressure to the trigger only when the crosshair is on their aiming point. These shooters all are using a light pull trigger that will break at under three ounces.

All of the top shooters are near fanatics about getting their rifle sighted in properly.

At the Canadian National Championships several years ago, three men were on the line at first light getting sighted in for the day's shoot. These men were Earl Hines, at that time American high-power and later smallbore silhouette champion; Lones Wigger, Jr., former Olympic shooting champion; and Dennis Martinen, then National AAA champion. Hines won the Canadian Championship, and Martinen and Wigger had a shoot-off for second place with Martinen, of Selah, Washington, shooting better that day.

At all smallbore matches, shooters have a half-hour to sight in. Few shooters are satisfied until they can hit a fly at one-hundred meters, with similar accuracy at all the other ranges.

"Here in the Northwest, we have the finest smallbore shooters in the country. Most of the national records have been held by Washington shooters. On any given day, there are a half-dozen shooters who can win the match. All have the physiological ability to shoot a match-winning score. The difference is in their mental attitude on that particular day," Blair feels.

"Confidence is the number one priority for the advanced silhouette shooter. He must have confidence that his equipment will shoot a tight group on every target from chickens through the last ram. He must also have confidence that he can clean off a bank of silhouettes on any given day at any range. Of equal importance is the ability of a shooter to concentrate for long periods of time. He must be able to clear his mind of all thoughts so that every muscle, bone and nerve is tuned to squeezing that trigger only when the crosshair is on that target point.

"Even more difficult, you must be able to clear your mind of those disturbing choke-up thoughts, especially

Air gun silhouette competition is gaining a foothold and manufacturers such as Target Master are manufacturing a complete set of silhouette targets for this type contest.

when you are under pressure and know that you need the last few silhouettes to win a match. It is the shooter who has control of his mind and is able to concentrate who will win the matches. Even though the shooter is working under a 2½-minute time limitation, it does not pay to hurry the

AIR GUN TARGETS
ALL FULL SIZE

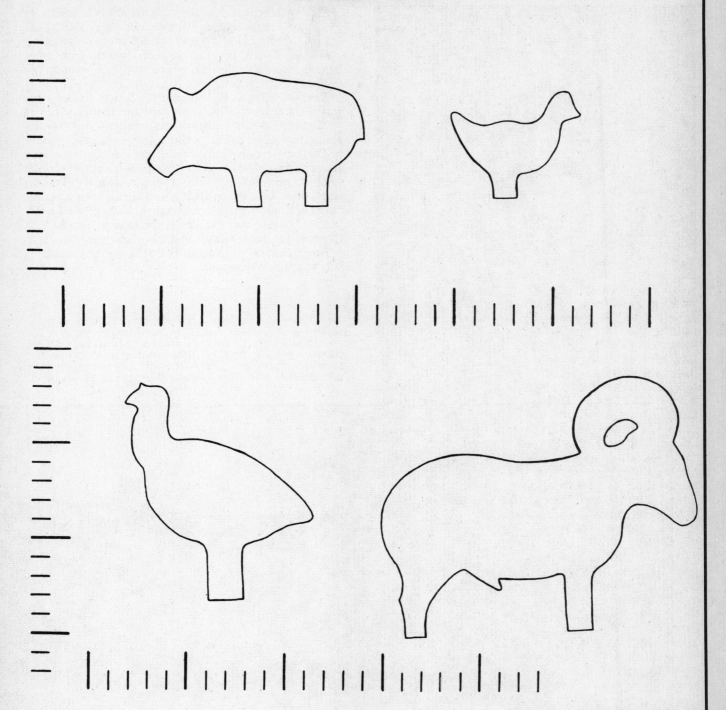

Courtesy of the National Rifle Association

shots. You are much better off to take your time to get four hits and leave one, than to hurry and knock only two or three over.

"Competition is fierce among rifle silhouette shooters. Most of use are shooting against ourselves, trying to improve our skills through the development of personal goals. It is not unusual to see two top shooters coaching and scoring for one another. Information is freely and correctly given. Silhouette shooting remains a fun sport; tops in a shooting challenge."

The Rimfire Fanciers Are Having Their Day, Too, In Long-Gun Silhouette Competition

"THE beauty of shooting the .22 rifle silhouette course is that you can take your favorite .22 rifle out of the gun cabinet and start shooting. The .22 program is divided into two categories, light or sporting rifle, and heavy rifle, ten pounds, two ounces."

That, at least, is the opinion of Wes Blair, who has watched this facet of the sport grow from infancy.

"In the light rifle category, one is able to compete with almost any rifle in the beginning stages, especially in the A or B classification. Some of the old hands in silhouette shooting have really been surprised when a novice shooter stepped up on the line with his Ruger autoloader or Stevens single-shot, bolt-action sporter and cleaned out a couple banks of silhouettes. At one match in the Northwest, a 23-year-old logger stepped up to the line, a big chaw of Copenhagen under one lip, and took the range record with a Ruger and a 4x scope. It's still the guy standing behind the rifle that counts."

Swinging metal targets such as these can be used for serious practice. For the .22 rimfire event, they are placed at 40, 50, 77 and 100 meters. (Below) Wes Blair competes in 30 rifle silhouette matches a year, large bore and rimfire. His Anschutz 64MS rifle is topped with Weaver T-16 scope, which he favors for .22 event.

Several manufacturers produce rifles for .22 silhouette shooting, but the Anschutz 64MS is favored by many. The two-stage trigger is adjustable and the stock offers it own advantages in the way of support for standing event.

The targets for .22 rimfire rifle competition are scaled at one-fifth the size of the traditional steel silhouettes used in big-bore competition. While the long-range heavy-caliber targets are made of three-eighths-inch steel, those for the rimfire variation of the game are made from thinner materials. For chicken and pig targets, the NRA requirement is quarter-inch steel; for turkey and ram targets, 3/16-inch steel is called for.

As for ranges, those used in .22 rimfire competition are decidedly shorter. The silhouettes may be set out at either yards or meters and still qualify under National Rifle Association rules.

The miniature chickens are set at forty meters or yards; the pigs at sixty meters or yards; turkeys at seventy-seven and the rams at an even one hundred yards — or meters.

The beginning shooter can, up to a point, compete with most rifles. However, quite possibly after the first season, he may reach that point when he can outshoot his rifle. If your .22 is shooting a two- or three-inch group at one hundred meters, you just can't compete with guys shooting rifles that will cut a half-inch group at the same distance.

Kimber makes an excellent quality .22 rifle that, if specified, will be supplied with a lightweight stock which will easily make the 7½-pound weight limitation, including sights. The trigger on this rifle is excellent and can be adjusted down to the two pounds allowed on the light rifle in NRA-sanctioned rimfire silhouette competition. The accuracy is superb, guaranteed by the company. If your rifle does not shoot as advertised, they will make it shoot without extra cost. The troubleshooter at Kimber is a silhouette shooter and personally takes care of any of the few complaints on this rifle.

The Anschutz 164 is widely used as a sporting weight silhouette rifle. It has been found to have an excellent trigger and is superbly accurate. The stock is ideal for off-hand shooting. "I have used the 164 in the lightweight competition and over the bench. Even when utilizing inexpensive target grade ammunition, it will shoot consistently under an inch. When using top-grade match ammunition, it will cut a ragged, one-shot hole at one hundred meters," Wes Blair contends.

Remington has produced a quality rimfire rifle in their

Mary Adkins has been one of the top .22 silhouette shooters in the Northwestern area of the United States. She favors the Remington 40X rifle with a fiberglass stock and a Leupold 24-power scope for holding on the targets.

Model 541S for a number of years. Silhouette shooters are using this fine rifle in increasing numbers and the 541S is appearing in the winner's circle frequently in smallbore matches.

"This rifle has all the features important to experienced silhouette shooters. It is superbly accurate, has a good trigger and a stock designed for off-hand shooting. One would not go wrong in purchasing one of these mid-range-priced .22s.

"The three rifles mentioned are ones most often seen on the firing line and have all proven to be excellent. Many shooters use their light rifle and also fire it in the heavy rifle category. When one considers the use he can get from a quality .22, it more than justifies the $300 to $500 one can spend on such a rifle, some shooters feel.

"If you are fortunate enough to have one of those superior grades of sporter, such as the Model 54 Anschutz Sporter, or the Remington 40X Sporter, which is just a little too heavy to make the weight limitation, there is still hope," according to Blair's research. Reinhart Fajen, the Missouri stockmaker, produces an excellent wood stock that is extremely light in weight. Blair's own Anschutz 54 Sporter was a bit more than ten ounces over the weight limit. Ivan Lindgren, a gunsmith from Olympia, Washington, who specializes in silhouette guns, fitted a Fajen stock to this sporter and produced a fine quality rifle capable of heavy-match rifle scores. One can also purchase a fiberglass stock that averages about one pound in weight less to ensure making the weight limit.

Anschutz has more or less taken the lead in the production of heavier rimfire silhouette rifles. Several seasons back, the West German firm came out with their Model 64 Metallic Silhouette rifle. This is an excellent, mid-price rifle with more than ample accuracy to shoot a possible over the silhouette course. The stock is designed specifically for standing shooting. It features an extremely high comb for the use of scope sights and a stippled forend and pistol grip. The trigger is two-stage and adjustable to a few ounces. This is quite likely the most popular silhouette rifle observed.

More world championships are held by the Anschutz Model 54 rifle than any other rimfire rifle. At the urging of silhouette shooters, Anschutz has introduced the Model 54 Metallic Silhouette rifle. This is an expensive rifle, but for the serious shooter, worth every penny. Accuracy is superb. With match ammunition, incredibly small groups are commonplace at one hundred meters. The trigger is superior and adjustable to an ounce or two. The stock of this rifle is identical to the 64. Combined with a quality scope, one could not have a better rifle.

Many shooters, especially men and women who were gallery shooters, had Model 52 Winchesters, 40X Remingtons or the Aschutz 54s. These rifles are overweight for silhouette competition. Rather than purchase another expensive rifle, shooters restock with either Fajen's silhouette stock, or one of the glass stocks such as those manufactured by McMillan in Phoenix, Arizona, or Brown Precision in San Jose, California. These fine-target rifles, restocked, make the ten-pound, two-ounce limit.

One addition a few dedicated shooters have added is a quality trigger capable of adjustments to grams. Ron Kesslering with his Model 52 Winchester, has broken many

Frank Newboles has been a top competitor on the West Coast in the light rifle category of silhouette competition. He favors a Model 541 Remington .22 rimfire that is mounted with a Weaver T-model scope. Rig weights 7½ pounds.

Some of the toughest .22 silhouette competitors have been found to be women and juniors, who take to the game.

records with this rifle that is equipped with a Green electronic trigger. This fine trigger has absolutely no travel — at least none can be felt — and is adjustable to a gram or two. Many shooters have Canjar's light-pull triggers on their rifles. This trigger is also excellent and is available for many rifles.

A silhouette scope must have the design characteristics for one to make fast and accurate changes in both elevation and windage, with a one hundred percent reliability in returning to zero. In a two-day, 12-shot match, one may change the elevation no less than a dozen times and also may make countless windage changes.

The elevation and windage adjustments on the Weaver T-Model scopes — discussed in the preceding section of this chapter — are large, target-like knobs that are easy to read. With just a glance you know if you are on zero. Range

Earl Hines, Jr. (in foreground) and Conrad Bernhard concentrate on downing silhouettes of turkeys during a hard fought shoot-off. Smaller targets become demanding.

adjustments can be made in a fraction of a second. Weaver T-Model scopes were available in powers from 6 to 30x, with a wide range of reticles available.

"Most silhouette shooters favor the crosshair and dot. Avoid extremely fine crosshairs; they are great for varmints and benchrest, but tend to fade out in bad light or shadowy conditions which we often have on the silhouette range," Blair advises from his own experience.

Lyman silhouette scopes are limited to 6-, 8- and 10-power, but many of the shooters are ordering 20, 30 or 35x models from other makers.

Redfield has produced silhouette scopes for years in both 10x and 12x. This is a good reliable scope. Redfield has made a fine 3-9x scope with Accu-Trac that a few high-power shooters use. For rimfire use, however, one should stick with 10x or 12x.

Leupold scopes have bright, quality optics and Blair recommends their 10x silhouette model for a light rifle.

As in big-bore silhouette shooting, Blair recommends that the beginning .22 rimfire silhouette shooter should stick with the lower-power scopes for the first year. Experienced shooters can better handle higher power optics. After a year or two of experience, some shooters are able to hold several seconds on the silhouette. Most try to get the shot off as they bobble past the silhouette.

Silhouette rifles are fickle critters. The price of top-grade match ammunition has skyrocketed. However, competitors are finding that CCI Mini-Group, Remington Target, and Ely Club will do a creditable job among the .22 rimfires. For serious shooting in match conditions, many shooters use target-type ammunition for chickens and pigs, and switch to the more expensive ammo for turkeys and rams. For practice, inexpensive .22 ammunition is okay for chicken and pigs and, with a good target rifle, will suffice at one hundred meters. You will get an occasional flyer at the longer ranges, but most will group well enough for practice.

When silhouette shooters gathered on the line for the second national outing at El Paso in 1976, there was a broad range of handguns and styles. Man standing in the white shirt is the late Tom Beall, the match organizer.

A VIEW OF THE PAST

CHAPTER 3

From A Blood Sport Of Mexico To Sophisticated Handgunnery Marks A Long March Of Progress

WHILE IT is difficult, if not impossible, to trace the beginning of any shooting sport, metallic silhouette shooting in general, and handgun silhouette specifically, can be pinned down almost to the year, if not the exact day, they were originated.

Rifle silhouette came first. It started in Mexico as a live-animal sport about 1914 when Pancho Villa and his men were raiding ranchos in the northern state of Chihuahua. An old account by one of Villa's men described how it came about.

With time on their hands, a contest was arranged to see who was the best shot. Livestock had to be slaughtered to feed the revolutionists, so according to the account, steers were tethered to trees at a distance. The men blazed away with their Mausers or whatever rifles they had, until the steers were killed and the best shooters had been determined in the process. A new shooting sport had been created even if Villa and his men didn't realize it at the time.

The practice of shooting at livestock continued and was refined as the years went by. Chickens, turkeys, pigs, sheep, cattle and whatever other domestic animals were available were used as targets. Smaller animals and birds were tethered and shot at closer distances, while the larger critters were placed at ranges of up to five hundred yards.

Shortly after World War II, the killing of live animals in this manner began to fade out and metallic silhouettes of the birds and animals were substituted. Even so, the original sport of shooting livestock would continue in the outlying areas of Mexico until the late 1950s, usually in conjunction with a fiesta.

My own introduction to the sport started in 1952, when I was a guest of Don Jose Joaquim Machado, a big-game hunting friend and an avid sportsman. He was conducting a fiesta on his ranch near Guadalajara and that was where I first saw the kind of shooting that ultimately would lead to our present sport.

Looking back over thirty-five years, my memory may be a trifle hazy, but as I recall the fiesta, there were a couple of dozen chickens, four sheep and two steers. The chickens were tied at stakes at distances I estimated to be seventy-five to one hundred yards from the big veranda of Don Jose's ranch house from which the shooting took place. The sheep were tied to posts at about two hundred yards and the steers an estimated four hundred yards.

I was probably the only one of the two hundred-odd guests who had not seen this type of shooting and didn't realize at the moment that the staked-out livestock would be part of the feast.

As the only *gringo* guest present and a personal hunting friend of Don Jose, I was given first shot. I selected the

Each participating shooter received one of these plates to commemorate first national silhouette championships.

Left: In the first formal match, Ray Chapman (right) and his partner won the two-man team event with the .44 Auto Mag. The author (center) and son garnered second. (Below) IHMSA adopted official buckles and their logo.

host's Colt *Woodsman* pistol, with which I had bagged ptarmigans the previous year when we were on an Alaskan sheep hunt together. At least the sight picture was a bit more familiar than those of the various rifles I picked up and examined.

Much to the surprise of the assembled guests — and to me, as well — my first shot bagged the nearest chicken. There was much applause and back slapping, and I wisely demurred taking another shot, knowing it likely would be a miss. Besides, having been a big-game hunter all of my life, shooting domestic animals tied to stakes didn't turn me on. At least I had the dubious distinction of being the only one present to bag something with a pistol. Everyone else used rifles.

As I quickly realized, the Mexicans were used to this kind of shooting and looked upon it as great sport. The tequila flowed, and, as the guests fired their rifles, hefty bets were wagered on individual performances. The chickens were dispatched first. Squawking and running about at the end of their tethers, wings flapping wildly as near misses stung them with dirt, they were not easy targets. When the last one went down, they were gathered up and taken to the kitchen. There was a short lull while points were posted, bets were paid off and more tequila consumed.

Then it was the turn of the sheep. With the increase in range, the bets increased porportionately. When the woolies finally had been downed, they also went to the kitchen.

Don Jose, himself, was the ultimate winner, making a magnificent shot on the last steer; a spine shot that dropped the animal in its tracks.

During subsequent trips to Mexico, I saw more live-animal competitions, including some that were pure loot shoots with all the manipulations that went with them. These were a far cry from the friendly fiesta gathering at Don Jose's rancho.

It was greed and cheating that finally ended the live-animal shoots, rather than any action by humane societies. The steel-plate silhouette targets were substituted for live animals as a means of better control.

Other Americans had seen or taken part in the rifle silhouette shoots in Mexico where the steel targets were used, and finally the sport was introduced into the United States.

Even though a lot of water has gone under the bridge and the silhouette sport has made enormous progress over the past thirty-five years, I'll always remember that long-ago fiesta at Don Jose's rancho. I was probably one of the first

Elgin Gates, Jr., prepares to fire on the first bank of chicken silhouette targets. The white strap around his back is part of the shoulder rig in which he packed a Smith & Wesson Model 29 .44 magnum for this competition.

Left: Tom Beall's .30/.223 Contender had markings on the side of forend for sight settings. Pad served as recoil protection. (Below) The late George Nonte was observer at match.

Americans to take part in a shooting sport originating in Mexico that ultimately would become the outstanding handgun sport of all time. That first chicken, bagged with a .22 pistol, would mark the beginning of a new phase of my handgun career that has exceeded my wildest dreams.

The first rifle metallic silhouette shoots in America were held about 1967 in the Arizona border towns of Nogales, Bisbee and Douglas. Six years later, in 1973, NRA entered the scene and sponsored the first rifle silhouette championships held north of the border. At the time there was no interest in metallic silhouette shooting with handguns, and it would be two more years before the first organized competition would take place in Tucson, Arizona, in September, 1975.

One of the fanciers of big-bore handguns was Lee Jurras, who had founded Super-Vel and had run that cartridge

At the first handgun silhouette championships, after a shooter fired, he kept score for the next competitor. Jane McQueary keeps score for James Herringshaw. At that match, most shooters carried handguns in holsters.

METALLIC SILHOUETTE SHOOTING

The author chose the sitting position for his competing during the early match in El Paso. He still uses it.

Terri Evjen was one of three women entered in the El Paso match, using one of the first rebarreled XP-100 pistols. (Below) This rifle silhouette match in Yuma was a forerunner of the handgun game. A number of the border towns held matches, inviting Mexican shooters.

company for a time before going on to other endeavors. At that time, he was involved in the sale of Auto Mag pistols and had formed the Club de Auto Mag Internationale, Incorporated. Since Jurras was pushing the idea of hunting with the Auto Mag, he obviously saw the logic of holding a shooting competition to promote the use of the big automatic on animal targets.

After a false start that led nowhere, early in 1975 a gent named Dutch Snow, who resided in Tucson, contacted Jurras and suggested his hometown as the logical site for the matches. He reported that he could reserve the range and the rifle silhouette targets.

Another Arizonian, Dale Miller, also became involved. He had been sponsoring combat matches in the area. Miller and Snow suggested that the course of fire be at 50, 100, 150 and 200 meters, adding to this a "surprise" segment that included silhouettes at unknown distances. It wasn't until May 1975 that it was announced the match would be slated for September 20-21 at the Three Points shooting range near Tucson. Sponsor, as originally planned, would be Jurras' Club de Auto Mag, but the name of the competition had been modified to become the First National Handgun Metallic Silhouette Championships.

The rules stated that the minimum caliber for competition would be the .357 magnum and there were six of these in the Auto Mag configuration along with seven Colt Pythons. The rest of the shooters elected heavier calibers in .41 magnum, .44 magnum, and .45 Colt, apparently feeling their heavier bullets would offer more knock-down power against the steel silhouettes.

My eldest son and I both were entered. We switched back and forth between my Smith & Wesson Model 29 .44

Rifle silhouette shooting predated the handgun game. It started in Mexico about 1914 as a live-animal sport. By the 1940s, metallic silhouettes were substituted for livestock. Competition crossed the border about 1967.

magnum with an 8⅜-inch barrel and the .357 Auto Mag. The Smith & Wesson was used for downing chickens and javelinas, while the .357 Auto Mag, because of its flatter shooting characteristics, was used for the turkey and ram silhouettes.

Oddly, I never had fired the Auto Mag before, but ended up in thirteenth place — tied with six others. I knew then that I was hooked on handgun silhouette shooting. My only claim to fame at that first match was to knock down five turkey silhouettes in a row at 150 meters, something nobody else was able to do. However, it should be noted that I missed all five turkeys in the first stage of competition.

The important thing was that a new handgun shooting sport was born that would spread all over the country in the weeks and months that lay ahead. Another important thing had been learned: Even the big magnum handguns were no match for those heavy steel silhouettes.

A year went by during which I spent a great deal of time resurrecting and reworking some of my old cartridge designs from the 1940s and 1950s that were used successfully on African hunting safaris. In addition, I developed a whole new series of cartridges to see how they would work in this demanding sport of handgun metallic silhouette shooting.

The second national silhouette championships were set for three days in October, 1976, at El Paso, Texas. The program I received from Tom Beall a month ahead called it the 1976 National Hunting Handgun Silhouette Championships. I had met this congenial Texas pistol shooter during the first match at Tucson in 1975 and, if ever there was an all-out enthusiastic one-man army, Tom Beall had to be it.

Before the end of the Tucson match the previous year,

The author spots for his son, who uses a .357 Auto Mag in first handgun silhouette match ever held. (Below) Lee Jurras, promoter of the first contest, observes a competitor during "surprise" match on targets set at unknown distances. Jurras was the match's chief referee.

In 1975 Arizona shoot, Janet McQueary (seated) was the only lady shooter. Firing S&W .45 Auto Rim, she dropped a ram at 200 meters and was applauded.

Kneeling, Hal Swiggett had a Colt Python for first handgun silhouette contest. Dutch Snow and Jeff Cooper were line officers then.

Beall had been talking about holding the next handgun silhouette championship in El Paso.

"I know I can get my friends at Fort Bliss to host the match," he had said. "Only thing is, I'd like to clear it with Lee Jurras."

At Tucson, Jurras had been enthusiastic about finding a permanent home for the handgun silhouette championships by making a deal with the Mescalero Apache Indians for a range on their reservation in southern New Mexico. After a great deal of negotiation, the deal fell through and the door was open to hold the second match somewhere else. Beall grabbed the opportunity and lost little time convincing the Fort Bliss Rod and Gun Club to host it.

Tom Beall had been working on his version of a silhouette pistol in .30 caliber on a Thompson/Center frame, just as I had been working on my own project, a Contender in my favorite 7mm. Both Beall's effort and my own were based on the Remington .223 case, his necked up to .30 caliber, mine to 7mm.

One thing in the match program bothered me. The program allowed for "any pistol of any caliber, weight not to exceed 4½ pounds, sight radius not to exceed fifteen inches."

My prototype 7mm/.223 weighed over 4½ pounds and

Shooter holds live chicken on silhouette stand to show the comparison in size. Live animals never have been used as targets in competitions conducted in the U.S.

The first major contest in Tucson in 1975 was marked by firing of a mountain howitzer by members of the 4th Artillery Memorial Regiment. This officially opened the first handgun metallic silhouette match ever conducted.

the lockup was loose. With an important business deal on the fire, I didn't have time to fix it right then.

I explained this problem to Tom Beall by telephone and he suggested we use his .30/.223 Contender for the match. I hurriedly accepted the offer. Incidentally, he had agreed earlier to put together another .30/.223 for me in return for one of my T/Cs in 7mm/.223.

There were fifty-three shooters entered in the match and each competitor was allowed to have a coach with him on the line, using a scope or binoculars to call each shot. At

Temperatures stood at more than 100°F in the shade and little shade was available at the 1975 Tucson contest. Friends and competitors sought the shade between shots.

In the 1976 championship shoot in El Paso, the prone position was not allowed; only sitting, kneeling and standing. Gates had modified his own sitting position.

the Tucson contest, we had been allowed to fire from the prone position, but in the El Paso tournament, this was not allowed. Shooters were limited to the standing, kneeling or sitting positions.

The first day of official competition, a Friday, was devoted to the two-man team event. As the silhouettes began to fall, it became obvious I wasn't the only one who had been practicing. Ray Chapman, renowned even then as a combat shooter, and his partner took the top honors with a score of 56X80. Jose Porras and Jose Calzada, up from Mexico for the championships, came in second with 52X80. My son and I came in third in the team event, scoring

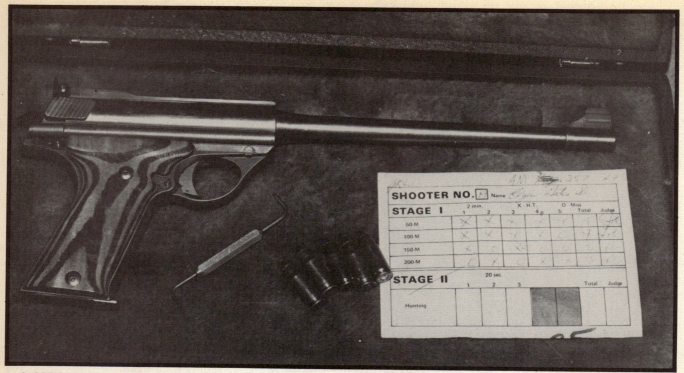

A .357 Auto Mag with 8-inch barrel was used by author in the first handgun silhouette championship in Tucson. It was used on the turkey and ram targets. For chicken and javelina silhouettes, he used S&W Model 29 .44 magnum.

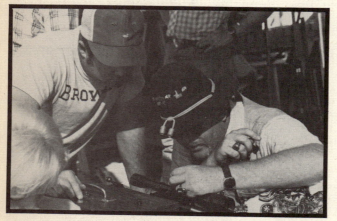

Tom Gatewood (right) checked scope setting on his rifle during 1978 NRA rifle silhouette championships. Some shooters use scope of 15-power for rifle silhouettes.

49X80. My individual score for the day was 29X40, second only to Porras' 33X40.

The following day was dedicated to individual championships and it had become obvious that Porras, Tom Beall and Ray Chapman would lead the pack. The rest of us would follow.

When the firing ended that afternoon, Beall and Porras were tied with 33X40 each.

Over the years, I've thought back to that day and tried to determine just who it was that came up with the idea of forming an organization devoted specifically to handgun silhouette shooting. It may well be that several of us had the idea about the same time. Whatever the beginning, more than a dozen of us crowded into a motel room that night of October 2, 1976, to dicuss the possibilities and the potential.

In addition to Porras and his partner from Mexico, we also had a Canadian marksman in our midst, Jim Bonsor, giving the match an international flavor. I made a motion that we name the organization the International Handgun Metallic Silhouette Association. The motion was carried unanimously.

Having noted the results of the high performance guns like Porras' rebarreled XP-100 and Tom Beall's .30/.223 Contender, as well as my own experiments with the 7mm/.223 and others at home, I moved that competition should be in two categories. One would be limited to stock production handguns as they come over-the-counter, out-of-the-box. Also, I felt there should be an unlimited category that

Rifle silhouette rules limit the stock's configuration. Competitor at right holds his rifle stock against the rules drawing to see if it's legal for NRA competition.

A variety of awards and prizes were part of the 1975 championships. (Left) Half of the scoreboard for the 1975 match carries names still familiar to the sport.

would allow tinkerers to experiment and develop long-range handgunning to its ultimate.

This motion, too, passed unanimously with two modifications. It was agreed to allow a trigger-smoothing job by honing the engaging surfaces of the hammer and the sear and to allow any standard grip to be installed as a replacement for the factory grip.

During that initial meeting, it was voted that all shooting would be freestyle with no artifical support. Administrative rules were instituted so that shooters could be classified through locally sanctioned matches.

On the final day of competition at Fort Bliss, the word was passed that a new organization, the International Handgun Metallic Silhouette Association, had been formed. Of the fifty-three competitors taking part in the championships, a total of thirty-four came on board with twelve of us being designated as founding members and the other twenty-two as charter members.

The match ended with Porras winning the title of national champion by one point over Tom Beall. I was lucky to get fourth overall and second in the fifty-meter championship.

That was the beginning of IHMSA. From those original thirty-four members, we grew to our present strength of over 45,000 from every state in the union and dozens of overseas countries.

An interesting side-note was the fact that the late George Nonte, throughout the founding meeting, had repeatedly insisted that we hand the new game over to the National Rifle Association. However, when such an approach was made, we were rebuffed. The NRA wanted nothing to do with us. That hasn't changed a great deal down through the years since our founding meeting, although the NRA has developed a handgun silhouette game of its own.

This update would not be complete without noting that Tom Beall, one of the real spark plugs in getting the organization off the ground, did not live to see its success. He died in an auto accident in February, 1977, only four months after the founding meeting of the association in that tightly jammed motel room. It was a great loss to his many friends, but his important efforts in getting the handgun metallic silhouette game under way have not been forgotten.

Jose Porras (left) is congratulated by the author on winning the overall championship in the 1976 contest. Porras also won the 50-meter competition at El Paso.

To put history in its proper perspective, the first national metallic silhouettes rifle championships were held in 1973 under the banner of National Rifle Association. At that time, there was no NRA interest in creating a handgun version of the silhouette sport.

In 1975, Lee Jurras promoted the first organized handgun silhouette match. A year later, at El Paso, Texas, in October of 1976, the International Handgun Metallic Silhouette Association was formed and a complete set of handgun silhouette rules were inaugurated. An attempt to hand the new handgun silhouette game over to NRA was rebuffed, but not for long. NRA expressed a desire to get into the act at their 1977 annual meeting.

On June 29, 1977, I received an official letter from Ed Andrus, manager of NRA's competition services. In essence, it advised that NRA intended to take up all types of metallic silhouette shooting for rifles and handguns and asked permission for NRA to adopt IHMSA's long-range handgun rules.

After consulting with other officers of IHMSA, permis-

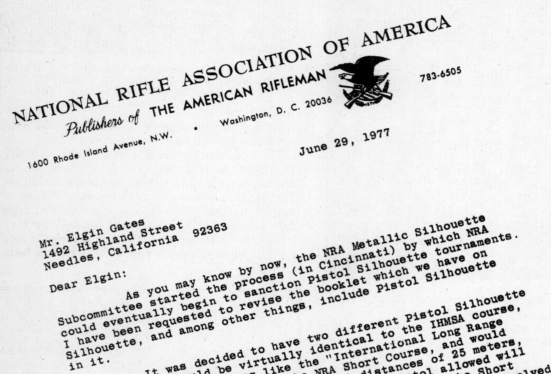

Page 2
Mr. Elgin Gates
June 29, 1977

Finally, we will be going ahead with promotion of a smallbore rifle Silhouette Course, which will utilize the High Power rifle rules, modified so that caliber restrictions are limited to .22 caliber short, long, or long rifle. Targets will be one-fourth scale, shot at one-fourth scale distances. This game looks like a sure winner to me, and barring any unforeseen problems, should also lead eventually to NRA sanctioned tournaments.

None of this that I have told you is by any means a secret; there simply has not been time to publicize it. However, it must be emphasized that all details of the rules are not complete, and that NRA is not sanctioning either Pistol or Smallbore Silhouette at the present time. Further Board action will be required before this can be done.

I look forward to hearing any comments which you may have and especially your reaction to the printing by NRA of the IHMSA rules. I certainly hope to meet you in September in Phoenix.

Sincerely yours,

Edward D. Andrus
Manager
Competitions Services
Department

EDA/md

sion was readily granted for NRA to copy IHMSA rules as requested. The feeling was that the more handgun shooters who were involved in an active shooting sport — whether it be IHMSA or NRA — all the better when it came time to battle the anti-gun forces. With handguns being the number one target, both organizations needed all the togetherness that could be generated.

A short time later, I was asked to fill a position on the NRA silhouette committee. I accepted, especially on the basis of NRA adopting our rules.

For a few years, IMHSA and NRA rules were virtually identical and there was a "gentlemen's agreement" whereby an IHMSA member could present this classification card at an NRA match and be allowed to compete. Likewise, NRA classification cards were accepted at IHMSA matches.

As long as possible, I attempted to influence the NRA silhouette committee to keep their rules as simple as possible and in line with IHMSA requirements. This was especially true insofar as the IHMSA production gun philosophy was concerned, so the handgun silhouette game would continue to be an Average Man's sport where anyone could compete on an equal basis, all competitors using standard, over-the-counter, out-of-the-box production guns.

With IHMSA's skyrocketing growth taking up to eighteen hours a day, often seven days a week, I felt I had to withdraw from the NRA silhouette committee in 1980 to devote full time to IHMSA.

In fairly short order, numerous NRA rule changes were implemented on a yearly basis to the point that, by mutual agreement, the interchange of classification cards between NRA and IHMSA had to be rescinded.

NRA's short-range pistol silhouette event, eventually called hunter's pistol, became quite successful. They also adopted a short-range .22 hunter's pistol course of fire, as well as several other versions of silhouette competition for black powder firearms, air rifles, and .22 rifles.

In 1979, IHMSA created a short-range course of fire for .22 pistols similar to our long-range game, except that the targets were shot at 25, 50, 75 and 100 yards. In 1986, IHMSA created a field pistol course of fire similar to the NRA hunter's pistol event. As in 1977, IHMSA has continued to allow NRA to adopt whatever IHMSA rules they wished. They have done so, repeatedly. The whole idea, insofar as IHMSA and NRA are concerned, is to provide as much competition as possible for all handgun aficionados, and in as wide a variety of competitions as possible.

A major point of departure between the current IHMSA and NRA rules for handgun silhouette competition lies in the fact that the NRA allows scope-mounted handguns in the standing event; IHMSA does not.

Author (kneeling) hunted Africa in 1957 with Roy Rogers. He was using experimental calibers, several of which had silhouette applications in the development of those rounds.

SILHOUETTE CARTRIDGE DEVELOPMENT

CHAPTER 4

The Author's Experiments Date Back To His African Hunting Safaris

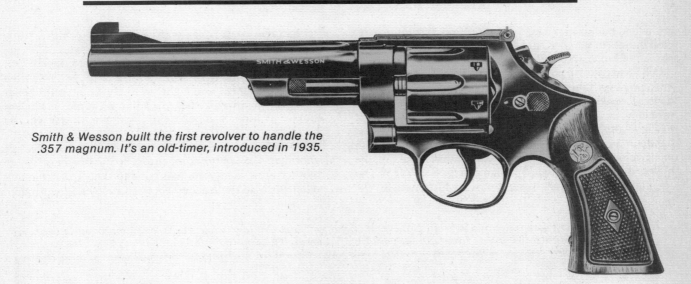

Smith & Wesson built the first revolver to handle the .357 magnum. It's an old-timer, introduced in 1935.

DURING THE long trip home from Arizona, after the first handgun metallic silhouette championships of 1975, I let my son drive. I had a head full of ideas and started putting notes and sketches on a lined yellow legal tablet. The one sure thing we had learned about this new game was that that the existing magnum handguns and cartridges available were not a good match for the heavy steel silhouette ram targets at two hundred meters.

The chickens, javelinas and turkeys weren't too difficult. While a low or marginal hit might leave a javelina or turkey standing — they had to be knocked down to count — a good solid center or high hit usually would topple either off its stand. It was the big, heavy rams that were the real challenge.

It should be noted here, in looking back, that the rams at that first match were made of soft steel; they had been hammered unmercifully with rifle fire in earlier contests. They were beat, warped, in bad condition and had oversize feet. As I recall, even the rail stands were wobbly and uneven, an overall combination that made these particular silhouette targets difficult to put down even with rifles, let alone handguns.

The heretofore invincible handgun cartridges such as the .357, .41 and .44 magnum were relatively slow in velocity and rapidly running out of gas at two hundred meters. During the first relay of the match, I had tagged rams repeatedly with my Model 27 S&W .357 magnum and the Model 29 S&W .44 mag, both with 8⅜-inch barrels, using factory ammunition. We were using 158-

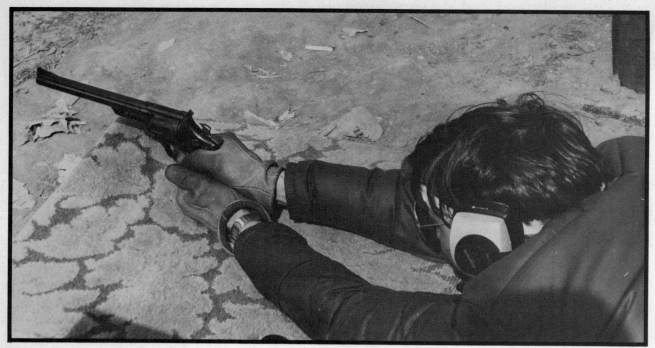
The author fired a Smith & Wesson Model 29 .44 magnum on some targets at first silhouette competition in 1975.

grain lead bullets in the .357 magnum and 240-grain jacketed bullets in the .44. In those days, there wasn't a large choice of bullets for these two calibers.

All I had gotten from hitting the steel rams was a series of musical pings. The rams didn't even quiver, much less fall down. Everybody at the match had more or less the same problem.

The Auto Mag, then the biggest and most powerful handgun available, did better. It put the bullets out with more velocity and the trajectory was flatter. Actually, the bullets themselves were not to blame in the S&W .357 and .44 magnum. They just weren't moving fast enough.

I had two Auto Mags at the match, one of the original .44s with a six-inch barrel and one of the newer .357 Auto Mags with an eight-inch barrel. I had chosen the .357 for the final bank of five turkeys and five rams, because I felt its better accuracy and higher velocity would offer better knock-down power. It did, to a point. Accuracy is vital, of course. You can't knock anything down, unless you hit it.

But looking back now, I have to chuckle at our collective ignorance — all of the competitors at that first match — in another area. Everyone had gone to that first silhouette match obsessed with accuracy, but no one had given much,

This .357 Auto Mag was equipped with an eight-inch barrel and was used by Gates in the 1975 match in Tucson. He downed turkey targets, five out of five, setting record in that meet. It's been repeated many times since then.

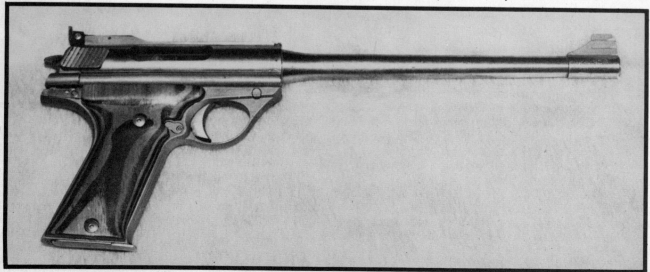

Lee Jurras, promoter of the first handgun silhouette meet ever held, converses with his spotter at the second championship shoot that was held in El Paso in October, 1976. The sport has expanded rapidly since that early era.

if any, thought to such things as remaining energy — a projectile's energy in foot-pounds at a given distance — remaining velocity or knock-down momentum.

On Lee Jurras' recommendation I had loaded all my .357 Auto Mag ammunition with one of his brand-new, highly touted, hunting bullets, a 137-grain hollow point.

Accurate? Yes, indeed. Flat trajectory? Yes. It was an ideal bullet for long-range hunting, but wasn't worth the proverbial damn for steel rams at two hundred meters.

I center-punched all five turkeys and down they went, the only 5x5 turkey score shot by anyone in the championships. Almost as easily, I center-punched the five

The steel rams, fired upon at a range of 200 meters, weigh 55 pounds each. Special cartridge development for these tough targets began about 1977 and has continued since, with silhouetters seeking the ultimate caliber.

METALLIC SILHOUETTE SHOOTING

Pistol at top is 1975 prototype experimental test gun in 7mm/06/1½ inches. That translates to a .30/06 full-length case cut to 1.5-inch length, necked to 7mm. This was forerunner of 7mm BR cartridge. Lower gun is a modern unlimited pistol on the XP-100 action in 7mm IHMSA International.

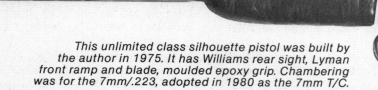

This unlimited class silhouette pistol was built by the author in 1975. It has Williams rear sight, Lyman front ramp and blade, moulded epoxy grip. Chambering was for the 7mm/.223, adopted in 1980 as the 7mm T/C.

rams. Only one went down. The other four hits with those 137-grain lead bullets produced nice, musical clangs.

During that long drive back home, I was pondering all of this. The old .357 magnum cartridge had been born in 1935 by the simple expediency of increasing the length of the .38 Special case from 1.155 to 1.290, an extra .135 or roughly, one-eighth-of-an-inch. It obviously was obsolete as far as knocking down fifty-five-pound steel rams reliably at two hundred meters.

Yes, with all the advertising hype, hoopla and public relations that went with it, you would think the 1935 .357 magnum was some kind of a fantastic new invention. In a way, I suppose it was. It was touted as the most powerful handgun cartridge in the world at the time of birth.

I was going on 14 in 1935, and had enough money from panning the tailings at the base of a stamp mill at one of Pop's mines in the Rocky mountains near Boulder, Colorado, that I could afford one of the new S&W .357 magnums. Pop ordered one, too. They cost sixty bucks then, a pile of

Black-maned African lion was taken during 1955 safari with 7mm/06 wildcat the author developed at the tender age of 13. Rifle is a sporterized Springfield which had been chambered for caliber.

money in the depression years, and it was about fifteen dollars more than the price of any of Smith & Wesson's other handguns. They didn't use model numbers then; it would become the Model 27 twenty-three years later, in 1957.

Pop was doing quite a bit of mining in those days. Gold had been selling for $20 an ounce up to 1933 when the Roosevelt regime raised it to $35 an ounce, so Pop reopened some of the old mines bearing low-grade ore that wouldn't pay a profit at $20 per ounce, but did pay fairly well at $35 an ounce. I spent the summers in the Colorado mountains hunting, fishing and panning gold.

When the new .357 S&W magnums came, both with six-inch barrels, we went over them with the proverbial fine-tooth comb. No doubt about it; they beat anything then on the market.

Phil Sharp, a well-known gun writer of the times, had been brewing up hot loads for the .38 Special during the early 1930s, looking for more power and urging S&W to build a stronger revolver to handle them. Winchester was

Author's first unlimited silhouette pistol was first fired in October, 1975. Frame was from a Thompson/Center Contender, while the barrel was a 7mm Mauser that had been cut off and rechambered to Gates' 7mm/.223 round.

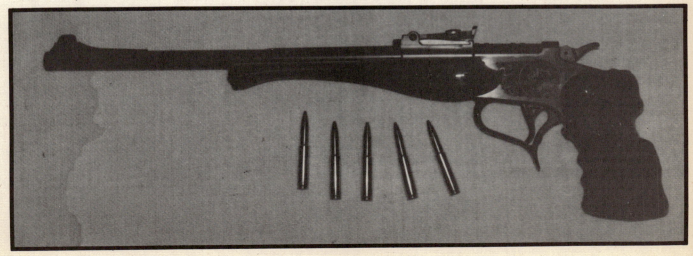

During 1957 safari in the Sahara Desert, the late Jack O'Connor used the author's 7mm/06, built in 1934, to bag several trophies. O'Connor is at right in photo.

Handmade dies were developed for loading special custom wildcat cartridges for early unlimited handguns. These dies are for the author's .30/.223 cartridge/gun combo.

brought into the act to develop a new cartridge, which they did. No great stroke of ballistic genius was involved; they simply lengthened the .38 Special case as described and that was it.

We measured the new .357 magnum case against the .38 Speical and Pop chuckled with delight. "A clever stunt," he said. "They lengthen the .38 Special case an eighth-of-an-inch so you can get more powder in it and, at the same time, the extra length will keep the cartridge from being fired in a .38 Special revolver and maybe blowing it up. Then advertise it as the most powerful handgun in the world and..."

"And everybody will want one," I finished for him, "Just like us."

"I think that's the idea," Pop said.

"Why not lengthen it some more and call it the .357 Super Magnum?" I asked.

"They might do that someday." Pop replied.

I would still remember our exchanged remarks thirty-five years later. They were prophetic.

In those early days of the .357 magnum, the revolvers came with a registration certificate. Ours were in the name of the dealer, but it didn't matter; we had the most powerful handguns available in hand!

The same stunt would be pulled twenty years later with the .44 Special, this time with Elmer Keith badgering Smith & Wesson. It was Remington instead of Winchester that would add an eighth-of-an-inch to the .44 Special case

Perhaps setting the trend for silhouette cartridges to come, Gates took these tusks from a huge elephant that he bagged with the old 7mm/06 wildcat of his youth. Tusks weighed 140 pounds each; the bullet was 165 grains!

and call it the .44 Remington magnum. More hype, PR and advertising would ensue and again we had "the most powerful handgun in the world."

Needless to say, I was a prime pigeon for the hype campaign and had one of the first Model 29 S&W .44 magnums to show up in Southern California, where I resided at the time.

When I showed it to Pop he grinned. "Same old trick," he said, "add an eighth-of-an-inch to the .44 Special, beat the drums, spend a million on advertising and we have another fantastic new invention, the .44 magnum!"

There was an interesting story at the time about how Bill Ruger got hold of one of the .44 magnum prototype cases that somebody picked up at the test ranges. That enabled him to get a jump on bringing out his own .44 magnum as the single-action Super Blackhawk. Chances are, only Ruger can verify the truth of this legend.

By the time the .44 magnum made its debut in 1955, I had done a fair amount of big-game hunting around the world since the end of WW II, and had enjoyed as a hobby the development of different cartridges of my own for hunting.

On most trips, I took as a spare rifle an old 7mm/06 sporterized Springfield that had been my first wildcat cartridge develpment in 1934 at the age of 13. With Pop's help I had rebarreled it with a 7mm Mauser military barrel and rechambered it to take a .30/06 case necked down to 7mm and shortened slightly to 2.250 inches. Wanting to keep it in its original configuration going back to 1934, for nostalgic reasons, I never was interested in putting a scope on it.

On a 1955 African safari, one of the gunbearers leaned my .300 Weatherby magnum against a tree during a lion hunt, while we took a quick lunch break. The rifle fell over, knocking the scope out of whack, so I had to use the old 7mm/06 for the rest of the trip. I bagged the lion with it, a beautiful black-maned specimen, using a 175-grain softpoint. Later, using some solid guilding metal bullets weighing 165 grains I had turned out on the lathe, I took a big elephant and other game with that same old rifle.

Two years later, I took it on a trip to French Equatorial Africa with Jack O'Connor as my hunting companion. As most sportsmen know, O'Connor was a small-bore fan, with the .270 Winchester his favorite. He wasn't too keen on the 7mm, but fell in love with my old 7mm/06 Springfield and used it to shoot several head of game when his .270 went on the fritz.

I also had used it and some other experimental rifles an cartridges to take smaller antelope and gazelle for t camp larder during a 1952 safari. These combinations h been worked up during the six months before the trip

Twenty-plus years after that trip, these would be s of the cartridges I would dig out of storage for the silhouette game. What prompted the development of wildcats in the first place was the fact that the .300 W erby magnum, while my all-time favorite long-range

METALLIC SILHOUETTE SHOOTING

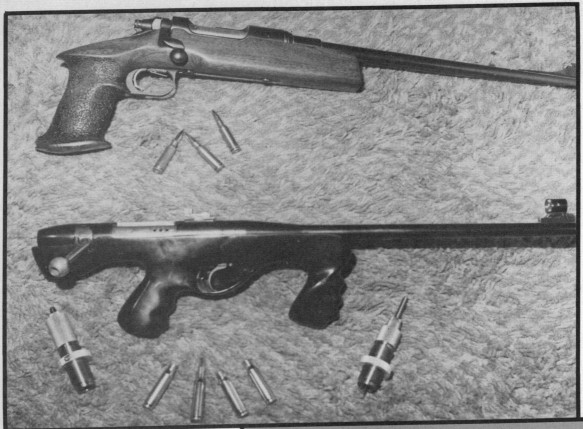

At top is early prototype unlimited gun on XP-100, chambered for the then experimental 7mm IHMSA International. Lower gun is on the Wichita action. Front handle was outlawed by BATF.

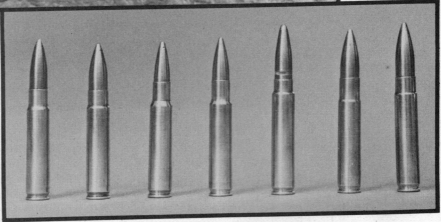

From left: 7mm/.223, the winningest cartridge in silhouette history; .30/.223; 6.5mm/.222 magnum; the 7mm/.222 magnum, 7mm/.222 magnum improved; .30/.222 magnum and the .30/.222 magnum improved caliber.

e, was too powerful for the small antelopes taken for meat or trophies. Sometimes, after being whopped a 180-grain soft-point or even a 180- or 200-grain partition bullet, there wasn't much left for the pot. military surplus rifles and equipment being imported merica from all over the world in that era, you em for as little as $10 each. It was a cheap way

o lightweight sporter-type rifles from these in my favorite 7mm and .30 calibers. For anish Model 93 Mausers chambered for 7mm, I simply set the barrel back and a cut-down 7x57 case. The measurewas 1.500 (1½ inches), but the final verall case length measured out to r rifle, I reworked a WWII Garauser action and chambered it to

the same intended length of 1.500. It came out at 1.528.

For loading dies, I simply cut off 7mm Mauser (7x57) and .30/06 dies with a carborundum cut-off stone at a carefully predetermined place. For cases, it was a matter of forming the shoulders back to the desired point, then trimming them to the correct length. The original shoulder angle of both parent cases was retained.

None of this cobblework on guns, dies or brass was to bench-rest precision and none of them would have won awards at a machinist's convention. Nevertheless, I had what I wanted: lightweight rifles with less than full-blown rifle cartridges. Many years later they would be effective in the handgun silhouette game.

At the time, having no thoughts of hanging a fancy name on these two creations, I simply called them the short 7mm and the short .30 cartridge when describing them to my hunting friends.

Perhaps setting the trend for silhouette cartridges to come, Gates took these tusks from a huge elephant that he bagged with the old 7mm/06 wildcat of his youth. Tusks weighed 140 pounds each; the bullet was 165 grains!

and call it the .44 Remington magnum. More hype, PR and advertising would ensue and again we had "the most powerful handgun in the world."

Needless to say, I was a prime pigeon for the hype campaign and had one of the first Model 29 S&W .44 magnums to show up in Southern California, where I resided at the time.

When I showed it to Pop he grinned. "Same old trick," he said, "add an eighth-of-an-inch to the .44 Special, beat the drums, spend a million on advertising and we have another fantastic new invention, the .44 magnum!"

There was an interesting story at the time about how Bill Ruger got hold of one of the .44 magnum prototype cases that somebody picked up at the test ranges. That enabled him to get a jump on bringing out his own .44 magnum as the single-action Super Blackhawk. Chances are, only Ruger can verify the truth of this legend.

By the time the .44 magnum made its debut in 1955, I had done a fair amount of big-game hunting around the world since the end of WW II, and had enjoyed as a hobby the development of different cartridges of my own for hunting.

On most trips, I took as a spare rifle an old 7mm/06 sporterized Springfield that had been my first wildcat cartridge develpment in 1934 at the age of 13. With Pop's help I had rebarreled it with a 7mm Mauser military barrel and rechambered it to take a .30/06 case necked down to 7mm and shortened slightly to 2.250 inches. Wanting to keep it in its original configuration going back to 1934, for nostalgic reasons, I never was interested in putting a scope on it.

On a 1955 African safari, one of the gunbearers leaned my .300 Weatherby magnum against a tree during a lion hunt, while we took a quick lunch break. The rifle fell over, knocking the scope out of whack, so I had to use the old 7mm/06 for the rest of the trip. I bagged the lion with it, a beautiful black-maned specimen, using a 175-grain softpoint. Later, using some solid guilding metal bullets weighing 165 grains I had turned out on the lathe, I took a big elephant and other game with that same old rifle.

Two years later, I took it on a trip to French Equatorial Africa with Jack O'Connor as my hunting companion. As most sportsmen know, O'Connor was a small-bore fan, with the .270 Winchester his favorite. He wasn't too keen on the 7mm, but fell in love with my old 7mm/06 Springfield and used it to shoot several head of game when his .270 went on the fritz.

I also had used it and some other experimental rifles and cartridges to take smaller antelope and gazelle for the camp larder during a 1952 safari. These combinations had been worked up during the six months before the trip.

Twenty-plus years after that trip, these would be some of the cartridges I would dig out of storage for the new silhouette game. What prompted the development of these wildcats in the first place was the fact that the .300 Weatherby magnum, while my all-time favorite long-range hunting

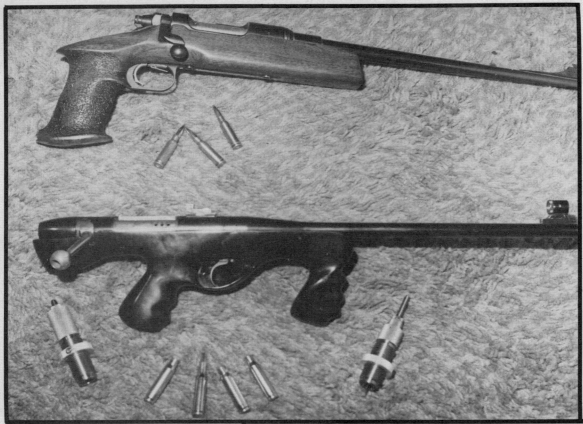

At top is early prototype unlimited gun on XP-100, chambered for the then experimental 7mm IHMSA International. Lower gun is on the Wichita action. Front handle was outlawed by BATF.

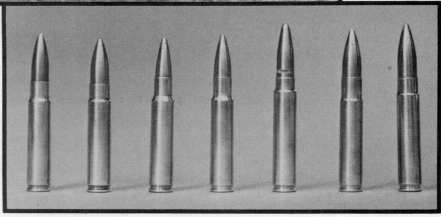

From left: 7mm/.223, the winningest cartridge in silhouette history; .30/.223; 6.5mm/.222 magnum; the 7mm/.222 magnum, 7mm/.222 magnum improved; .30/.222 magnum and the .30/.222 magnum improved caliber.

rifle, was too powerful for the small antelopes taken for camp meat or trophies. Sometimes, after being whopped with a 180-grain soft-point or even a 180- or 200-grain Nosler partition bullet, there wasn't much left for the pot.

With military surplus rifles and equipment being imported into America from all over the world in that era, you could buy them for as little as $10 each. It was a cheap way to experiment.

I made up two lightweight sporter-type rifles from these old military guns in my favorite 7mm and .30 calibers. For both I used old Spanish Model 93 Mausers chambered for the 7x57. For the 7mm, I simply set the barrel back and rechambered it to take a cut-down 7x57 case. The measurement I was aiming for was 1.500 (1½ inches), but the final chamber depth for the overall case length measured out to 1.532. For the .30 caliber rifle, I reworked a WWII Garand barrel, fitted it to the Mauser action and chambered it to the same intended length of 1.500. It came out at 1.528.

For loading dies, I simply cut off 7mm Mauser (7x57) and .30/06 dies with a carborundum cut-off stone at a carefully predetermined place. For cases, it was a matter of forming the shoulders back to the desired point, then trimming them to the correct length. The original shoulder angle of both parent cases was retained.

None of this cobblework on guns, dies or brass was to bench-rest precision and none of them would have won awards at a machinist's convention. Nevertheless, I had what I wanted: lightweight rifles with less than full-blown rifle cartridges. Many years later they would be effective in the handgun silhouette game.

At the time, having no thoughts of hanging a fancy name on these two creations, I simply called them the short 7mm and the short .30 cartridge when describing them to my hunting friends.

Early silhouetters wanting to use the XP-100 had to start with .221 Fireball (bottom). Gun at top has been converted to .30 IHMSA Intl.

Unlimited kit was available to IHMSA members. It consisted of XP-100 .221 barreled action, a Peterson wood stock, Douglas barrel from JGS Machine, dies by RCBS, cartridge brass from Federal. Cartridge boxes contain various calibers in International chambering series.

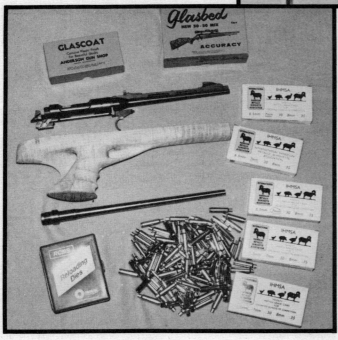

Nine years later, in 1961, Frank Barnes would produce his own version in .30 caliber, known as the .308x1.5-inch Barnes, which received wide publicity at the time. Barnes' design and dimensions certainly were more precise than my own crude cut-off cases. His .30 case came out exactly at 1.500 with a shoulder angle of twenty degrees, while mine was 1.528 with a seventeen-degree shoulder angle.

In 1976 and 1977, I rebarreled XP-100s to take my own short 7mm and .30 caliber versions. In 1979, Remington met the overwhelming demand for an economy, unlimited silhouette pistol by bringing out a new version of their XP-100 with fourteen-inch barrel chambered in what they would call the 7mm BR cartridge. Remington used their .308 full-length, small primer pocket case as the parent and wound up with a 1.520-length case with a thirty-degree shoulder angle as compared to my 1952 creation of 1.532 with a twenty-degree shoulder.

I probably had as much influence as anyone in getting Remington to bring out the 7mm BR XP-100 silhouette pistol. In the 1977-1979 period, we had to buy the complete XP-100 in .221 Fireball just to get the needed action. I tried time and again to get Remington to sell us XP-100 actions only, but they declined on the basis that it was company policy because of potential liability, et al.

Finally, in early 1979, I had a talk with Jack Preiser, one of the Remington officials. I had sent them a drawing previously of my short 7mm cartridge. What I wanted at the time, seeing as how they wouldn't sell actions separately, was to buy a quantity of barreled actions which do appear on their parts list. Obviously, no manufacturer the size of Remington would be interested in a small order on a special basis, so I was prepared to give them a substantial order when I called Presier.

At the time I gave him quite a spiel — all true — about how the silhouette game was coming on strong and what demand there was for XP-100 actions for rebarreling into something more powerful than the .221 Fireball. I emphasized that we needed it in 7mm or .30 caliber with a fourteen- or fifteen-inch barrel for our unlimited game.

Sure enough, one of his first questions was how many did I want, just in case they would consider the matter as a special or contract order.

I told him I would give him a firm order for 1000 on an exclusive basis, if they would supply it as described, with a short cartridge like the one on the print I had sent, 7mm preferred, and factory formed brass to go with it.

Preiser said he would put it before the board. He said it was obvious the silhouette game was coming on as I described and that we were getting serious about the matter.

Remington put their research and development department to work on the project and, while my order for 1000 barreled actions was never officially accepted, I did cut a deal to get the first two hundred of the new XP-100 7mm BR silhouette pistols that came off the line in the spring of 1980.

The bottom line was that they refined my short 7mm cartridge slightly, reducing the case length from 1.532 to 1.520 as previously described, changing the shoulder angle

METALLIC SILHOUETTE SHOOTING

Jim Stekl was a member of the R&D team that developed the XP-100 7mm BR silhouette pistol. It was added to the Remington line-up in 1980, with its longer barrel.

IHMSA headstamp with a ram on the base of brass for the 7mm IHMSA International cartridge was produced by Federal under contract. More than half a million rounds have been sold throughout the free world to silhouetters.

from twenty to thirty degrees. Also, they used their own small primer pocket .308 full-length BR case as the parent. This proved to be the one fly in the ointment, so to speak, about the whole project. They kept promising to make ready-to-load brass on a month-to-month basis, but it never came. It would be six years later — May 1986 — before Remington would supply formed 7mm BR brass.

In the meantime, it was a nightmare for individual silhouetters to form the full-length .308 BR brass down to the 1.520 length for the new XP-100 7mm BR pistol. The custom set of form dies alone cost about $100 and the forming process was long and complicated.

In the face of this, what I did was to rechamber most of the two hundred guns to my own 7mm IHMSA International cartridge. It not only had more horsepower, but factory-formed brass was available. I had persuaded Federal to run off an order of 500,000 rounds; a special order with the IHMSA headstamp that included an imprinted ram.

Another short rifle used on a 1957 African safari with a hunting friend, Roy Rogers, was an old falling-block Remington Hepburn No. 3 single-shot from the 1880s. I had picked it up at a gun show to get the action. The barrel was rusted out. I rebarreled it with a .358 caliber barrel for a deliberate reason: that long ago discussion with Pop about a still-longer .357 magnum case. The best available parent case was the old .32-30 Remington which, though a collector item by then, was fairly easy to convert to a long .357 magnum. This case was 1.640 inches in length, the measurement which was later to be the basis of an entire series of 1.600-inch silhouette cartridges I would develop as Super Mags.

For the African trip I had only eighteen .32-30 cases converted, plus a set of hand-made dies, powder, primers and bullets for reloading.

Over the years, I worked on dozens of other cartridges as a hobby during periods of spare time. None of them were earth-shaking and most didn't amount to anything. I've specifically described the genesis of the short 7mm and .30 caliber cases and the long .357 Super Mag from those early days, as they would become somewhat popular in the handgun silhouette game.

To say it again, I was thinking of all this during that long drive home from Arizona in 1975. What I felt we needed for those heavy steel rams was some higher velocity car-

Author chambers XP-100 pistol to 7mm IHMSA International caliber under supervision of Jim Cuthbert, owner of JGS Die & Machine. This firm makes excellent reamer line.

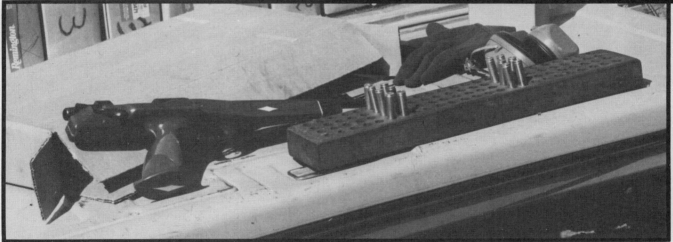

Below: In background is a part of shipment of 200 XP-100 Silhouette BR guns that the author chambered for 7mm IHMSA International round.

tridges and the handguns to handle them. There had long been a big gap where handgun cartridges stopped and rifle cartridges took over. It was time to fill it.

Going back first to my 1952 developments and using the .308 case this time, I cut it down from its 2.015 length to 1.750 and 1.500. This latter case, known as the .308x1½, is the one I've described as being created by Frank Barnes in 1961. It originally was intended for military use. Eventually, benchrest shooters tried it. I then necked these .30 caliber versions down to 7mm, as described previously. As a sort of afterthought, I also shortened one of them to 1.860.

Over a year later — after a great deal of testing, experimentation, load development and even computer analysis — I settled on the 1.860-inch length with a thirty-eight-degree shoulder angle as being the ultimate unlimited cartridge. The long, painstaking work was not in vain. The 7mm IHMSA International quickly became, and remains to this day, the most popular and successful unlimited cartridge in use.

The first gun I crudely cobbled together during the last days of September and early October of 1975 was a gunsmith's nightmare, but it worked. I used an old 7mm Mauser military rifle barrel cut down to 16½ inches and adapted it to fit a T/C Contender frame. This rig was what I intended to use in experimenting with some of the smaller rifle cases like the .223 Remington for which I had lots of experimental brass.

Back in the 1957-59 period, I lived in Newport Beach, California, about two miles from Costa Mesa, where the Fairchild Company was developing the AR-15 rifle. From a friend who worked there, I got a plentiful supply of prototype test ammunition and brass which I played with and kept.

Obviously, the .22 projectiles would be ineffective against the rams, so I used a standard .223 body reamer to chamber the barrel and a 7mm neck reamer. After some initial frustrations I had a pistol that would take the full-length .223 case expanded to 7mm. It is known today as the 7mm/.223, its correct generic name, or as the metric 7x45. Four years later, as the silhouette game began to shift into overdrive, Thompson/Center would adopt it as the 7mm TC.

That prototype gun, which I still have, was crude and ugly and weighed about five pounds, as did most of the

Author's early experiments include (from top) Ruger frame handling a .223 case cut to 1.5 inches, necked to 6.5mm; unlimited revolver in .50 short magnum caliber; a bull barrel Contender .338 IHMSA International.

This kit for an unlimited XP-100 allows rebarreling to IHMSA .270 International. Kit included needs for bedding factory Zytel stock.

other prototype guns I cobbled together for other test cartridges.

The first shot out of my 7mm/.223 prototype was fired on the morning of October 7, 1975. Unless someone built an unlimited silhouette handgun between September 21 and October 7, 1975 — and no one has ever made that claim — then mine was the first.

Being between projects as a land developer, I was able to spend the better part of four months working up cartridges for this exciting new silhouette game.

As military brass was cheap and plentiful, I chose the aforementioned two basic cases to work with: the .223 and the .308. Somewhere in that unknown area between existing pistol cartridges and rifle cartridges there had to be potential cartridges that would be ideal for shooting silhouettes.

Using a variety of jury-rigged dies and home-made expanders, I started with the .223 case at its full length of 1.760 inches and first expanded the neck to 7mm as described. I also expanded it to 6.5mm and .30 caliber. Then I shortened a batch of .223 cases to 1.500 and repeated the neck expansion process used for the longer cases. I also made up several similar versions from the commercially available and slightly longer .22r Remington magnum.

The same basic procedure was followed with the .308 case, although I must admit I did not consider using it as a full-length case for handgun silhouette at the time. These experiments were carried out with rebarreled XP-100

The author fires the .44 Auto Mag at silhouettes at the Black Canyon range in Phoenix, Arizona, using his standing position. Such experience showed that the game called for more impressive calibers in order to win.

actions, as I was somewhat apprehensive about using these larger, more powerful cartridges in the Contender frame. At that time, I believed that full-length rifle cartridges of the .308 type would be too powerful to use in handguns. I was wrong. In the years to come, XP-100s would be rebarreled and chambered in every full-length rifle cartridge known, inluding the .458 Winchester magnum!

By the spring of 1977, eighteen months after my initial cartridge experiments and developments, word of the new silhouette game and the new unlimited pistols was spreading like wildfire. Every shooter and every gunsmith in the country was getting into the act and the great unlimited cartridge and pistol race was on.

It quickly became popular — and it still is — for some gunsmith to change the taper of a case body a degree or two, add or subtract .010 from the length — even the big companies do it — change the slope of the shoulder a degree or two; or move it up or down a few thousandths and then send a print in to one of the die making companies and have their name stamped on the dies. Presto! A new cartridge: The 6.5mm Garfinkle, the .297 John Doe or the .344 MacNamara. There's nothing wrong with this. It's the spice of the sport, a sense of accomplishment and the fun of the game — not to mention the personal satisfaction that comes from knocking down the rams with your own creation from case to dies to the final bullet, primer and powder combination.

During the great unlimited gun race of the late 1970s, custom Douglas barrels chambered for the unlimited International series of cartridges were contoured and threaded to fit the XP-100 action that was then popular.

In a personal sense, I never considered hanging my own name on the cartridges I created and developed, but I have no problems with those who do. It's just a matter of personal preference. Maybe I just never believed anyone would be interested in buying a 7mm Gates, a .322 Basull, or a .305 Edsel. Ford Motor Company learned a lesson on that one thirty years ago!

Whatever the merits of naming cartridges may have been in those early days of the silhouette sport, the floodgates had been opened on a new world of long-range handgunning. A new dimension had been added in the form of potent and exciting unlimited pistols that would change the handgun world, the firearms industry and the very art of reloading, itself.

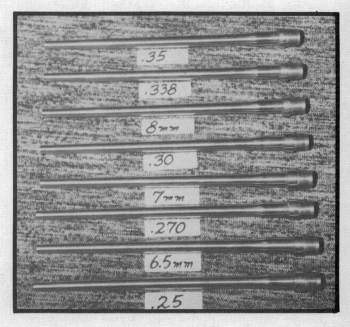

David Bradshaw demonstrates classic Creedmoor position used in silhouette shooting. Revolvers require use of a blast shield made of Kevlar body armor to protect against cylinder gap blast, lead shaving. Gun is M29 .44 magnum.

TIPS & STRATEGIES FOR WINNING

The Basics Are Simple, But Concentration Is A Must!

HOW SHOULD a beginning silhouette shooter practice? Answer: Live in the present. Apply the ethic of the hunter — one shot. Identify the target; fix it in your mind. Focus your eyes on the sights, concentrating finally on the front sight. Be absolutely specific about where the bullet will go.

Relax as you draw your bead on the target. The gun must "hang naturally" on the target. If it does not, adjust your position until it does.

Remember, if you force the gun, you expose yourself to flinching and a rude awakening on recoil, as the target stands in regal contempt of your fire!

Creedmoor Position: Stand, facing the target squarely. Spread your feet approximately two feet apart. Sit. Recline with knees drawn up. Let the knees drop together.

Reach your off-hand behind your head as though to touch behind your shoulder blades. Rest your knowledge box on your forearm. With the elbow of your gun hand a few inches to the side of your hip, place your gun against your thigh. Again, if the sights do not align naturally upon the target, adjust your position until they do. Do not touch the trigger, nor put your finger into the trigger guard, until you are *on target, ready to fire.*

Inhale through the nose, exhale through the mouth. When everything "smells magic," then fire. That is to say, gently build up pressure on the trigger until it breaks. If you

CHAPTER 5

Bradshaw demonstrates the proper hold for the standing position for silhouette. He has Ruger silhouette model.

are locked on the target and start the trigger squeeze, you will not know yourself when the trigger is going to release the firing pin or hammer. If you consciously "pull" the trigger, this is a form of flinch and your chances of hitting the target are not good.

Ride the gun on recoil. You have gripped it lightly, not with a white-knuckle death grip. Your mind is on the purity of holding the gun on target and "squeezing" the trigger. Do not resist or otherwise worry about recoil. Above all, do not anticipate recoil. To do so is an error. Go for the ride when the recoil comes. "Going for the ride" is called follow-through.

Standing Position: Stand facing the target squarely. Lead slightly with our left foot (right-hand shooters). Extend both hands toward the target for maximum eye relief. Support the weight of the gun evenly in both hands. Think and shoot with exactly the same confidence and determination you bring to freestyle — Creedmoor — shooting.

Dry fire and live fire are the same thing, with the exception that you can trace the cleanliness of your letoff when you dry fire. Live fire, of course, is the measure of marksmanship.

What effect does changing light have on sight settings? The high-power rifleman knows "sun high, sights high." However, IHSMA silhouette has thrown some wrenches into the art and science of iron sighting that have permanently damaged the teachings of Camp Perry. One thing holds true: the sun does pull POI (point of impact) toward itself.

The unique problem facing the silhouetter is that his targets are unique — each and every single one is different than the one before. The target shooter has a bull and circles printed on the same paper on the same plane.

A .44 magnum, sighted for rams in Vermont, may shoot twenty inches to two feet high in Arizona. By the same token, you may need more elevation as the day's light ends, for to engage a target, reliably, it must be seen; when you drop your sight picture to fix your target in fading light, you must crank your elevation up to compensate.

To know what effect light plays upon your eyes and mind, you must be confident of your marksmanship. Otherwise, adjustments will be made purely in reaction to one's own poor marksmanship.

See always the same sight picture. *Focus brain on target. Focus eyes on sights.*

What is the effect of wind blowing, either from behind or onto the shooter? Wind from behind lifts the POI. A wind from either three or nine o'clock is a "full value" wind and will bend the path of a bullet more than any other wind of the same velocity.

My windage rule: Read and believe wind on the javelina targets at one hundred meters. Chickens at fifty meters are met by bullets traveling at their best velocity. Thus, the wind has minimal time to deflect a bullet at fifty meters. Light is much more likely to displace POI at fifty meters than is wind.

Taking advantage of rugged terrain, this silhouette target layout is situated so several shooters can compete.

METALLIC SILHOUETTE SHOOTING

Four sets of turkey silhouettes are arranged on wooden rails. Each of the targets is of three-eighths-inch steel.

Javelinas, on the other hand, offer a broad surface on which to read wind drift. Believe the wind at the javelinas and adjust the rear sight accordingly. Always move a rear sight in the direction you want your shots to go. This is a fundamental that must be ingrained.

A windage adjustment for javelina targets must be doubled for turkeys, tripled for rams. The effect of wind on revolver bullets is vastly greater than is the same wind on single-shot pistols firing rifle bullets. Bullets from unlimited guns are even less affected.

Believe you can hit the target. Then hit the target.

One shot at a time, think of the target you have your sights on. At this moment, neither the last target nor the next target exists. A perfect 40x40 does not exist in the present. A 40x40 is an event that has transpired. A 40 is forty separate, single shots, one shot at a time. Over and over, again.

Marksmanship requires such fearsome concentration. Marksmanship is the structured application of art and science to reach out and touch and permanently change a target beyond the immediate reach. It is done with a bullet. You can only control the bullet before it leaves the barrel. After that it is on its own.

For the veteran handgunner, participation in silhouette matches stimulates the refinement of technique. For the beginning silhouetter, competition affords a rapid acquirement of basic marksmanship skills.

Veterans and beginners alike will benefit from a periodic examination of their shooting habits. Without this self-assessment, sloppiness is almost certain to infect shooting behavior; a collapse of technique will result.

Gun preparation, ammo preparation and shooter preparation all must be in order before match time. Preparation of gun and ammo is beyond the scope of this piece; I place it in front of the shooter to emphasize that for the shooter unsure of his gun and ammunititon, it will be virtually impossible to concentrate on the business of dispassionately dispatching silhouettes!

Nevertheless, a few gun notes won't hurt. Presuming the gun meets the accuracy standard of IHMSA silhouette — at fifty meters: bolt pistol, one-quarter-inch to one inch; single shot, one-half inch to 1½ inches; revolver, one inch to two inches — some basics much be adhered to.

a. Keep all screws snugged. Check the screws on a revolver after every match and following each practice session; likewise T/C forends.

b. Return rear sight to chicken adjustment after coming off rams. If windage has been moved, return it to zero.

c. Clean bore periodically with twenty to forty strokes of a solvent-saturated bronze brush; let stand at least one night before cleaning with flannel patches. Keep muzzle downhill of action.

d. Lubricate sight adjustment screws. Lubricate bolt locking lugs of XP-100 to prevent galling.

e. Keep T/C bolt dry.

f. Do not over-lubricate any handgun.

g. Shoot the match with ammunition of known performance and for which sight settings are established.

Shooter preparation: For one month leading up to the regional championships, I had almost no opportunity to practice or compete. I didn't worry about it, for to fret over competition leads only to disaster. My confidence sprang from the fact that during that time I kept a reasonably serious mind to the tasks at hand, knowing that when the blue chips were in the pot, my long-practiced shooting techniques would become instinctive.

Coach versus Spotter: Spotting is an activity of surprising difficulty in that it requires constant watch be kept for exactly where each bullet strikes its target and, when that fails to happen, exactly where it misses. The spotter should use a spotting board to convey to the shooter the exact whereabouts of each shot immediately after it is fired. My spotter, David Bradshaw, not only is a top champion in his own right, but is a coach and spotter of no mean ability.

Whereas spotting is passive or, at most, suggestive, coaching involves giving directions. Shooters new to silhouette shooting especially will benefit from thoughtful instruction. Both shooter and coach must be open-minded and flexible for the relationship to work; the shooter must learn to repeat over and over the fundamental acts of marksmanship and, for instance, to be unafraid of adjusting his sights when it becomes necessary; the coach to patiently steer the shooter into a confident performance.

It is a sin for a spotter or coach to exclaim, "That bullet went over the turkey's back, one foot out at two o'clock!" when, in fact, he failed to see the shot and had no earthly idea where it went.

A competitor should not be interrupted during the course of fire for any reason other than a safety violation. The rules so specify. It is the job of the spotter/coach to keep wellwishers, friends and those bearing political messages away from the shooter.

But it was politics that did me in. David Bradshaw, as chairman of the IHMSA safety committee, received an urgent message that drew him from the firing line after I had downed the first five chickens. Ten more chickens to go. Chickens usually are easy and I did not lose my concentration. Then, while the second bank of targets were being reset, a runner from the stathouse, ignorant of the rule to not disturb a shooter, came and handed me a note. Yes, it was a poitical problem. I tried to shut it out of my mind, but did not quite succeed. The first chicken of the last bank remained in place after my shot.

Bradshaw got back when I was on the second bank of javelinas, but it was over for me. A 59x60 — it was a sixty-round match — in the International class would be good for only fourth place.

Then it was Bradshaw's turn and we got down to the business of getting him through the course of fire without interruption, if possible.

Everchanging light conditions and shimmering mirages plagued all shooters as high noon came upon us. Temperatures hovered near the 100-degree Fahrenheit mark. The range faced north, fortunately, and the sun was almost directly overhead. There was no cover over the firing line. Competition in the morning had enjoyed a measure of pro-

A range officer spray paints a ram target to eliminate the bullet splashes from the previous relay. Note that the feet of the rams overhang the rear edge of stands. This rule tends to reduce overloading of cartridges.

METALLIC SILHOUETTE SHOOTING

Many spotters prefer binoculars to spotting scopes. Use of both eyes makes it easier to follow bullet flight.

Shooter uses the Creedmoor position, while his spotter waits with spotting scope to tell him where he hit.

tection from a flat gray haze that did not burn off until noon. Then came the mirages that tortured sight pictures and caused many bullets to sail wildly away from where they were aimed.

The early afternoon sun also made it difficult — sometimes impossible — to see bullets in flight. Yes, when conditions are normal, and the spotter is correctly positioned behind his shooter, you can actually see the bullets in flight as they seem to rise above the target, then slope down to hit — or miss.

This is why I prefer to spot with a pair of quality binoculars rather than a spotting scope. Spotting with binoculars works the eyes evenly and keeps them balanced and sharp for shooting. I used a pair of Zeiss 10x40 armored binoculars. These feature fully internalized central focusing. The Zeiss is incredibly sharp, has great depth of field and, for the observation of bullets in flight, is an excellent combination. Light transmission of the Zeiss leaves spotting scopes in the dust.

To spot chickens, I focus right on. At one hundred meters, I focus on the javelina, then draw in the focus about ten meters. For the turkey, I draw in twenty meters or so by focusing on grass or ground objects in front of the targets. Focus is set at about thirty meters in front of the rams. These adjustments permit focal interception of a bullet's flight to the target. The Zeiss 10x40 is lashed to a tripod with rubber bands.

I issued commands and reminders, as Bradshaw relentlessly knocked down one silhouette at a time with carefully timed, deliberate fire. His concentration was awesome. He followed the dictum laid down at the beginning of this chapter. After all, he was the one who compiled it.

It would be tedious to describe each shot, but each one

was a hit. Not all were perfect center punches, but under the conditions of light and heat, his performance was incredible as was that of two other International class shooters. All three of them shot perfect 60x60 unlimited category scores.

Then it was time for the shootoffs. Shootoff targets at that time were the option of the match sponsor. Some clever club member had hatched up plaster-of-paris chickens of standard size. They had been poured in a mould and were about one-inch in thickness. As the background was green grass, they were left their natural white color.

Bradshaw's gun was a Remington XP-100 rebarreled and chambered for the 7mm International. The stock was an H-S Fiberthane contour stock with thumbhole. It has a Bo-Mar rear sight and a Redfield International globe front sight with a .075-inch post mounted to the barrel via a Redfield .200-inch base. The load was Hornady's 175-grain spire-point with 30.8 grains of H4895, Federal IHMSA Ram headstamp brass and a Federal 210 Match primer.

The plaster chickens were set on the two-hundred-meter stands. To the naked eye they were barely visible. Through the Zeiss, they stood out clearly.

Bradshaw carefully prepared himself again and was the last to fire after the command was given. He was aware that the other two competitors had missed, but he was not distracted. His bullet rose up and over the target at its peak of trajectory, then arced down to explode the plaster chicken with a hit where the leg joins the body. I put a pin in the spotting board at that location and held it down where he could see it. He nodded, and proceeded to explode the other two chickens with two more deliberate shots to take the title and the trophy.

A matter of concentration.

David Bradshaw uses a Thompson/Center Contender in the standing position, the most difficult type of shooting. (Below) In the early days of the sport, most shooters used the front-facing prone position in silhouetting.

During an early match of the International Handgun Metallic Silhouette Association, author was drafted as a line officer.

FIRST MATCHES, EARLY HANDGUNS

Thousands Of Rounds Through A Hot-Loaded Handgun Makes It Obvious Which Will Last!

If you wonder about form, this was called freestyle, shooting in the forward facing prone position. The relay was firing at chickens during second sanctioned match of the new organization. Photo was taken in March, 1977.

ONCE THE International Handgun Metallic Silhouette Association was founded and its rules created, the privilege of holding the first sanctioned match was offered to Tucson. However, because of internal problems, they couldn't agree to abide by the new IHMSA rules and lost the opportunity.

Thus, the honor of holding the first IHMSA match went to the Angeles range located in the hills just north of Los Angeles, and was scheduled for January 8-9, 1977.

Sixty-six shooters from all over the Southwest went through the forty-round course of fire in the two categories created for IHMSA competition, production and unlimited. Production competition was in four classes: Unclassified for brand new shooters, class B for novices and classes A and AA for the more experienced handgunners.

Guns were mostly Model 29 S&W revolvers in .44 magnum with six- and eight-inch barrels. There were a few Rugers and Auto Mags. It was at this inaugural IHMSA match that the first inkling came that the much-touted S&W .44 magnum revolver had met its match, and then some.

As one of the official line officers for both days, I still bear a scar on the right side of my face from a chunk of lead shaved from a .44 magnum Smith & Wesson Model 29 that was starting to come apart, and two more scars on my left forearm from another S&W .44 that was out of time and shaving lead badly with every shot.

Until the silhouette game came along, S&W pistols — with their beautiful finish, had been highly respected in law enforcement work where practice was done with light, cream-puff wadcutter loads. To knock down fifty-five-pound, three-eighths-inch steel rams at two hundred meters required more firepower, consisting of heavier bullets and powder charges. The hard facts learned from the results of those early IHMSA silhouette matches quickly proved that some guns couldn't cut the mustard.

They did win at those first few matches simply because that was what just about everybody was shooting. Usually

METALLIC SILHOUETTE SHOOTING

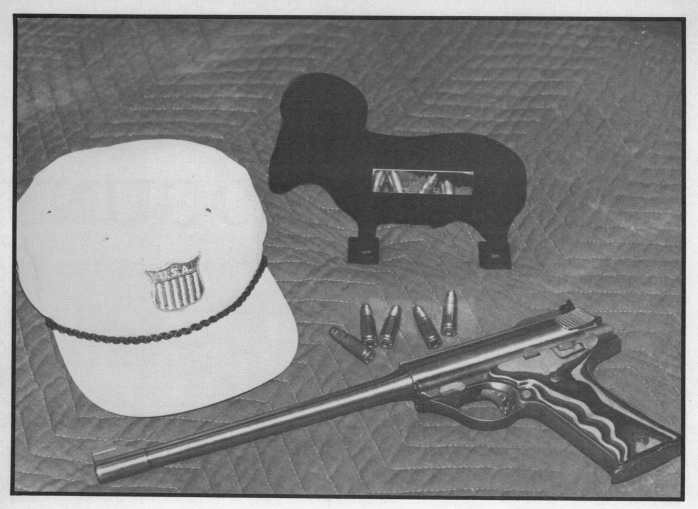
This .357 Auto Mag with an eight-inch barrel was used by the author during early IHMSA matches. He later used it to set the production gun record of 31X40 in the Canadian championships in June, 1977, winning the ram trophy.

it was a competitor with lighter loads whose S&W would get through the forty-shot course of fire. The sad fact was that S&Ws were not designed or built to take the rugged use they were being put to in shooting thousands of maximum loads at the steel silhouettes. That, of course, was not the intent when they were designed.

The ratio of S&Ws used in those first few matches was at least two to one over all other brands combined. I had retired my own S&Ws after the 1975 match at Tucson. They had begun to shoot loose, shave lead and lose accuracy. Careful examination after arriving home from the 1975 match had convinced me that, in spite of their reputation in law enforcement, they would never be in serious contention in the new silhouette game.

Ten yers of silhouette shooting have proved my contention. The only S&Ws seen in the game now are those used occasionally by brand new shooters just coming into the sport. Invariably, they soon switch to one of the more ruggedly built pistols that have been improved steadily by their makers. In the IHMSA .22 game and the new field pistol course of fire, where less power is required, some S&W revolvers are being used.

The real tragedy in those early years of silhouette shooting was that management of Bangor Punta, who owned S&W, refused to listen to silhouette shooters. They spurned the idea of building stronger, more rugged revolvers. To S&W officials of that era the silhouette sport was an oddball, flash-in-the-pan game that never would get off the ground. They had done quite well, of course, in building a menagerie of pretty guns for well over a hundred years and why should they waste money improving what they felt was already the ultimate revolver?

The more rugged, but not so pretty, Ruger Blackhawk did hold together under the grueling punishment of silhouette competition. Within three months of those first IHMSA matches, the switch-over was patently obvious. Ruger

With his son, Robert, acting as spotter, the author shoots at rams across the valley, 200 meters away. The turkeys at center right in photo were placed at 150 meters. The photo was taken during the first California IHMSA match.

pulled even with S&W and within six months it became a no-contest situation.

The thing that no one realized — including the manufacturers — was that, before the silhouette game came along, the man who bought a .357 or a .44 magnum probably would fire less than fifty rounds of factory ammunition through it during a lifetime. Revolvers didn't have to be all that rugged for this kind of minimal use. The thousands of rounds fired by silhouette shooters during practice and in official matches quickly brought out the design and workmanship flaws in any pistol.

There were a few exceptions, of course. Elmer Keith was one of them, firing thousands of rounds in the big magnums. While few knew it, he carried a crippled hand around for many years as a result of one revolver coming apart from some of his fancy loadings.

Dan Wesson, one of the newer revolver makers in the early days of handgun silhouette, listened to silhouette shooters and built a rugged, accurate, big-frame revolver that today totally dominates the revolver competition.

Unlimited competition at those early matches was a study in rapid development. Jose Porras, who won the 1976 championship at El Paso, had set the record then by knocking down thirty-three silhouettes out of forty. This stood for three months, until the first IHMSA-sanctioned match at Angeles range where I raised the record one point to 34x40 using a .30/.223 T/C Contender. Second place went to an XP-100 rebarreled and chambered in .308 full length, with third and fourth places going to S&W Model 29 .44 magnums.

For a production gun, I used a .357 Auto Mag with fair success. The action of the Auto Mag was strong enough; it was the small parts like firing pins, springs and other parts that would break and put the shooter out of the match.

The Thompson/Center Contender was slow in getting established in the early days. A single Contender in .44

Ray Chapman (left) was one of the co-match directors at the Angeles range meet. Gates was line officer for event.

magnum was used by Tom Beall in the 1975 match. A few were fired in the 1976 championships, mostly in unlimited-type configurations. During those first IHMSA-sanctioned matches of 1977, only three Contenders were in the first four places.

Neverless, it wasn't long before shooters realized that the single-shot Contender would be the wave of the future in silhouette competition. The designer, Warren Center, listened to us closely and soon began making excellent improvements in his pistol. As a result, the Contender came to be the winningest production pistol in the sport.

At the second IHMSA-sanctioned match in March, 1977, the first four places in unlimited went to XP-100s chambered for the .308x1½, which was the unlimited cartridge of that moment in time. The 34x40 record I had set in January was tied by Paul Boren of Los Angeles. Two months later, at the third IHMSA-sanctioned match, I had my 7mm International prototype working and raised the unlimited record to 38x40. A month after that, at the Canadian National Championships, I set the production gun record at 31x40 with the .357 Auto Mag. Neither record would last long. The new IHMSA handgun silhouette game was off and running and most of us felt the handgun world would never be the same again.

The results of these first IHMSA-sanctioned matches were published in the first and second issues of *The Silhouette,* which was created to report match results, test reports and other news for IHMSA.

Results of the first match sanctioned by IHMSA, January 8-9, 1977, at the Angeles Range, California.

UNLIMITED OPEN

1. Elgin Gates, Sr., Needles, CA	T/C .30-223	34
2. Buck Toddy, La Puente, CA	XP-100 .308	33
3. Al Seropian, West Covina, CA	S&W .44	24
4. Paul Boren, Montebello, CA	S&W .44	22

PRODUCTION AA

1. Paul Boren, Montebello, CA	S&W .44	29
2. Ron De Rosier, West Covina, CA	AMP .44	19
3. George Papac, Los Angeles, CA	S&W .44	19
4. Al Seropian, West Covina, CA	S&W .44	18

PRODUCTION A

1. Dave Whitman, Grand Terrace, CA	S&W .44	23
2. King Dalton, Ontario, CA	S&W .44	19
3. Mickey Fowler, Glendale, CA	S&W .44	17
4. Joe Garcia, Burbank, CA	S&W .44	16

PRODUCTION B

1. Al Leventoff, Sunland, CA	Ruger .41	20
2. Phil Harris, Walnut, CA	Ruger .44	13
3. Herb Haller, Los Alamitos, CA	AMP .44	12
4. Rod Guzman, Sylmar, CA	Ruger .44	11

UNCLASSIFIED

1. Jeff Dye, LaVerne, CA	S&W .44	24
2. Duane Otis, San Francisco, CA	S&W .44	18
3. John Adams, Jr., Torrance, CA	D. Wesson .357	16
4. Jim Licking, Los Angeles, CA	S&W .357	16

Results of the second match sanctioned by IHMSA, March 12, 1977, at the Angeles Range.

UNLIMITED

1. Paul Boren, Montebello, CA	XP-100 308x1½	34
2. Buck Toddy, LaPuente, CA	XP-100 308x1½	33
3. Mil Blair, Burbank, CA	XP-100 308x1½	33
4. Elgin Gates, Needles, CA	XP-100 308x1½	32

AA CLASS

1. Paul Boren, Montebello, CA	S&W .44	26
2. Al Seropian, West Covina, CA	Ruger .44	26
3. Elgin Gates, Needles, CA	AMP .357	25
4. John Adams, Redondo Beach, CA	Ruger .45 LC	15

A CLASS

1. King Dalton, Ontario, CA	S&W .44	26
2. Mickey Fowler, Glendale, CA	S&W .44	24
3. Dave Whitman, Grand Terrace, CA	S&W .44	22
4. Rene Zamorano, Huntington Park, CA	T/C-30H	22

METALLIC SILHOUETTE SHOOTING

B CLASS

1. Fred Darling, Lennox, CA	S&W .44	24
2. Mary Lindars, San Bernardino, CA	S&W .44	15
3. Al Leventoff, Sunland, CA	Ruger .41	14
4. Mil Blair, Burbank, CA	S&W .44	14

UNCLASSIFIED

1. John Sabol, Simi Valley, CA	S&W .44	24
2. Richard Frantz, Simi, CA	S&W .44	22
3. Jeff Dye, LaVerne, CA	S&W .44	22
4. Charles E. Green, Torrance, CA	T/C .30-30	21

Results of the third match sanctioned by IHMSA, May 14-15, 1977, at the Angeles Range.

UNLIMITED CLASS

1. Elgin Gates, Needles, CA	XP-100 7mm	38
2. David Engram, Flagstaff, AZ	T/C .30-223	34
3. Alan McKee, Los Angeles, CA	XP-100 7mm	32

PRODUCTION - AA CLASS

1. Paul Boren, Montebello, CA	AMP .357	27
2. Jeff Dye, Los Angeles, CA	S&W .44	23
3. Mickey Fowler, Glendale, CA	S&W .44	21
4. Buck Toddy, La Puente, CA	S&W .44	21

A CLASS

1. King Dalton, Ontario, CA	S&W .44	29
2. Fred Darling, Lennox, CA	S&W .44	29
3. Mark Yamamoto, Alamitos, CA	S&W .41	25
4. Duane Otis, San Francisco, CA	S&W .44	24

B CLASS

1. Rod Buzman, Orange, CA	S&W .44	21
2. Phil Harris, Walnut, CA	Ruger .44	15
3. Susan Stoops, Carson City, NV	S&W .357	9
4. Herb Haller, Los Angeles, CA	AMP .44	6

UNCLASSIFIED

1. Ron Rune, Los Angeles, CA	S&W .41	23
2. Jerry Montgomery, Montebello, CA	S&W .44	22
3. Jeff Dye, La Verne, CA	S&W .44	21
4. Herb Cox, Burbank, CA	S&W .44	20
5. Sam Wammock, San Fernando, CA	S&W .41	20

TOP PRODUCTION LADY

Sandy Bobich, Los Angeles, CA	S&W .44	18

Trophy winners at the first match ever sanctioned by IHMSA gathered with officials for group photos. Top row, fourth from left, is Dave Whitman, who has been a continuing force and won the IHMSA international revolver title in 1987.

An interesting sidelight to early reports on the matches was a letter that probably reflected the thinking at the time:

>I want to let you know there is a guy up here in Idaho (his initials are E.K.) who could make mincemeat out of your silhouette game. Among other things, he invented the .44 magnum and invented and designed all kinds of other guns, bullets, etc., and can he shoot! He bumps off deer and elk at six hundred to eight hundred yards with his sixgun regularly and used to practice on an outhouse at 1000 yards, hitting it with every pistol he picked up including a two-inch Colt slip gun. He has shot 250 jackrabbits at over two hundred yards with sixguns without a miss. I could go on and on and, if you don't believe any of this, why all you have to do is read about it as he has written it all up.
>
>Like I say, I could go on and on, but you must have the idea by now. He probably doesn't want to make any of your amateurs look bad, but if there was something to make it worthwhile, he might come down and take you to Tap City.
>
>R.S.

METALLIC SILHOUETTE SHOOTING

In the earliest days of handgun metallic silhouette, many contestants used the Smith & Wesson Model 29 .44 magnum. The maker even designed this version for the sport. Consensus, however, is that the Model 29 has not been engineered for thousands of heavy loads.

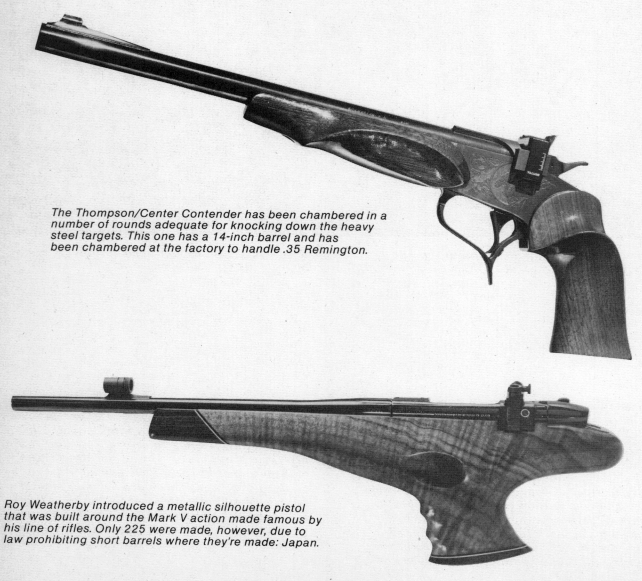

The Thompson/Center Contender has been chambered in a number of rounds adequate for knocking down the heavy steel targets. This one has a 14-inch barrel and has been chambered at the factory to handle .35 Remington.

Roy Weatherby introduced a metallic silhouette pistol that was built around the Mark V action made famous by his line of rifles. Only 225 were made, however, due to law prohibiting short barrels where they're made: Japan.

As the sport progressed, there was rapid development in unlimited guns. Optical sights were not legal, but tube sights were. Top gun is an XP-100 Remington chambered in .308x1½. Lower gun is chambered for the 7mm International, which was pioneered by the author. He set what then was a record for unlimited guns — 38x40 — in early history.

The tenor of the thinking among avid silhouette shooters of that era is reflected in another letter received in rebuttal:

We sure would admire to see some fancy shooting like that and while we realize he really could make mincemeat out of our silhouette game and win the silhouette national championships with one hand tied behind him with a two-inch snub-nose, we got some of the fellows together to work up a friendly wager at $1000 per shot. E.K. can fire the forty-shot handgun silhouette course with any gun and load of his choice, freestyle, as per IHMSA rules, against any one of the five shooters we will pick. E.K. can select one of the five or we will draw a name out of a hat. Anyway, E.K. and our shooter each fires through the course. At the end, the winner gets $1000 per shot for the difference in scores. For example, if E.K. knocks down 40x40 (well, hell, let's say he is human and misses one and ends up with 39x40) and our man only gets, say, 31. Then we will pay E.K. $8,000, as he would win by eight shots. Surely, this ought to make it worthwhile.

And on the same basis, a couple more of the guys would like to go the same route, so I reckon E.K. could tap the boys for an easy twenty-five to thirty Big Ones before they learn their lessons.

Of course, we reserve the right to sell tickets (and split the proceeds with E.K.) to this event as it ought to draw every gun owner in the Los Angeles basin and the fifty states, as well, to see in person the kind of shooting they have been reading about for forty years.

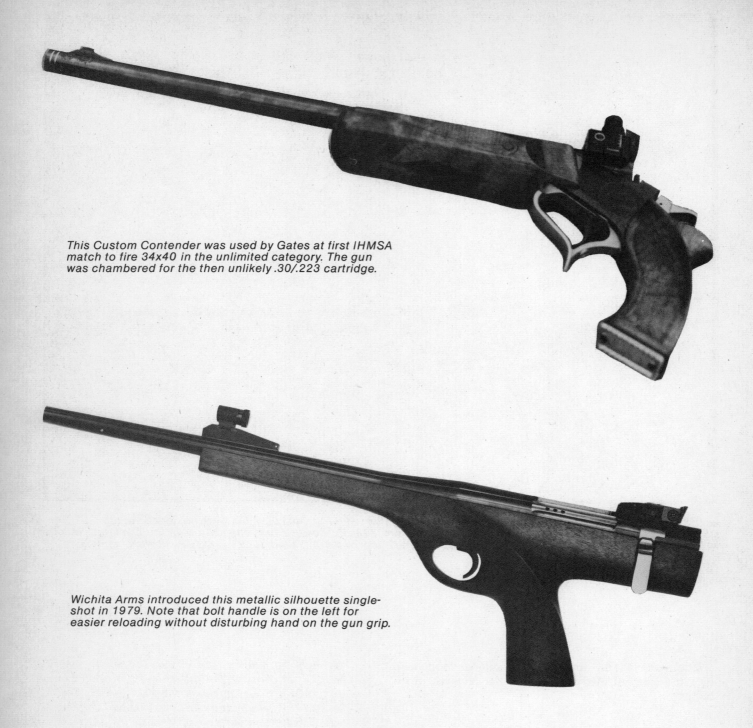

This Custom Contender was used by Gates at first IHMSA match to fire 34x40 in the unlimited category. The gun was chambered for the then unlikely .30/.223 cartridge.

Wichita Arms introduced this metallic silhouette single-shot in 1979. Note that bolt handle is on the left for easier reloading without disturbing hand on the gun grip.

It can be assumed that the critic of our infant sport was referring to the late Elmer Keith, a noted handgunner in his own right. The claims that the correspondent made for E.K. were drawn from the recorded feats of the late shooter and gun writer. There is no doubt that Elmer Keith — if that is the individual to whom the writer referred in his letter — deserved every iota of his fame. We all respected and admired him.

As far as is known, however, Elmer Keith never tried his talents on handgun silhouette shooting. At least, there is no record in the official records of the organization to show that he fired any sanctioned match.

But the spirit shown by the young silhouette shooters is reflected in the reply to our critic. The same spirit continues to this day.

At the Angeles range in California, three shooters on the right are firing downhill at turkey silhouettes set out at 150 yards. Relay on the left is firing across the valley, where the ram-shaped targets are at 200 meters.

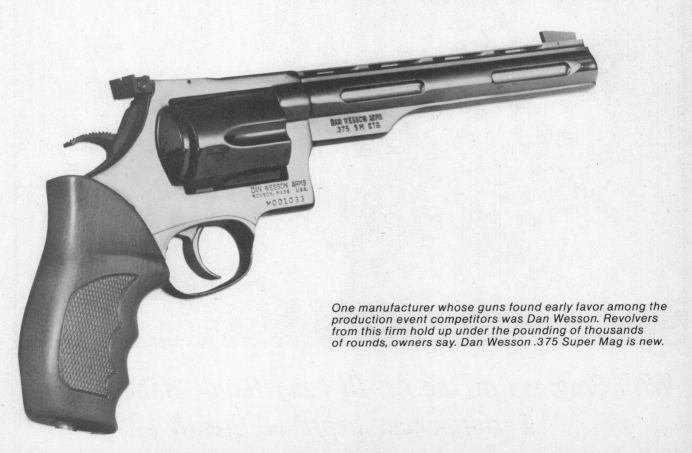

One manufacturer whose guns found early favor among the production event competitors was Dan Wesson. Revolvers from this firm hold up under the pounding of thousands of rounds, owners say. Dan Wesson .375 Super Mag is new.

METALLIC SILHOUETTE SHOOTING

CHAPTER 7 Outstanding Silhouette Records

With Progress In The Art Of Long-Range Handgunning, Performances Improved Greatly

Left: While many 40x40 unlimited category scores have been fired in IHMSA competition, 11-year-old Christy Smith of Alice, Texas, holds the record as the youngest to accomplish the feat. (Below) Bob Mijares (left) was first to fire 40x40 with a production handgun. Jack Beaumont presents him with an engraved T/C Contender.

Dave Whitman used a .44 magnum Ruger revolver to shoot the first IHMSA 40x40 score with a cylinder gun. This shooter has won All American honors in the organization.

SINCE THE IHMSA was formed in October, 1976, a great deal of progress has been made in long-range handgunning as to accuracy, shooting procedures, better equipment and loading techniques, not to mention improved bullets and other components.

While no attempt has been made to keep silhouette records at every club or even at the state level, IHMSA headquarters has kept track of the top records set at the national and international levels.

Shooting perfect 40x40 scores with unlimited guns started early in the game and soon became commonplace. Not so easy was the first 40 fired with a pure out-of-the-box genuine production gun. Some of the top competitors gave it their best shot from Day One, but it was almost three years before the first production gun 40 was fired.

The breakthrough came on July 28, 1979, at the West End Club near Ontario, California, when Bob Mijares fired the first production gun 40x40. In doing it, he baffled all the experts who felt you had to have everything perfect; tight gun, carefully trimmed and sized brass of the same lot number, exact powder charges to the tenth-of-a-grain, selected bullets of perfect concentricity, polished cases and so on.

Yes, Bob Mijares had luck, but he could shoot and he did, too. Here is the account as related in the official match report:

"On July 28, in the beautiful valley of the West End Gun Club, the sun was shining and the temperature warm enough for record-breaking weather. The weather didn't break any records, but Bob Mijares did with his standard, old-type Thompson/Center Contender in .357 Herrett. Bob shot an official production 40x40 for a new international record. He accomplished this extraordinary feat in the supine position on his back with his pistol between his knees and without a spotter or coach! And his Contender didn't have the new-fangled locking bolt that everybody is hot for.

"Bob, an AAA shooter, was asked about his ammunition and stated that he used Speer 250-grain spire-point bullets with whatever brass he had and without even trimming all the cases to any certain length. Load was 32 grains of IMR 4895.

"There were plenty of witnesses to Mijares' feat, and so there would never be any question about it, he offered his gun for tear-down inspection. Three of the range officers checked the gun thoroughly and reported it as being 'long-out-of-the-box' with the old-style skinny barrel, loose-as-a-goose in lockup with wobbly sights. His brass was what he bought in a sporting goods store grab bag and contained four different brands. It was dirty, untrimmed and Bob had been shooting it for about a year. Primers were standard large rifle, brand unknown. For the uninformed, .357 Herrett brass is made by cutting down and reforming stan-

Josie Engle, match director at the Piedmont Sportsman Club in Virginia, displays the standing form with which she fired a new record of 36x40 for the standing position. She used Thompson/Center .30-30 Contender to rack up score.

dard .30-30 Winchester cases."

Once the ice was broken with Bob Mijares shooting the first production 40x40, the feat has been duplicated numerous times over the years. All the same, shooting a perfect production gun silhouette score under IHMSA rules still isn't all that easy, and the ratio is about one perfect production gun 40x40 to every fifty shot with unlimited guns.

Through 1987, a perfect 40x40 score has never been shot from the standing position wherein shooters use the same production guns used in freestyle competition. Imagine, if you can, shooting from the standing position with the pistol extended straight out, held in both hands, with no support, such as resting elbows on the side of the body allowed, or any other such thing, and trying to knock down forty steel silhouettes from fifty to two hundred meters. This feat may never be accomplished, but IHMSA shooters have shot some scores that would have been declared impossible not many years ago.

The first truly remarkable standing score was a 36x40, shot in 1980 by a lady shooter in Virginia, whose score exceeded the previous standing record by four points! Here is the account of her remarkable performance written at the time:

"In a fantastic exhibition of shooting skill, All-American Josie Engle of Orange, Virginia, set two new handgun silhouette records, and did it in style!

"In June, 1980, at the Piedmont Sportsman Club, Gordonville, Virginia, Match Director Engle, after tending to the paper chores of the match, shot her standing event and proceeded to smash the standing record by a full four points with an unbelievable 36x40! (That qualifies as a Triple-A freestyle unlimited score!)

"If that wasn't enough, Josie already had shot a 39x40 in unlimited plus a 34x40 in production freestyle, totaling up to a sizzling all-round total of 109x120, another record, which puts her at the top of the President's 100-Club list.

"Josie using a standard, out-of-the-box Thompson/

Illinois competitor Carter Jones displays record-setting style that enabled him to set all-time 37x40 standing score.

Center Contender chambered in .30-30 with a ten-inch barrel, calmly mowed down nine of ten chickens, ten of ten pigs, and ten of ten TURKEYS! She bobbled just a bit on the first stage of rams, missing three of the five, but she came right back and cleaned the rail of the last five in a row!

"As a family-oriented handgun sport, and the most popular shooting game in the country, IHMSA boasts a whole cadre of the fair sex who are shooting up a storm, east, west, north and south. I've written before that handgun silhouette is a woman's game too. Does anyone need any more proof?

"And guys, you had better get your acts together, or Cool Hand Josie Engle and any one of a dozen or more gals from Maine to California will take you to tap city any weekend in the year.

"Loads were 20 grains of 4759 with Hornady 150-grain spire point bullets on chickens, pigs and turkeys; and 37 grains of H380 with 168-grain Hornady match bullets on rams."

Josie Engles' record was tied in August, 1981, by Tom Colassanto, IHMSA's Connecticut state director, with ten chickens, ten javelinas, nine turkeys and seven rams.

The standing record held until June 23, 1984, when Carter Jones of Champaign, Illinois, raised it by one point to 37x40 at a regular IHMSA-sanctioned match using a

METALLIC SILHOUETTE SHOOTING

Allen Kirchner, a silhouette shooter from South Carolina, was the third contestant ever to shoot an official 40x40 score with a revolver. To accomplish this feat, he used a Colt Python revolver featuring 8-inch barrel.

Thompson/Center Contender chambered for the 7mm/.223 and called the 7mm TC.

Jones used 24.5 grains of IMR 4895 with a Hornady 162-grain HPBT bullet and a Remington 7½ BR primer. When asked about his ideas on successful standing performance, Jones said the heart of his system was trigger let-off which he rated as more important than stability. Carter Jones' record remains the highest standing silhouette score ever shot, and may last for many years — if not for all time.

One of the long awaited IHMSA silhouette records was a perfect 40x40 fired with a revolver. Experienced silhouette shooters know that single-shot pistols are inherently more accurate than revolvers for reasons that are too obvious to go into.

Partial proof of this was the prolonged delay in achieving a revolver 40x40. The first single-shot 40 was fired in July of 1979 as related above, and while revolver-fired 37s, 38s and 39s were the proverbial dime-a-dozen, it would be December, 1981, before the long-awaited revolver 40 would make silhouette history. Following is the official account:

"Three-time All-American Dave Whitman of Colton, California, IHMSA Life Member No. 19, shot the first and long-awaited perfect 40x40 at an IHMSA sanctioned match with a revolver. To be exact, Dave did it with a new out-of-the-box .44 magnum Ruger Super Blackhawk with a 10½-inch barrel. The date was December 19, 1981.

"Needless to say, it was a delightful Christmas present. But that wasn't all. Dave shot a standing 30 on Saturday the 19th to go along with his revolver 40, then on Sunday, the second day of the match, he whipped off two more 40s in unlimited and production for the long coveted 150 four-gun aggregate, a feat that was part of, and barely overshadowed by his six-gun 40."

"In case anyone thinks it was a fluke or an accident, let's start at the beginning and let Whitman tell the story:

"The revolver was a new Ruger 10½-inch Super Blackhawk .44 magnum with Pachmayr grips. I had just taken possession of the gun on December 10 and fired twelve rounds through it to get sighted in at fifty meters on the morning of the 12th. Later that same day I went to a small match in Meyers Canyon to get sight settings for the pigs, turkeys and rams. When I arrived, Ray Stafford, the new

Philip Braud, a resident of Louisiana, was the second member of IHMSA to score a 40x40 perfect with a wheelgun. This particular score was shot with his Dan Wesson .357 magnum. Not all revolvers shoot with consistency.

match director, agreed to spot for me.

"The next day I went to another silhouette club match full of high hopes and great expectations which lasted until three turkeys in a row just stood and laughed at me.

"My last chance for 1981 came on December 19-20. I went on the line in standing class first with a T/C 7mm and lucked into a 30.

"At approximately 1:45 p.m. on Saturday, I went on the line with the Ruger and Ray Stafford again as my spotter. Everything went pretty well up to the last bank of rams with no misses and only one really marginal hit on a turkey, which was so slow in falling that I had time to say 'aw heck' before it fell over. When I hit number 4 ram in the last bank, number 5 fell with it and I had to call for an alibi shot. By this time I was wound tighter than a ten-day clock and I had a strong urge to go to the bathroom. When the range master called me to fire the alibi shot the range got so quiet you could have heard a mouse sneeze. I said four Hail Marys and some stuff I made up and squeezed it off. It was a center punch that took its own sweet time to go over, but fall it did. Ray Stafford let out a war whoop and I had a nervous breakdown.

"On Sunday I slid through a 40x40 in unlimited and managed to squeeze a 40x40 out of the T/C 7mm in production for a four-gun aggregate of 150."

Whitman's load data was as follows:

For the .44 magnum Ruger revolver, he used 24 grains of 296 Ball powder; a 240-grain Sierra JHP bullet; Federal case; and the CCI 350 primer.

For the production single-shot and standing competition, he chose a Thompson/Center 7mm; for chicken, pig and turkey targets, his load combined a 140-grain Sierra spitzer bullet, 23 grains of Reloder 7, CCI 400 primer. For the rams, his load was a 160-grain Sierra boat tail spitzer bullet, 22 grains of Reloder 7 powder and a CCI 400 primer.

METALLIC SILHOUETTE SHOOTING

David Bradshaw displays the .44 Dan Wesson VH8 he used, with Federal JHP ammunition, to shoot the first officially recorded revolver score of 60x60. Russell Aldridge (left) was his spotter for this event.

In the unlimited category, Whitman used a Sako 30 Jirsa custom pistol with a 150-grain .30-caliber Sierra spitzer bullet, 25.5 grains or Reloder 7 and the CCI 400 primer.

As often happens when the psychological barrier of such "impossible" feats as the four-minute mile and the revolver 40x40 are accomplished, someone else soon gets on the bandwagon.

Within three months of Dave Whitman's perfect 40 with his .44 magnum Ruger Super Blackhawk, Phillip Braud of Louisiana turned the trick at a Mississippi match using a Dan Wesson .357 magnum, with 16.5 grains of WW 296, behind a 160-grain Hornady FMJ bullet in a WW nickel case backed up by CCI 550 primers. A month later, Allen Kirchner, IHMSA's Region Two director from South Carolina, shot a revolver 40 with his eight-inch barrel Colt Python .357 magnum. His load was 13.5 grains of WW 296; Speer 180-grain flat nose .358 rifle bullet, Federal magnum cases and CCI 550 primers.

The first revolver 60x60 score — one of only a minor few that have ever been shot — was fired by David Bradshaw on September 11, 1982, at the Vermont state championships. His account of the feat is interesting enough to relate here:

"As I drove down the highway toward a fateful IHMSA Vermont championship, nursing a powder headache from having spent the previous day blasting power-line trenches through a granite ledge in a rain that held the fumes to the ground, I mulled over which category to shoot first. It was standing, again with my Dan Wesson M-44 VH 8-inch. As it turned out, my control of the trigger was not up to snuff and 41x60 was the result.

"It is imperative to exercise the same gentle accumulation of pressure on the trigger in standing that freestyle requires. Many competitors think they can — indeed must — squeeze faster in standing. That misconception results in panic on the firing line.

"Revolver was next and I recruited Russell Aldridge to spot. Using a combination of push-in spotting boards and a set of lucite recording spotting boards, Russ kept track of

The author, Elgin Gates, (left) accepts the trophy from Ray Chapman for setting the ultimited handgun record of 34x40 in the first match the International Handgun Metallic Silhouette Association ever conducted.

my every shot.

"Nervousness struck early. With the chickens cleaned and the first bank of pigs down, Russ said of the pigs, 'The first four shots were right on top of one another. The fifth was a couple of inches high. They're in there, David.'

"The thought of a perfect score danced in my mind. It had been a fixation. But it was now remanded to the custody of my back brain, away from the critical business of shooting one silhouette at a time. To think of the target just shot is to romance the past. To think of the next target is to dream of the future. Both sins will destroy one's performance.

"Between relays I looked at my revolver, my notebook and, most especially, the ground. Since a competitor must focus eyes on the sights, particularly the front sight, I didn't want the lenses of mine hardening way out there on those ever-changing silhouettes.

"It must have paid off. As the last turkey fell, Russ said 'You're grouped up in the back, but those last five shots were inside six inches. Keep it up!'

"Needlesss to say, the pressure chewed on my nerves through three banks of rams. After fifty-nine shots, my gun hand trembled more than ever. Russ watched helplessly as the bullet of the sixtieth shot rose over the ram, then dropped back down to strike the ram in the medulla oblongata — the base of the skull. 60x60. There is no feeling quite like the fleeting kiss of perfection."

Federal 240 JHP ammuition was used.

While no important handgun silhouette big bore records have been set or broken since 1984, there are still a few out there, and there's that old saying: "Records are made to be broken."

Time will tell.

GOODS FOR SILHOUETTE RELOADERS

CHAPTER 8

These 7mm International rimmed cartridges — 7-R in the silhouetter's vernacular — are the results of reload expertise. They are backgrounded by author's scoped Thompson/Center which is chambered for this cartridge.

This Sport Eats Up Thousands Of Rounds; To Compete, Handloading Is A Must!

ONE THING about handgun metallic silhouette stands out above all else: the perpetual consumption of loading components.

Many IHMSA silhouette shooters attend matches on a weekly basis and shoot an average of three guns per match. This means he is shooting 480 rounds per month in actual competition and probably the same amount in practice. Add to that a similar quantity that may be fired by his wife and children and the total adds up to a lot of bullets, powder and primers being used, not to mention the brass that has to be replaced periodically.

With the price of factory ammunition out of sight, the only practical and economical way to stay in the sport is by handloading. More than that, the essence of the game — and a lot of fun to boot — is the satisfaction of brewing up your own pet loads and the delightful gratification of knocking down the steel silhouettes with ammunition created by yourself.

Make no mistake about it, the IHMSA handgun silhouette sport is one hundred percent a reloader's game. Nobody — and I mean, nobody — uses factory ammunition, except for the .22 rimfire branch of the sport.

One major manufacturer of bullets, components and handloading equipment has no hesitation in crediting the IHMSA handgun silhouette game with twenty percent of his sales. Handgun silhouette also has been an important incentive in stimulating the industry to develop more and better reloading tools and accessories.

Some of the more recent developments that are finding wide acceptance in the silhouette game are described here, starting with the Hornady Pro-7 progressive press.

The long-awaited Hornady progressive press for loading handgun and rifle ammunition is in production. Called the Pro-7, the new Hornady is a five station O-frame press featuring compound leverage. The frame is constructed of aluminum with the "O" section heavily webbed for rigidity. The ram bearing area is long and thick to support the ram and hold the shell plate in precise alignment during loading.

Like most progressive loaders, the Pro-7 is designed for right-hand operation; the handle is on the right. I can't

The powder measure is mounted on the Hornady Pro-7 press via a drop tube that features a floating bushing unit.

The shell plate is adjusted with a lock nut on the Hornady Pro-7 press. Spring washer hinders free rotation of the shell plate, flush seating of primers. The author has found it is best to remove this from machine.

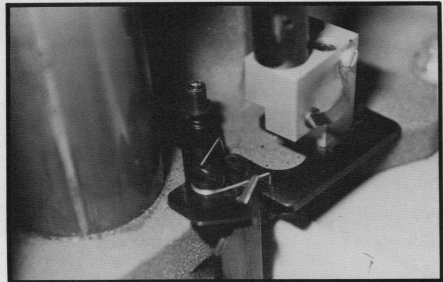

Automatic primer feed is adjustable for pick-up, timing, seating depth. The primer tube has been shielded by the author for safety reasons.

Loaded round is in left foreground and Hornady 7mm 175-grain SP that is about to be seated is in charged case for rimmed 7mm International.

imagine that this should pose a problem for southpaws, who are compelled to learn the use of many right-hand tools, including truck transmissions and chainsaws.

The "tolerance package" for the Pro-7 must be sharp, for F&F (Fit 'n Finish) is excellent. This is a most important characteristic of any press that serves for loading match ammunition. On a progressive loader fit 'n finish is critical to its very functioning.

Shell advance and priming are automatic. Powder is metered through a drop tube, which is threaded for standard powder measures such as Hornady, Redding, RCBS or Lyman. Two powder bushings are supplied, one for pistol, the other for rifle. The appropriate bushing is inserted into the drop tube before screwing drop tube in the powder measure. In loading, as the shell plate is raised, the case to be charged enters the drop tube, contacts the powder bushing — which is held to the bottom of the tube by gravity — and pushes it up until the press ram reaches the top of its stroke.

When the handle of the powder measure is whacked up and down, powder is funneled through the bushing into the cartridge case.

The massive ram of the Pro-7 is hollow and houses a "drive shaft." At the bottom of the drive shaft there is a star wheel — a spoked disc. The toggle — to which the ram, linkage and handle are attached — has two adjustable fingers (called cams) that rotate the star wheel.

With the ram in the down position and the operating handle up, the shell plate will rotate one-half station at the beginning of the ram's upward stroke. The shell plate will advance the second half-station as the ram completes the downstroke. The ram remains stationary during the top two-thirds of the ram stroke.

The shell plate rotates clockwise. The stations work in this way:

Station 1. Located at rear left of press. Remove loaded round. Insert case to be loaded. Pull handle. Case is sized and decapped.

Station 2. Push handle. Case is primed. Pull handle. Case mouth is belled (straight wall cases).

Station 3. Push handle. Pull handle. Whack powder measure. Case is charged.

Station 4. Push handle. Set bullet in case mouth. Pull handle. Bullet is seated.

Station 5. Push handle. Pull handle. Bullet is taper-crimped. (Station 5 is specifically for taper-crimping bullets loaded for auto pistols and separate roll crimping of bullets to be fired in revolvers.)

Primer tubes and seating cups for small and large primers are supplied. Capacity is over 100 primers, so one pack may be loaded at a time. The primer tubes fit inside a steel sleeve that must be in place or the automatic primer feed will not work. The sleeve serves as a blast shield in case of a primer tube detonation. The likelihood is remote, but it is always better to be safe than sorry.

CAUTION: Shooting glasses, safety glasses or other protective eyewear should always be worn when loading ammunition. It is plain common sense.

As cases are sized, spent primers are decapped through a hole in the base plate, where they drop down a tube into a plastic bottle. This manner of handling fired primers is much cleaner than having them pop out indiscriminately, with the abrasive residues collecting on the ram.

Shell plates are interchangeable and available in most popular rim sizes. A locknut is used to secure and adjust shell plate tension. If the shell plate is loose it will tip during primer seating, causing primers to seat crooked or be crushed. If the shell plate is too tight, it will not rotate and index properly.

The Pro-7 comes equipped with a continuous ring-type spring lock washer between the adjusting nut and the shell plate. The first thing you do with the Pro-7 — after reading the excellent instruction manual — is to remove this goofy ring and offer it to some clown to wear on his nose. Hornady Manufacturing will save itself three cents and a Tylenol headache by omitting this spring washer from the press.

I like to lubricate the underside of the shell plate and underside of the adjusting nut with military graphite grease. This black graphite grease is thick and will not flow. Nevertheless, keep it away from the outer area of the shell plate, where it could contaminate primers.

As delivered, my Pro-7 was mildly out of time. (This I blame more on the deliterious presence of the spring washer than on whoever assembled the unit at the factory. However, two other Pro-7s that I have used showed correct timing out of the box.

As with other quality progressive loaders, such as the Star Universal and the RCBS 4x4, operation of the press takes some getting use to. But once you get the hang of it, you may once again find you actually enjoy reloading!

To date, I have loaded .357 Super Mag, .44 magnum, .45 ACP, 7-R and 7 INT (7mm IHMSA) on the Pro-7. Ammunition produced on the press is excellent. The secret of smooth operation of the press lies in the selection of quality dies, properly adjusted, and in the development of a rhythmic working pattern, with smooth strokes of the handle.

RCBS has introduced a four-station progressive loading press. The 4x4 inherits three noteworthy characteristics from the older A-2 Rockchucker presses: (1) cast iron frame and linkage, (2) "O" frame to resist flexing and consequent case distortion and (3) compound leverage with massive ram and ram-support.

As we all know, quality control has been sadly lacking

Priming is accomplished manually by flicking a thumb button. Primers seat effortlessly on the down stroke.

For the RCBS press, shell plates are available for most cartridges. They are fully adjustable for the tension needed to prevent the cases from tipping when primer is seated.

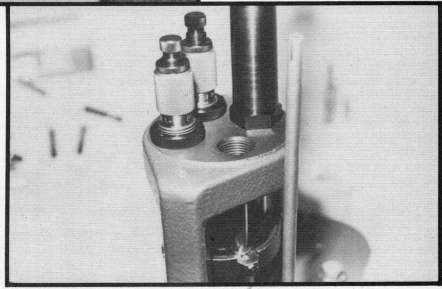

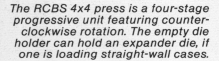

The RCBS 4x4 press is a four-stage progressive unit featuring counter-clockwise rotation. The empty die holder can hold an expander die, if one is loading straight-wall cases.

on a number of products in recent years. If the new RCBS 4x4 and Uniflo Measure are any indication of the present, quality control is excellent. The 4x4 is beautifully made.

Salient features of the 4x4 include:

(a) Shell plate tension is adjustable to compensate for any variations between different shell plates, rim thickness, etc., to compensate for wear, to hold shells straight as they are pulled over the expander ball and — very important — to hold the case head flat for primer seating.

(b) Spent primer catcher at station #1.

(c) Quickly interchangeable primer seating cups (station #2).

(d) Effortless primer seating — exceptionally sensitive "feel" (station #2).

(e) Steel powder drop tube with three precision fitted bushings for rifle and pistol cases (station #3).

(f) Adjustable shell detents to keep the various case sizes positioned in the shell plate. Spring-loaded detents make shell removal at any station a snap.

(g) Great leverage — easily full-length sizes difficult cases, such as .308s fired in machine guns, .375 H&H, etc.

(h) Relatively short handle throw — no more than Rockchucker. "Shovel handle" spreads leverage effort over width of user's palm — very comfortable.

Precision finish and alignment of components.

Primer seating is one of the crucial steps in loading accurate ammunition. Shells must be held perfectly straight lest primers be tipped or crushed. Primers must be seated below flush with the case head or ignition of the powder charge will vary from shot to shot. In addition, the very important "feel" is lost when components of the seating tool (or press) are loose or misaligned, causing excessive force to be required for seating.

Recently, a competitor for whom I was spotting found it impossible to cock his revolver. I immediately suspected high primers and told him to remove the cylinder from the gun (it was a single-action). Sure enough, the primers were high, but they were high because they had been seated crooked. The ammunition had been loaded on a Dillon 450 progressive loader. That design does not allow for adjusting the tension of the shell plate. The shell plate lifted, under pressure of the shell being primed, with the result that the primer had to be "crush fit" into the "tilted" primer pocket.

Misaligned priming components pose the threat of priming tube detonation in a progressive loader. High primers in loaded ammunition can "slam-fire" in heavy recoiling guns — such as magnum revolvers — when the cylinder slams against the standing breech on recoil or, with autoloading weapons, when the bolt slams against a round with a high primer. In some instances the action is not fully locked. In the case of revolvers, the round that slam fires almost invariably is to the left or right of the barrel!

The point is this: High primers are bad! If your primers are not seating flush or below flush, stop loading and ascertain the cause immediately.

Occasionally an individual will give me ammunition to chronograph. The first two things I check are the appearance of a resized case and whether the primer is seated below flush.

I have experienced nothing but easy, precise priming with the RCBS 4x4. The 4x4 primes every bit as well as — if not better than — the RCBS bench priming tool, which is the standard among priming tools.

The shell plate must be rotated manually and rotation is counter-clockwise. The primer seater is charged manually with a smooth flick of the thumb. Dave Andrews of Omark Industries explained that the manual staging of the 4x4 is designed into the press to give the reloader more deliberate control of the operations. The 4x4 is not intended as a high-volume progressive. Nevertheless, it most assuredly beats loading on a single-stage or turret-type tool.

The first rule for operating a progressive loading press — any progressive — is no conversation, no distractions, no interruptions!

Each stroke of the handle produces a loaded cartridge. Neglect to charge one case with powder and you will pay for it later when a bullet sticks in the throat of your single-shot, or lodges in the forcing cone of your revolver. When you operate a progressive loader you must pay attention every second. If you have any doubt whether you charged each and every cartridge with powder, you are instantly obliged to weigh each and every cartridge of that batch. Any round that is light will bottom on the scale. Then you must pull the bullet and reload the case.

The RCBS 4x4 is a progressive loader of exceptional quality. I shot a revolver 40x40 and 143x160 revolver aggregate with ammunition loaded on the 4x4.

The Lee 1000 is a recent entry into the reloading market and is also the lowest priced true progressive loading press, a bargain that the serious handgun reloader can't pass up. For your money, you get the press already set up and assembled when you take it out of the box, except for putting the handle on whichever side you feel comfortable with. Also included is a deluxe powder measure with four measuring disks, each containing six cavities. When you buy or order the 1000 in your chosen caliber, a set of carbide dies is included. In the box you will also find the obligatory set of instructions — they are helpful, so go ahead and spend three minutes reading all the way through — the charge disk tables and the warranty. The warranty is self-explanatory: two years or 100,000 rounds, whichever comes first. That's what I call a warranty!

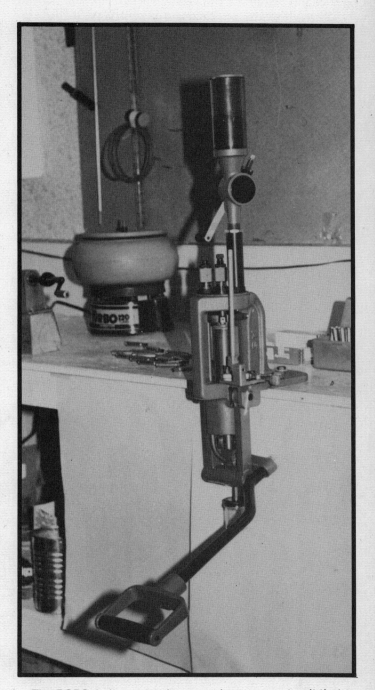

The RCBS 4x4 progressive press is a compact unit that requires little space to set up. The handle is in the bottom-of-the-stroke position. Note heavy construction.

Being that mine is a silhouette shooting family, I wanted to find a press that would cut down on the time that I spent reloading before every match — five to seven hours — yet had an affordable price along with reliability.

I've checked out the other progressive loaders on the market, but all the affordable ones required manual indexing and feeding of cases and primers, therefore, making them "semi-progressive" loaders. The big-bucks loaders were true progressive loaders, even though you placed the bullets in the cases by hand. The closest-priced one of these lists for $230 more. That savings sure can buy a lot of powder and bullets!

When I removed the 1000 from the box, I started a stopwatch to see how long it would take a ten-thumbed wonder to set it up and get it running.

Using the instructions, I drilled the three mounting holes and primer discharge hole in my reloading bench and had the press mounted and solid in 4½ minutes; not bad so far. I then set up the case feed cylinder and plate with the four feed tubes — long enough for forty-eight .357 Super Mag cases — in three minutes. Next was setting the dies for my cases — no different than in my Jr., as far as time. The Lee Powder Through Expander Die must be used if you intend use the powder measure.

So, let's load. Insert the primer tray and make sure the primer trough is full. Fill the powder measure reservoir and put the top on. The first pull of the handle inserts the first case into the shell plate ready for sizing. The next pull sizes and deprimes the case, with the spent primer being held in the ram body. When the handle is returned to its beginning position, the shell plate is rotated 120 degrees, a new case is inserted by the case feed and the resized case is reprimed. On the next stroke the resized case is charged with powder and the second case is resized. Return the lever to its original position and the shell plate is rotated 120 degrees, again placing the charged case under the seating/crimping die and repriming the second case and feeding in the third case.

Now comes the only non-machine function, wherein the bullet is placed in the belled mouth of the charged case. When the lever is pulled, the bullet is seated and crimped into the case. Returning the lever to its starting position

Redding dies are being used in this loading session for the 7-R silhouette cartridge, which the author favors.

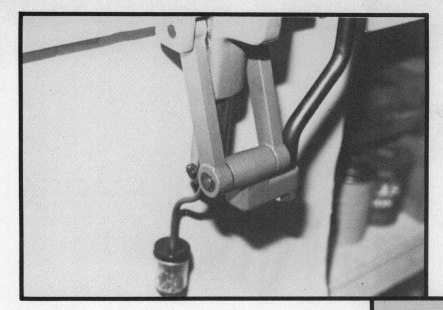

The RCBS progressive press features a massive cast iron frame. The ram and leverage components are heavy.

Uniflo measure being manufactured today shows a return to quality the author feels was lacking previously.

cycles the plate another 120 degrees, thereby dropping the loaded round into the discharge chute. From now on all that is necessary is to place a bullet into the charged case and pull the lever.

I was able to load eighty-five rounds of .357 Super Mag in nine minutes the first time out of the blocks! Just be careful and watch your primer tray and powder measure, since it can be so enjoyable loading at this rate, you could run out of powder or primers like I did! One feels foolish having to pull bullets because you didn't notice that the powder measure was empty.

The only two problems I encountered with the Lee 1000 was that the ball on the lever came off after 187 rounds. I replaced it with judicious use of Super Glue. The other glitch was the discharge chute and the .357 Super Mag cases. The sides of the chute were made for the shorter cases such as .45 ACP and .357 mags, so when the longer Super Mag cases were ejected they tended to fall over the chute rail and onto the floor. This was remedied by using a short piece of coat hanger attached to the feed stand-off bolt and paralleling the chute side only half an inch higher. Works like a charm, even for the 7mm T/C.

It is my opinion that this is the best progressive loader for the money and possibly the best progressive loader available outside of the commercial loaders at ten to fifteen times the cost. At present, the 1000 is available in the standard pistol calibers and their variations. Lee says that there will be a .223 plate assembly available so that we can load our 7mm TC, using the 1000! When that plate is available it will only take me 1½ hours to do what used to take six hours!

Let us fade back in time for a brief but very important moment. A family of Yankees by the name of Lyman, in Middlefield, Connecticut, made a receiver peep sight for rifles that revolutionized marksmanship at a time when rifle ballistics had exceeded established sighting methods.

The Lymans built a range in Wallingford, Connecticut, called Blue Trail, the scene of many grand marksmanship tournaments. The Blue Trail Range is where, not halfway through high school, I learned the subtle ways to the Garand M1 rifle; it is the range where, at age 15, I tied the great high-power rifle master, Sam Burkehalter, in the end to be edged by chisel-trigger Sam with 4-Vs.

Lyman Turbo 1200 vibrating tumbler works on a portion of 800 7mm IHMSA cases the author was reloading. The brass (foreground) has been cleaned.

Reloading powders favored by most silhouette shooters include Du Pont IMR 3031 and 4895, Data MP744, the Winchester 680 and 296 concoctions, Hodgdon H4198, BL-C, H322, Hercules Reloder 7, as well as some others.

Lyman still is serving American marksmen. Lyman reloading dies are top rate, being the only readily available .38/.357 dies that reliably and precisely handled those .357 Super Mag and .357 Maximum cartridges during that turbulent formative period of its inception.

No matter what the manufacturers would have us believe, without organized sport there can be no direction given the development of arms to equal this compelling knowledge that IHMSA-sanctioned competition has unleashed upon handling.

Were it not for a set of Lyman Super Deluxe .38/.357 dies, my work on the Super Mag/Maximum project would have fumbled forward without silhouette handloads crucial to the evolution of the revolver. As it was, I was restricted to totally inadequate available .357 revolver bullets and a few .358 rifle bullets built for the .35 Remington — a cartridge neither here nor there.

The Lyman Multi Deluxe dies handled the prototype Federal and Remington brass with true seating of every available bullet; it was a task that other makes of dies could not address. With the many grim developmental inhibitions afflicting this project, I am compelled to award Lyman a powerful recognition for enabling me to press information distilled from IHMSA competition into the development of the .357 Super Mag.

Remington concentrated on a conventional 158-grain JHP .357 Maximum loading. Federal, bearing heavily upon the infusion of silhouette knowledge provided by shooters, leaned swiftly toward the production of a 180-grain JHP loading for the .357 Super Mag/Maximum that would capture the heart of silhouetter and hunter alike. Federal strode the correct path, as the Super Mag/Maximum is a cartridge that favors heavy bullets.

So let's take a look at Lyman's Turbo 1200 tumbler.

This is a brass-cleaning machine which, in its Halloween costume of orange and black, perfectly matches the "explosives" signs that accompany transportation of dynamite products.

The Lyman 1200 is the best machine available to the handloader for cleaning brass. It comfortably absorbs 130 .308 cases or 140 7mm IHMSA cases and, within a span of two to four hours, buffs a shine upon the tarnished brass. My 7mm IHMSA cases, which have not been polished since they were formed in early 1978, were in such an evil state of repair that I was reluctant to throw them in the Lyman 1200. Veteran competitors will recognize the heavy coating of carbonized propellant residues that build up on the inside walls of a bottlenecked cartridge case as it is reloaded between ten and thirty times. This caking may be cut with a dentist's pick, as it should.

Four to five hours of vibration in the Lyman tumbler will bring most of the recalcitrant cartridge cases into line, restoring to life even my beat-to-dirt 7mm IHMSA brass.

The two best preservers of cartridge brass are the bolt-action rifle/pistol and the revolver. Yet, regardless of the arm we use, brass attrition soon rears its stubborn head.

The Lyman tumbler may be used day in and day out, hours and days at a time, to rectify and salvage brass that has been lost in the mud and grime of life.

The Lyman comes with a modest sack of what appears to be ground corn cobs as the polishing medium. As the tumbler warms up, a mild ultrasonic wave develops which folds brass into the hub of the tumbler. A few hours of this organic commotion polishes cartridge brass into a state of cleanliness aproaching that of brand new cases.

Cleaning time, advises Lyman, is about half that required to accomplish the same job in other tumblers. This is borne out by experience with several other rotating-drum tumblers.

It is important to check the flash hole of every single case that has been tumbled, since the polishing media seems to have been carefully ground to the exact size for wedging in there. Use a fine punch or a dentist's tool to remove media from the flash hole.

The Lyman Products Corporation (Route 147, Middlefield, CT 06455) has in the Turbo 1200 a most useful product. The Turbo 1200 will efficiently clean and polish 260 .357 magnum, or 130 .308, or 140 7mm IHMSA, or 200 7mm TC, or 100 .30/06 cases.

Lyman also makes a Turbo 600 model, which has half the capacity of the 1200.

This unlimited silhouette pistol is chambered for the 7mm IHMSA International cartridge. This round was developed specifically for handgun silhouette competition and, to date, is not available as a factory-loaded cartridge.

David Bradshaw holds two Ruger Redhawk double-action revolvers, with two more in his belt. Obviously he is a fan of this model. Bradshaw does extensive handgun field-testing developed for silhouette shooting.

A MATTER OF PHILOSOPHY

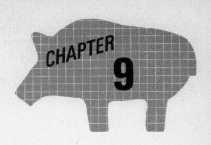

In Silhouette Shooting, A Production Gun Must Be Just That: A Production Handgun

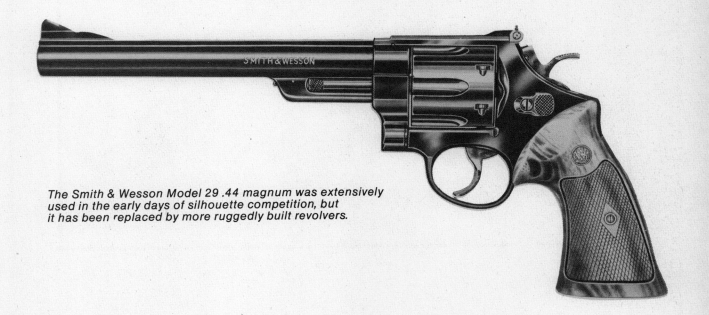

The Smith & Wesson Model 29 .44 magnum was extensively used in the early days of silhouette competition, but it has been replaced by more ruggedly built revolvers.

HAVING PARTICIPATED in a number of sports using mechanical equipment, such as speedboat racing, motorcycle and stock car racing and several of the shooting sports, I've long been acutely aware of what is called the "equipment race."

Simply stated, it is the modification of said mechanical equipment to improve its performance. In other words, do whatever it takes to gain a mechanical edge over the rest of the competitors, thus making it easier to win.

As stated, I've been through several sports where the Equipment Race philosophy prevails. I am intimately familiar with it just as I am intimately familiar with how it first prostitutes, then spoils said sport and eventually stunts its growth and participation to the point where only a handful of hardened "professionals" with the bucks for the best or an unlimited subsidy from some greedy manufacturer are left in the game. History is full of these equipment race sports that started with a good idea, blossomed, then fell victim to the legal cheats who wanted to win at any price and snorted derisively at the doctrine of having a set of rules that would provide genuine and equitable stock production equipment for all competitors on an equal basis.

All this was fresh in mind the night we founded the International Handgun Metallic Silhouette Association in that motel room in El Paso, Texas, October 2, 1976.

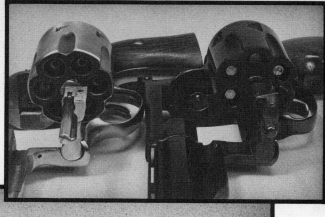

Cylinders of Ruger Redhawk (left) and Dan Wesson .44 magnum are the heaviest on the market; long and fat. Another strong point for these guns is that both cylinders lock up both fore and aft.

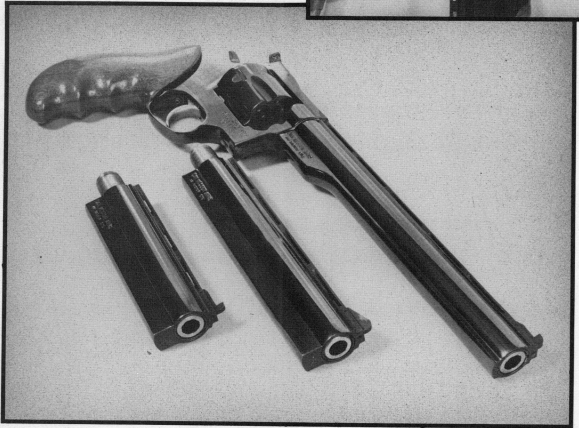

The heavy but interchangeable barrels of the Dan Wesson .44 magnum contribute greatly to the gun's accuracy. Optional combat stock absorbs recoil.

In order to keep this brand-new shooting sport from going down that same old highway to the rocky oblivion caused by the unbridled Equipment Race, I proposed two basic rules: One for the genuine over-the-counter, out-of-the-box production gun that would allow *all* shooters to compete equally with one another, with only shooter ability counting. In short, we wanted an everyman's shooting sport — something that never before had been created. But recognizing the latent desire inside most men to gain that mechanical edge over the rest of the competitors, if they could, I proposed a separate "unlimited" category, with the sky the limit as to modifications and price of equipment. The only limitations in this category would be weight, barrel length and sight radius.

I was well aware, as in any sport, that there would be a few misguided souls out there — the legal cheats — who would swear, with one hand on the Bible, that equipment did not count; it was only the man who counted. These are shooters who want to convince the world that they are right, at the same time insidiously maneuvering and manipulating to get that desired mechanical edge, either by buying it in the form of custom-built, high-cost, precision equipment or by undetectable internal modifications. And at the same time, they endlessly play their trite little recording about how the thousand dollars' worth of modifications in their guns don't count; it's only the man who counts. There is no use in asking them a straightforward question as to why they spent a thousand dollars for modifications, if they don't count. You will not get an honest answer.

IHMSA's production gun philosophy is simply stated:

Stainless steel Dan Wesson 740V8S (top) is chambered in .357 Super Mag. Blued model is in .375 Super Mag. Both are equipped with silhouette sights and new style silhouette grips.

Big-frame Dan Wesson is the most successful silhouette revolver marketed today. It is chambered (from top) for .357 Super Mag, .375 Super Mag and .44 Magnum.

We *want* all manufacturers to improve their products. Following the rigidly enforced IHMSA production gun rule, some have done exactly that. At the same time, this makes the better gun equally available to *all* IHMSA members as well as to handgun hunters and the general public, at the same price.

The total industry, with one or two exceptions, respects this IHMSA production gun philosophy. Manufacturers know they can build a standard production gun that is safe from their standpoint of liability exposure and that it will not be modified perpetually from the moment it is delivered over the counter. They know also that, under this IHMSA rule, their guns will be competing equally against the standard production guns of other manufacturers. And important to them is the fact that, if they build a better gun, IHMSA members will buy them by the thousands.

Gunmakers know their liability exposure is much less when their guns are shot as they come over the counter and out of the box. As intimated, there is a clear-cut incentive for any manufacturer to build a better gun as a result of IHMSA's production gun rule. Makers like Thompson/Center and Dan Wesson, to name just two of the more responsive handgun builders who listened to silhouette shooters, have improved their guns enormously over the past ten years as a direct result of the IHMSA production gun requirement. Hefty increases in sales have more than repaid their efforts.

What makes a handgun desirable for silhouette shooting? Shootability, the concept that handgun manufacturers often misunderstand and sometimes ignore. The

METALLIC SILHOUETTE SHOOTING

Bob O'Connor, then president of Dan Wesson Arms, examines first 40V8S Super Mag to handle the .357 Super Mag cartridge that was created by author. Chief engineer Bob Domain (right) accepted Gates' specifications for long cylinder in designing the gun.

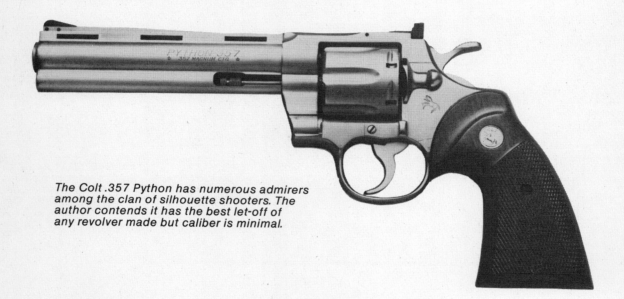

The Colt .357 Python has numerous admirers among the clan of silhouette shooters. The author contends it has the best let-off of any revolver made but caliber is minimal.

other reason is durability, the handgun quality that is most important to marksmen.

I am convinced that it is no accident that major manufacturers ignore freely available knowledge developed by competitive marksmen. An intrinsic flaw of egos attracted to the corporate ladder seems to prevent management-type individuals from considering anyone else's opinions.

But there are exceptions. Two men who immediately come to mind are Hugh Reed of Federal Cartridge Company and Duane Small of Dan Wesson Arms. There are others, of course, who understand the benefits of listening and who know that performance is the purpose of innovation. Without guys like Hugh Reed and Duane Small, we still would be shooting steel with the same revolvers and cartridges with which the game began.

Manufacturers use words like "ergonomics" — which means human engineering — to describe how well a gun fits the hand, how easily the action opens, et al. Seldom considered within the context of ergonomics are such qualities as trigger pull, sights and grip. Yet, these are the qualities that determine the shootability of a revolver or pistol.

Based upon experience and my own evaluations, I have composed a chart that ranks revolvers and pistols on the following criteria of shootability:

1. Durability.
2. Accuracy.
3. Letoff (weight and cleanliness of the trigger pull).
4. Lock time (in practical terms, the perceived movement between trigger-break and primer ignition).
5. Sight picture.

Standing shooter fires his big .44 magnum Ruger Super Blackhawk at 150-meter turkey targets. Rams, set at 200 meters, on extreme left, are a greater challenge.

Modular triggers of the big-frame Dan Wesson revolver (left) and the Ruger Redhawk (right) obviate the need for side plates. Respective assemblies are closer in conception than execution. The DWA trigger carries the hand, the hand carries the connector. With the Ruger, the trigger carries the hand, transfer bar separately.

6. Sight adjustments.
7. Felt recoil (.44s are ranked only against .44s, .357SM against .357SM, etc.).
8. Grip (a subjective quality; nevertheless, some grips facilitate marksmanship, while others detract from it. For example, the Pachmayr Gripper for the Thompson/Center Contender represents an extraordinary advance in handgun stocks).
9. Lockup (in revolver, cylinder tightness; in a single shot, bolting).
10. Cylinder-to-bore alignment.

I have omitted balance from the list because it is such a subjective quality and, when discussing powerful handguns, balance should be discussed in the context of felt recoil.

Single-action revolvers are ranked as a group, as are double-action cylinder guns. Production single-shots form still another group.

Letoff ratings are determined by trigger pulls safely achievable under IHMSA rules. It should be apparent that the lighter action and shorter hammer-arc of a small-frame revolver gives it a lock-time advantage over large-frame revolvers.

The Colt Python, properly tuned, has the best letoff of any revolver made. Unfortunately, the Python is limited to the weak .357 magnum. The Elliason sight of the Python is also the best made, most accurately adjustable sight to be found on a production handgun. (The excellent Bo-Mar has some of the advantages of the Elliason.)

The Dan Wesson .357 is the only double-action chambered for the .357 Super Mag. That automatically gives it the lock-time advantage over the similarly chambered

This is the original prototype of the big-frame Seville stainless silhouette model in .44 magnum with its 10½-inch barrel. This was the forerunner of the Seville with a longer cylinder to handle .357 Super Mag round.

Interarms' Dragoon model is the basic single-action of the old Peacemaker design. Rifling is 1-to-18, with a right-hand twist and is smooth; lock-up is excellent.

Seville and Ruger single-actions.

Individual features of a gun are ranked according to their place among guns now in production. Number one is the best of guns in production. Under felt recoil, number one would be "the most comfortable to shoot."

Under barrel/cylinder alignment, three different guns share the number two rating. This is because, with numerous examples measured with a Sheldon Williams Revol-A-Gauge, the amount of chamber-to-bore misalignment averages about the same for the Colt Python and the Smith & Wesson models 27 and 686.

Anywhere the Elliason sight is used, it tops the field for accuracy of adjustment, as noted in the Colt Python and Mossberg Abiline. Elevation and windage screwheads of the Elliason are scalloped about the edge to hold adjustments — which are determined by the pitch of the thread.

Virtually all other sight screws incorporate a fan of detents on the underside of the screw head. These are subject to manufacturing irregularities. If the detents on the underside of the screw head are not accurately placed, or the screw head is bent, uniform adjustment of the sight will be impossible. Have you ever come up one click and found you were shooting lower? Now you know why!

Among production single-shots, the Wichita ranks behind

Competitor fires a .44 magnum Ruger Super Blackhawk at a distant target. The model has been among the most popular for the iron target game.

Top gun is 10½-inch Seville chambered for .357 Super Mag. Lower model is the new Seville .32 H&R magnum with scope for IHMSA field pistol competition.

the T/C and BF Silhouette. The Wichita grip is a great mass of steel; while it adds weight to the pistol, the concentration of this weight in the hand causes the gun to recoil straight back. This condition is aggravated by the relatively low bore line of the pistol — a feature appropriate on a free pistol, but out of place on a powerful handgun.

During development of the Dan Wesson Model 44, a frame with an exceedingly low bore was tried. Muzzle-whip was reduced, but recoil into the shooter's palm, wrist and elbow was so severe that the design was abandoned.

When Sig Himmelmann split the sheets with Harvey Kahn, Himmelmann took the single-action El Dorado (which later evolved into the vastly superior Seville), and Kahn got the Abilene. Later, Mossberg would buy out the Abilene. The Abilene .44 barrel is excellent, with a .426-inch groove diameter. Accro and Elliason sights were purchased from Colt. Grips tend to be a high grade of walnut.

So much for that. The Seville frame shows no evidence of heat treatment. Dry firing will peen the metal around the firing pin until it seizes forward to prevent cylinder rotation. Chambers are bored with watermelon exit-holes. The sear-tip on the trigger is about as thick as a baby's fingernail and metalurgically impure, with alternating lumps of

Both guns are Ruger stainless steel single-actions. Top is Model KS411N, with patridge-type front sight blade and a 10-inch barrel. Other gun is KS47N with a ramp front blade and a 7½-inch barrel length.

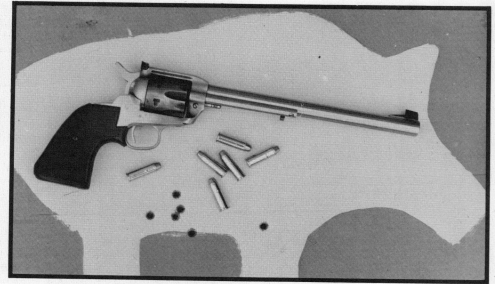

The six-shot group was fired by David Bradshaw on javelina test targeted with Interarms' stainless steel silhouette model in .44 magnum. Standard equipment is the patridge front blade and Pachmayr grip.

hard and soft metal — making it just about impossible to stone. Camming of the loading gate is near-nonexistent. The weak extractor spring allows the extractor to pound the cylinder face when the gun is fired.

The coarse-threaded screws seem specially designed to back out under recoil. The anvil ignition (designed to circumvent the Ruger transfer-bar patent) allows the trigger to be pulled with the hammer down.

When I first shot the Llama Super Commanche revolver in the so-called "silhouette" version, I was unable to put a bullet on the paper at fifty yards. Ditto at twenty-five yards. Finally, at ten yards, I managed to print some holes in the vicinity of a cardboard chicken. This was with the Federal 240-grain JHP, the most accurate commercial handgun ammunition on the planet. Shooting Creedmoor style at twenty-five yards, six-shot groups averaged twelve inches! Now, were these bullets to fly to two hundred meters without further deviation (a virtual impossibility), we would have a spread of nine feet.

Quality control continues to be a major problem with all makes. Perhaps another criteria — factory service — should be added to the list. However, reports on factory service vary widely. Some guns are returned to the factory two or three times and still come back unsatisfactorily repaired. Other guns receive excellent repairs the first time through.

Obviously, a frame with the barrel hole drilled off-center

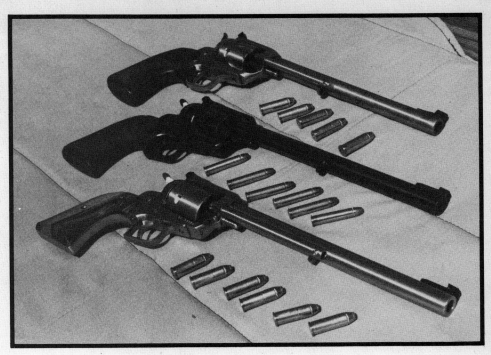

From top: Interarms' Dragoon silhouette .44 magnum; Ruger SRM .357 Maximum, discontinued early in its life; the Ruger KS411N .44 magnum, made from stainless steel for silhouette.

Both single- and double-action guns are used in silhouette competition. Calibers range through .357 magnum, the .357 Super Mag, .375 Super Mag, .357 Maximum, .44 magnum, and even the old .45 Colt!

cannot be repaired; it must be replaced. A gun in which the tolerances accumulate in the wrong direction is junk, no matter who made it. Without special tools and experience, these flawed guns can be hard to spot when you're buying one across the counter.

In 1985, I was told by a competitor that he and three companions had gotten together and bought a total of twenty copies of one popular big-bore revolver in order to find one that was silhouette-accurate.

For those who have a gun in which the tolerances accumulate in the right direction, the best advice is Keep It!

I have felt for some time that single-action revolvers are on the way out, because of the faster lock time of the double-action. However, there certainly should be room for a single-action built on a double-action frame. The big Dan Wesson .357 Super Mag, .375 Super Mag and .44 magnum frames are naturals for conversion to single-action or installation of a single-action kit. This would eliminate the need for a heavy double-action rebound spring.

As single-actions go, the Seville stainless .357 Super Mag silhouette model and its big brother chambered for the .375 Super Mag rank well above the rest of the field. They were designed specifically for the silhouette game and manufactured with the intent of providing tight-fitting cylin-

The new BF silhouette pistol is a single-shot falling block with a match-grade barrel. First calibers are the .32 H&R magnum and the older .32-20. Both of these are eligible calibers for IHMSA field pistol competition.

Initial run of BF silhouette pistols has an eight-inch match barrel with a Bill Jordan style grip. Author says the trigger is the most crisp of any factory handgun. This model is drilled, tapped for Thompson/Center mount, scope, as well as any standard one-inch handgun scope.

Shooter fires a Merrill pistol. Author blames lack of parts, service for the fact that the gun is not popular in sport. The price is $635!

ders with minimum gap and all holes successively aligned to the barrel breech opening.

Just as important is the fact that the Seville is the only single-action model that is being chambered currently for the enormously successful .357 Super Mag and the only single-action ever that has been chambered for the .375 Super Mag.

The .357 and .375 Super Mags are simply superior cartridges for silhouette shooting and hunting when ranked against than the old .357 magnum first introduced in 1935 and the .44 magnum from 1955. The .357 Super Mag, in use now for half a dozen years, has proved to be virtually unbeatable in the big-frame double-action Dan Wesson and the Seville single-action silhouette model.

In late 1982, Ruger introduced the SRM Blackhawk chambered for what they and Remington called the .357 Maximum. Unfortunately, some mistakes were made. One of the more serious was in trying to compromise the potential of the cartridge with a too-short cylinder. The resulting problems in forcing cone erosion and top strap cutting

Ron Carter displays his 40x40 score shot with 7mm Thompson/Center Contender. Such single-shots appear to have outranked revolvers in popularity for contesting.

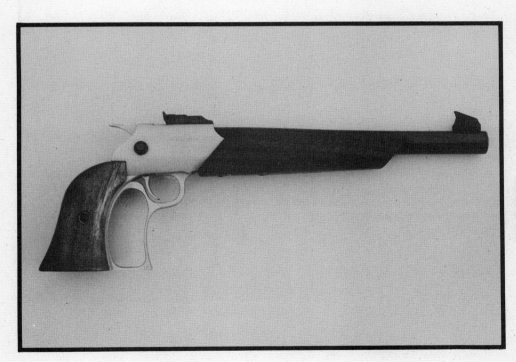

Single-shot, falling-block M.O.A. Maximum pistol is made in a wide variety of silhouette calibers, but $499 price tag hurts sale.

caused Ruger to cease production of this particular chambering.

Sig Himmelman, owner of United Sporting Arms at that time and maker of the Seville, and Robert O'Connor, president of Dan Wesson Arms, accepted the longer cylinder specifications I had worked out for maximum performance for the .357 Super Mag and each brand now occupies the top silhouette ranking for single-action and double-action revolvers respectively.

The Interarms .44 magnum Virginian Silhouette Dragoon is an exceptionally accurate revolver, hampered by the longest hammer arc of any single-action. Rod Sward, who was responsible for the improved Dragoons, explained the long hammer arc of this specific model variation as necessary for cocking the revolver since, by design, only one dog of the pawl is used in rotating the cylinder. Most single-actions "double-dog" the cylinder ratchet.

One highly touted single-action which shall remain nameless is little more than a copy of the old Colt Peacemaker design — like virtually all of the other single-actions in

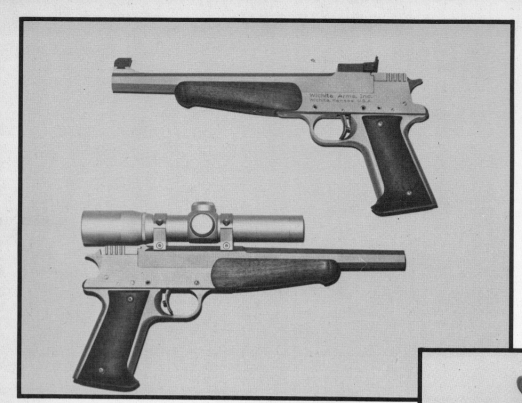

The Wichita single-shot has made little impact on the silhouette scene, according to the author. He blames a lack of service, high price.

Curt Williams of Bakersfield, California, poses with a trophy antelope, which he took with the .357 Super Mag Thompson/Center Contender. This is the same gun with which he shoots silhouette.

existence — turned out to be a bust in the silhouette game.

The promoter was pushing it as the world's most powerful handgun, a claim that crops up two or three times a year from other individuals and manufacturers of handguns. Said claim is based on shooting holes in soft boilerplate steel and blowing up plastic gallon jugs of water. But even a .22 magnum gives a satisfying shower of spray when fired into a jug of water.

This super hot dog cartridge is, in reality, the old Winchester line-throwing cartridge from way, way back that was made fractionally longer than the old .45 Long Colt so it couldn't be shot in a .45 revolver by error.

All the press agent stunts and the oohs and aahs are simply a glorified attempt to justify the $1000-plus price tag put on this piece.

For handgun silhouette competition however, the real and useful ballistics of this cannon are sub-standard. Several novice shooters have forked over big bucks for one of these highly touted guns, thinking they could shoot perfect 40X40 silhouette scores right and left. None of them ever came close. These big boom creations are no more suited to the silhouette game than a Mack truck is suited to race at Indianapolis. After one or two attempts to use one of these boomers in a silhouette match, the poorer but wiser owner usually passes off the piece — at a considerable loss — to some gullible collector as a conversation piece to hang

Shooting the Ruger Redhawk, David Bradshaw downs a metallic chicken at 50 meters during a match. Chick is off the stand, still in the air. Other than trigger smoothing, no other modifications are allowed on production guns.

over the mantel.

Who's next? Well, there's a lineup of applications out there waiting in the wings for the title of the world's most powerful handgun. They range from the .44 Sooper Dooper double-mag to the .45-70 Government full-length. The heck of it is that big booms, by themselves, don't mean automatically that such boomers are good silhouette guns. You need good mid-range ballistics and two-hundred-meter accuracy that none of these big handguns seems to possess.

Single-shots are difficult to rank in order of accuracy. The Contender, the Wichita and the Merrill all have proven to be remarkably accurate in individual instances. The problem, obviously, is one of individual boring, rifling and chambering characteristics, along with quality of parts and assembly.

Here is where the matter of price comes in. For the price of a Merrill — or XL, as it now is called — you can buy two T/C Contenders or three of the brand-new BF silhouette pistols.

If we take the word of the would-be experts who claim that only the man counts, not the equipment, then the Contender, with its lifetime warranty, or the new BF silhouette pistols are super bargains. Year after year, match after

From left: Bert Stringfellow, designer of the new BF silhouette pistol; Tom Colasanto, Connecticut state IHMSA director at the time; the author; and David Bradshaw of the IHMSA board of directors met to discuss attempts to destroy the rules governing eligibility for production guns in silhouette competition. The rules still stand!

match, championship after championship, the Contender has been the winningest gun in IHMSA competition. This has been true over the past eleven years by an unbelievable margin. The price is fair and parts are cheap. If you attend any of the IHMSA International championships, Thompson/Center provides expert gunsmiths to repair or rebuild all Contenders while you wait; parts are free.

The Merrill has been at the center of a political controversy. Most IHMSA members consider it to be an expensive handmade pistol that is totally outside of the basic production gun perimeters and, therefore, legal only for the unlimited category. Only because it was approved at the time IHMSA was chartered is it still allowed to compete in the production categories. Performance-wise, if it breaks down on the firing line, a non-workable extractor requires a rod, and sometimes a mallet, to drive out fired cases. Knowledgeable silhouette shooters contend this is caused by rough, poorly finished chambers.

The Wichita also seems to suffer from a lack of parts, service and warranty work, with months of waiting for repairs, not to mention price. Such factors have kept this pistol out of serious silhouette contention.

A bright spot in the world of single-shot pistols is the new BF silhouette model manufactured in Grand Island, Nebraska. The BF Silhouette pistol is the brainchild of Bert Stringfellow, vice president of IHMSA, who has been an active competitor for decades and was one of the original shooters at the 1975 match.

Stringfellow deliberately designed this pistol to avoid the mistakes made by the others. In so doing, he has provided a rugged, high-performance pistol with a falling-block action and simplicity of design. The BF has only twenty-one parts, including the grip and forend, versus thirty-one part numbers for the Wichita and sixty for the T/C Contender. This handgun has an air-gauge match grade barrel permanently fitted to the frame for consistent and superior accuracy. The action is held open, held closed — and fired — by means of a single spring and follower. All parts are made from solid bar stock steel and heat treated under the newest available technology. No castings are involved. Most important, the simple, rugged design allows the gun to be sold at a real bargain price: under $200. As it gains acceptance in the silhouette crucible, it has the potential of being one of the big winners.

Another single-shot that has been established as legal for IHMSA production gun competition — and which is being well accepted — is the M.O.A. falling-block pistol called the Maximum. It is available in a wide variety of

RATINGS CHART

Gun	Durability	Accuracy	Letoff	Lock Time	Sight Picture	Sight Adj.	Felt Recoil	Grip	Lockup	Chamber To-Bore Align't
DOUBLE ACTION										
DW .44/.375, .357 Super Mag	2	1	1	1	1	1	1	1	2	1
S&W .44	3	2	2	2	2	2	3	3	4	2
Redhawk .44	1	3	4	4	4	3	2	2	1	2
Llama .44	4	4	3	3	3	4	4	4	3	3
Python .357	2	2	1	1	1	1	3	1	1	2
DW .357	4	1	4	2	2	3	1	3	2	1
S&W M686	3	2	2	3	3	2	4	2	4	2
S&W M27	1	2	3	4	3	2	2	4	3	2
SINGLE ACTION										
Seville .44/.375, .357 Super Mag	3	2	2	3	3	3	1	1	2	1
Ruger .44/.357 Maximum	1	3	1	1	4	4	2	1	3	4
Dragoon .44	2	1	3	4	2	2	3	1	3	2
Abilene .44	4	4	4	2	1	1	4	2	4	3
SINGLE SHOT										
T/C	1	1	2	2	3	3	1	1	2	2
BF SILHOUETTE	1	1	1	2	1	1	1	2	1	1
Wichita	3	2	3	3	2	2	3	3	3	2
Merrill	2	2	3	3	3	3	3	3	3	2
M.O.A. Maximum	1	1	2	3	3	2	2	3	1	1

Note: Chart above is based on 1 to 4 rating with 1 the best, 4 the worst of guns listed.

Warren Center (right) and the author discuss the T/C Contender and its place in the silhouette scene. The single-shot has become highly popular in competition.

legal production cartridges as well as in unlimited class rounds.

It's single-piece receiver is made of chrome-moly steel rated at over 100,000 pounds of tensile strength. Douglas barrels are used and, by means of a special spanner wrench, barrels of different lengths and calibers are interchangeable after first being fitted to the receiver at the factory.

The receiver is Armoloy-treated to resist corrosion and wear. It also is drilled and tapped to accept M.O.A. ridged scope mounts. Open factory sights feature Millett-type adjustments and a unique safety is provided by a manual transfer bar. The transfer bar button must be in the *Safe* position in order to load and unload the pistol. To fire the pistol, the button must be moved to its downward position; this can be accomplished only after moving the hammer to the rear.

The two things going against the M.O.A. Maximum are its slow rate of production, with eight weeks or more for delivery; and its rather high price for a production gun; retail is $499.

The ratings chart above outlines the shootability of virtually all of the available production guns used for silhouette competition, double-action and single-action revolvers and single-shots. By adding up the ratings in the chart for a particular gun you will get a fair index of the shootability of that model. The lower the total, the better the rating.

As a final comment, please bear in mind that no manufacturer has yet been able to produce that perfect gun and probably never will. Even the best rated manufacturer will produce guns among which there are individual lemons. And sometimes a gun from the worst rated will be a pearl. The point is, when you get your hands on a handgun that performs well, don't let it get away!

Competitive silhouette matches are the acid test for newly developed cartridges. Knock-down power may result in an overall loss in accuracy. The one that succeeds achieves that narrow line for both.

SILHOUETTE LOADS FOR SINGLE-SHOTS

CHAPTER 10

A Lot Of Experimentation Went Into This Info Which Actually Was A Search For Safety!

AS STATED in a previous chapter, some of the first potential handgun silhouette cartridges I formed for testing were based on the .223 Remington and the .222 Remington magnum rifle cases.

Old military rifle barrels cut to lengths of fifteen to sixteen inches were used. I machined T/C-type locking lugs and heli-arced them on, so the barrels would readily fit the T/C Contender frame for testing.

It was apparent right at the beginning, that cutting down the cases from the overall 1.750 length of the .223 Remington and the 1.850 length of the .222 Remington magnum to 1.500 inches was an ineffective approach against the heavy steel rams, as was the old 1935 .357 magnum.

After firing about five hundred rounds each of the cut-

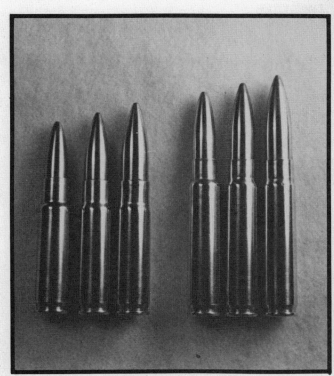

Initial prototype silhouette cartridges created by author in 1975 included (from left) 6.5mm/.223, 7mm/.223, .30/.223. Rounds on left have shortened cases; the three on right are in full-length .223.

Cartridges used in 7mm prototype testing program are (from left): 7mm/.222 and 7mm/.30/06x1½. The bullets (from left) are Speer 115-grain HP, the 139-grain Hornady spire-point; 160-grain Speer BT.

METALLIC SILHOUETTE SHOOTING

down 1½-inch versions of each of the .223 and .222 magnum cases necked to 6.5mm, 7mm and .30 caliber, I abandoned this line of testing and went back to the full-length versions of each, necking them to the same three calibers.

The results were better, but even then I realized the case capacities of the .223 and even the .222 magnum were marginal for loads and bullets that would take the heavy rams down without fail. Consequently, after about 4000 rounds had been fired at full-size rams, I set them aside.

One important equation needs to be mentioned. These tests were made in late 1975 and early 1976, using rams set full-foot on the stands, as we had shot them at Lee Jurras' first handgun silhouette competition in September, 1975. This meant that the full surface of the bottom of the ram's feet were in contact with the stand — a railroad rail set upside down. In short, set full-foot, they were too difficult to knock down with the then available handgun cartridges, such as the .357 magnum, .41 magnum and .44

Author recommended "overhang" rule that allowed rams to be set with feet overhanging the stand to make them easier to knock over with the handgun.

6.5mm/.223

CARTRIDGE: 6.5mm/.223. Developed by E. Gates, Oct. 1975, adopted by Thompson/Center 1982 as the 6.5mm T/C
GUN: T/C Contender
BARREL AND LENGTH: 10-inch, Factory 1982
TWIST: 1:8
PRIMER: Federal 205M
CASE: Federal .223

These tests are based on ten-shot groups fired at fifty meters from sandbag rest position.
* Asterisk indicates maximum load. Work up to these slowly.

POWDER	WEIGHT IN GRAINS	AVERAGE MUZZLE VELOCITY FPS	STANDARD DEVIATION FPS	GROUP SIZE
120-GR NOSLER				
Win-748	28.0	1872	12	.71
Win-748	29.0	1983	9	.38
Win-748	30.0	2065	16	.77
120-GR SIERRA				
Win-748	28.0	1866	13	.65
Win-748	29.0	1930	9	.44
* Win-748	30.0	2051	15	.73
140-GR HORNADY				
Win-748	25.5	1787	10	.93
Win-748	26.5	1856	7	.84
* Win-748	27.5	1924	12	1.14
IMR-3031	22.0	1727	9	.83
IMR-3031	23.0	1797	7	.41
IMR-3031	24.0	1877	8	.56
* IMR-3031	25.0	1924	14	1.06
* IMR-3031	25.5	1973	12	1.12
IMR-4895	23.0	1720	9	.45
IMR-4895	24.5	1832	14	.57
IMR-4895	25.0	1868	8	.62
* IMR-4895	25.5	1915	19	1.17

Note: All load data and information in this book is the result of safe and careful testing by the author and other contributors submitting the material contained herein. Since neither the author, DBI Books, Inc., nor any of the contributors has any control over the components, equipment and techniques used with this published information, no liability or responsibility for any injury or damage that occurs is either implied or assumed.

Custom T/C Contenders were used to test early cartridge developments. Changing barrels, grips, forends, they were used to test short cartridges such as the 6.5mm/.223x1½; 7mm/.223x1½; .30/.223x1½ as well as same calibers on the .222 Remington magnum case and in the full-length versions of the same calibers.

6.5mm/.223

CARTRIDGE: 6.5mm/.223. Developed by E. Gates, 1975; Adopted by Thompson/Center 1982 as the 6.5mm T/C
GUN: T/C Contender
BARREL AND LENGTH: 10-inch, Factory 1982
TWIST: 1:8
PRIMER: Rem 7½
CASE: Federal .223

These tests are based on ten-shot groups fired at fifty meters from sandbag rest position.
* Asterisk indicates maximum load. Work up to these slowly.

POWDER	WEIGHT IN GRAINS	AVERAGE MUZZLE VELOCITY FPS	STANDARD DEVIATION FPS	GROUP SIZE
HORNADY 129-GR SPIRE PT				
Win-748	24.5	1732	6	.64
Win-748	26.0	1822	8	.43
Win-748	27.5	1905	4	.72
* Win-748	28.5	1964	12	1.03
* Win-748	29.5	2043	19	1.31
IMR-3031	22.5	1686	5	.53
IMR-3031	24.0	1788	4	.41
IMR-3031	25.0	1923	12	.86
* IMR-3031	26.0	1993	14	1.12
RL-7	19.5	1677	8	.52
RL-7	20.5	1793	10	.72
RL-7	21.5	1917	9	.27
* RL-7	22.5	1986	16	1.34
IMR-4895	24.0	1723	6	.41
IMR-4895	25.0	1840	8	.37
* IMR-4895	26.0	1907	11	.72
* IMR-4895	27.0	2004	14	1.07
H-322	22.0	1720	12	.43
H-322	23.0	1827	14	.57
H-322	24.0	1924	6	.32
* H-322	24.5	1952	8	.47
* H-322	25.0	2010	11	1.07

Note: All load data and information in this book is the result of safe and careful testing by the author and other contributors submitting the material contained herein. Since neither the author, DBI Books, Inc., nor any of the contributors has any control over the components, equipment and techniques used with this published information, no liability or responsibility for any injury or damage that occurs is either implied or assumed.

magnum; that included the .357 and .44 Auto Mags. The old .357 magnum was virtually useless and the rest of the magnum loads and bullets would leave about half of the full-foot-set rams standing after solid hits.

On this basis, my tests of even the full-length 6.5mm, 7mm and .30-caliber versions of the .223 and .222 magnum rifle cases were unsatisfactory, so I moved on to the larger diameter and longer rifle cases as related in an earlier chapter.

In the meantime, shooters were going to what I called "dynamite loads," in desperate attempts to knock the rams down. This is when we went through the period of having guns shoot loose and start coming apart.

I could see the writing on the wall: The silhouette game was entering a dangerous phase that could lead to real tragedy. When a gun blows up from an overload, the result can be akin to a hand grenade going off. Pieces fly everywhere.

The author tests an early 7mm/.223 prototype on Contender frame. Gun features a 15-inch unlimited barrel. Round later was adopted as the 7mm T/C.

6.5mm/.223 Unlimited

CARTRIDGE: 6.5mm/.223. Developed by E. Gates, Oct. 1975
GUN: XP-100 Rebarreled
BARREL AND LENGTH: Mannlicher Military, 15 inches
TWIST: 1:9
PRIMER: Federal 205 Match
CASE: .222 Rem Mag

These test are based on ten-shot groups fired at fifty meters from sandbag rest position.
* Asterisk indicates maximum load. Work up to these slowly.

POWDER	WEIGHT IN GRAINS	AVERAGE MUZZLE VELOCITY FPS	STANDARD DEVIATION FPS	GROUP SIZE
129-GR HORNADY				
H-4895	26.0	2290	5	.32
H-4895	26.5	2320	3	.43
H-4895	27.0	2348	4	.51
140-GR HORNADY				
H-4895	25.0	2270	5	.47
H-4895	25.5	2310	7	.64
H-335	25.0	2132	11	.61
H-335	25.5	2194	9	.58
120-GR NOSLER				
H-335	25.5	2265	5	.52
H-335	26.0	2304	12	.68
140-GR SIERRA				
H-335	25.0	2237	7	.55
160-GR HORNADY				
H-4895	28.0	1903	12	1.03

Note: All load data and information in this book is the result of safe and careful testing by the author and other contributors submitting the material contained herein. Since neither the author, DBI Books, Inc., nor any of the contributors has any control over the components, equipment and techniques used with this published information, no liability or responsibility for any injury or damage that occurs is either implied or assumed.

From left: 7mm/.223, adopted in 1980 by Thompson/Center as the 7mm T/C; 7mm/.222 Remington magnum; 7mm/.30/06x1½, adopted in 1979 by Remington as the 7mm BR with minor changes of shoulder angle and the smaller primer pocket .308 FL case as its parent; 7mm IHMSA International, which is the most winning round in the history of unlimited silhouetting; 7mm International Rimmed, called the 7-R that now is a production cartridge with several of the major manufacturers; 7mm/.225; 7mm/.308. All but last of the cartridges shown were developed by the author in 1975-76.

7mm/.223

CARTRIDGE: 7mm/.223. Developed by E. Gates, October 1975. Adopted by Thompson/Center 1980.
GUN: T/C Contender Tested 1982
BARREL AND LENGTH: Standard Factory 10-inch
TWIST: 1:9
PRIMER: CCI 400
CASE: Military Headstamp 1973

These tests are based on five-shot groups fired at twenty-five meters from sandbag rest position.
* Asterisk indicates maximum load. Work up to these slowly.

POWDER	WEIGHT IN GRAINS	AVERAGE MUZZLE VELOCITY FPS	STANDARD DEVIATION FPS	GROUP SIZE
120-GR HORNADY SP				
IMR-4198	22.2	1934	16	.83
IMR-4198	23.2	2048	23	.77
IMR-4198	24.2	2170	12	.53
Win-748	27.4	1813	14	.43
Win-748	28.4	1920	26	.72
Win-748	29.4	2010	17	.54
120-GR SIERRA				
IMR-4198	22.2	1984	5	.47
IMR-4198	23.2	2037	3	.49
IMR-4198	24.2	21.55	22	.73
IMR-4895	20.8	1805	21	.51
140-GR SIERRA				
Win-748	25.2	1720		.56
Win-748	26.2	1793		.47
Win-748	27.2	1847		.34
168-GR SIERRA MK				
Win-748	21.0	1423	20	.31
Win-748	22.0	1508	12	.48
Win-748	23.0	1573	6	.29
Win-748	24.0	1610	7	.32

Note: All load data and information in this book is the result of safe and careful testing by the author and other contributors submitting the material contained herein. Since neither the author, DBI Books, Inc., nor any of the contributors has any control over the components, equipment and techniques used with this published information, no liability or responsibility for any injury or damage that occurs is either implied or assumed.

METALLIC SILHOUETTE SHOOTING

The potential for serious injury to shooters and spectators alike was frightening in those early sanctioned matches of 1977.

Consequently, in July 1977, six months after IHMSA's first sanctioned match was held, I suggested we go to what would be called the "overhang rule." In short, we would set the rams on the stands so that the back of the feet extended over the back edge of the stand from three-fourths of an inch to an inch. This would establish a balance that would allow the ram to topple off of its stand with a less powerful hit.

The proposal was approved unanimously and went into effect on July 11, 1977. The main reason this was done was for safety purposes; to stop the rapidly growing trend toward the maximum-plus loads that were being used.

With the new rule in effect, considerably less striking

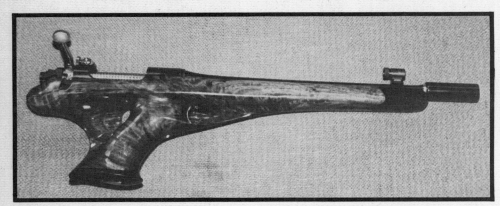

This unlimited gun from the author's collection has been chambered for the 7mm IHMSA International cartridge. It has dominated competition for the 11 years of its existence.

7mm/.223

CARTRIDGE: 7mm/.223 (7mm TC)
GUN: T/C Contender Super 14
BARREL AND LENGTH: 14-inch Factory
TWIST: 1:9
PRIMER: Federal 205M
CASE: Remington .223

These test are based on ten-shot groups fired at fifty meters from sandbag rest position.
* Asterisk indicates maximum load. Work up to these slowly.

POWDER	WEIGHT IN GRAINS	AVERAGE MUZZLE VELOCITY FPS	STANDARD DEVIATION FPS	GROUP SIZE
130-GR SPEER				
IMR-4198	22.4	2097		
IMR-3031	26.2	2073		
IMR-4895	27.5	2040		
140-GR SIERRA SPITZER				
IMR-4198	22.2	2011		
IMR-3031	24.6	1934		
IMR-4895	25.6	1927		
150-GR NOSLER PARTITION SPITZER				
IMR-4198	21.5	1907		
IMR-3031	24.5	1936		
IMR-4895	25.6	1927		
160-GR SIERRA BT				
IMR-4198	20.5	1823		
IMR-3031	22.6	1720		
IMR-4895	23.6	1734		
H-4198	21.5	1846		
H-4895	21.5	1704		

Note: All load data and information in this book is the result of safe and careful testing by the author and other contributors submitting the material contained herein. Since neither the author, DBI Books, Inc., nor any of the contributors has any control over the components, equipment and techniques used with this published information, no liability or responsibility for any injury or damage that occurs is either implied or assumed.

This silhouette range at Scottsbluff, Nebraska, illustrates the types of terrain that can be utilized. There is no requirement for table flatness.

7mm/.223 Unlimited

CARTRIDGE: 7mm/.223 Unlimited Configuration
GUN: XP-100 Rebarreled
BARREL AND LENGTH: Douglas Airgauge
TWIST: 1:9
PRIMER: Federal 205M
CASE: Military .223

These tests are based on ten-shot groups fired at fifty meters from sandbag rest position.
* Asterisk indicates maximum load. Work up to these slowly.

POWDER	WEIGHT IN GRAINS	AVERAGE MUZZLE VELOCITY FPS	STANDARD DEVIATION FPS	GROUP SIZE
120-GR HORNADY SP				
IMR-4198	22.5	2185	12	1.03
IMR-4198	23.5	2290	9	.74
IMR-4198	24.5	2348	14	.97
139-GR HORNADY SP				
RL-7	21.5	2260	12	.81
H-322	24.5	2248	19	.63
IMR-3031	25.5	2220	9	.70
IMR-4895	27.3	2207	23	.47
Win-748	28.5	2712	17	.58
145-GR SPEER FLAT BASE				
Win-748	26.0	1985	12	.73
Win-748	27.0	2021	8	1.54
Win-748	28.0	2078	11	1.08
150-GR NOSLER SB				
Win-748	26.5	2056	12	1.06
Win-748	27.5	2087	17	.87
154-GR HORNADY SP				
IMR-4895	25.0	1863	11	.93
IMR-4895	26.5	1930	23	1.07
IMR-4895	27.5	2010	7	1.63
IMR-4895	28.0	2107	16	.87
IMR-4895	28.5	2164	9	.76

Note: All load data and information in this book is the result of safe and careful testing by the author and other contributors submitting the material contained herein. Since neither the author, DBI Books, Inc., nor any of the contributors has any control over the components, equipment and techniques used with this published information, no liability or responsibility for any injury or damage that occurs is either implied or assumed.

METALLIC SILHOUETTE SHOOTING

force and momentum were needed to knock down the overhanging rams. A solid high or center hit from the old .357 magnum had a fair chance of knocking down the ram.

Just as important, this brought many of the cartridges I had abandoned the year before — such as the 6.5mm/.223, 7mm/.223, .30/.223, and the same versions on the .222 magnum case — back into the game. A whole new area of cartridge development was reopened and, all over the country, shooters and gunsmiths alike got into the act.

My 1975 tests were repeated and refined with the best and latest bullets and components available. The data is presented here for silhouette shooting. This data, incidentally, is perfectly valid for hunting purposes.

At the first IHMSA match held in Fresno, California, in June 1977, author used prototype 6.5mm/.223 round that he fired in a T/C Contender with 15-inch barrel.

7mm BR & 7mm/.222 Magnum Unlimited

Bullet	Powder	Charge	7mm BR Avg	7mm BR Var	7mm/.222 magnum Avg	7mm/.222 magnum Var	Remarks
							(All 7 BR loads shot in 110° temp, 7x47 loads in 70° temp.)
Speer 115-gr Hp	RL-7	26.0	2326	26	2439	72	Not top, either gun
	H322	28.0			2590	50	
Hornady 139-gr sp	H4198	22.0	2000	10			
"	H322	25.0	2117	52	2226	64	
		27.0	2239	82	2231	73	Top in 7x47, near top in 7mm BR
"	BL-C2	28.0	1994	58	2008	20	
		29.0	2067	17			
Speer 145-gr S	RL-7	24.0	2120	25			Slight primer crater-top Near Top
"	H335	27.0	2064	79			
"	H4895	26.0	2076	33	2213	34	Top in 7x47, near top in 7mm BR
"		27.0	2166	38			Slight primer crater-top
Speer 145-gr BT	748	27.0	1974	42	2055	34	Mild
		28.0			2120	79	Top
Sierra 160-gr SBT	748	25.0	1814	30			Real mild
"	H335	25.5	1929	27			
Speer 160-gr BT	H335	27.0	2023	23	2086	17	Very slight crater (both) Top
"	H4895	25.0	1977	56			Same
"	IMR4895	25.0			2010	57	Same

*Velocity information for one five-shot group measured ten feet from muzzle with Oehler M33 Chrontach and sky screens. All loads used Federal's small rifle thick gap match primer (#205M). Overall lengths were: 115 Speer HP — 2.22 inches; Hornady 139 SP — 2.34 inches; 145 Speer S — 2.21 inches; Speer 145 BT — 2.24 inches; Sierra 160 BT — 2.26 inches; Speer 160 SBT — 2.23 inches.

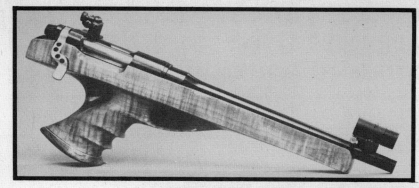
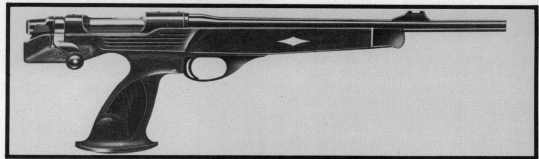

Left: Unlimited silhouette pistol on an XP-100 action was built by Jack Dever of Oklahoma City. It is chambered for the 7mm/.223, which author considers to be marginal. (Below) Remington's 7mm BR silhouette pistol, available at an economy price, has allowed anyone to compete in silhouette at a fair price.

7mm IHMSA INTERNATIONAL

Load data:

TEST GUN: Custom XP-100
BARREL LENGTH: 15" 1 in 10" RH twist
BULLET DIAMETER: .284
PRIMER SIZE: Large Rifle Standard
MAX. CASE LENGTH: 1.875
TRIM CASE TO: 1.865

POWDER	WEIGHT IN GRAINS	BULLET IN GRAINS	CASE	VELOCITY
H-4198	28.0	140 Sierra	Federal Case	2196 fps
H-322	30.0	140 Sierra	Federal Case	2215 fps
H-4895	30.0	140 Sierra	Federal Case	2099 fps
H-4198	28.0	154 Hornady	Federal Case	2136 fps
H-322	30.0	154 Hornady	Federal Case	2162 fps
H-4895	30.0	154 Hornady	Federal Case	2074 fps
H-322	30.0	168 Sierra	Federal Case	2165 fps
H-4895	30.0	168 Sierra	Federal Case	2071 fps

7mm INTERNATIONAL PRESSURE BARREL TESTS

One of the major industry maufacturers ran some load data test using a special pressure barrel for the 7mm IHMSA International cartridge as follows:

Bullet	Powder Type	Powder Wt. Grs.	Velocity Ft./Sec.	Ex. Var. Ft./Sec	Pressure Lbs./Sq.In.	Ex. Var. Lbs./Sq. In.
140 Sierra	H-4227	20.0	1877	24	42,200	2,700
154 Horn. SP	H-4227	20.0	1825	8	45,180	2,100
162 Horn. Match	H-4227	20.0	1837	31	55,580*	2,200
162 Horn. Match	H-322	29.0	1992	51	37,200	1,500
154 Horn. SP	Win-748	31.0	1933	96	30,900	5,000
145 Speer	Win-760	35.0	1790	32	29,660	1,500
154 Horn. SP	H-4895	30.0	2018	21	36,360	2,300
175 Sierra BT	H-4895	32.0	2092	21	44,480	1,700
160 Speer SP	RE-7	26.0	1927	27	35,780	2,200
145 Speer SP	IMR-4198	26.0	2088	98	40,380	6,400

*This load is too high in pressure to be practically recommended.

As Experience Progressed, the 7mm Family Became An Obvious Silhouetting Choice

DURING THAT hectic period of cartridge design and development of late 1975 and early 1976, I came up with four major series of cases. Two of them were what I had worked with in the early 1950s for hunting, the short 1.500-inch 7mm, .30 and other experimental calibers of the same length; and the longer series based on lengthening such cases as the old .357 magnum, .44 magnum and a number of others for the 1.600 series, most to be straight-wall cases.

Of the other two which first saw the light of day in 1975, one was the 1.860-inch IHMSA International series made from larger rifle cases such as the .308, 30/06, 7x57 and so on. I ended up with seven of these, all with the exact same overall length, neck length, shoulder angle and case capacity. Only the calibers were different. They were .25, 6.5mm, .270, 7mm, .30, 8mm, .338 and .35 caliber.

I made up the fourth group with rimmed cases which I called the International Rimmed series, mostly using the old Winchester .30-30, as well as the newer .225 Winchester as parent cases. Then, when the .375 Winchester came out in 1978, I revised the cartridge drawings to use it. The .375 Winchester was the best and toughest of this series because of its higher CUP (copper units of pressure) rating of 53,000 as compared to the 38,000 CUP rating of the .30-30 case.

After the "overhang" rule was put into effect, some of the marginal cartridges like the 7mm/.223, 7mm/.308x1½ and others of similar capacity proved to be successful.

Phil Briggs, a member of the IHMSA field test staff, is checking out a version of the 7mm International Rimmed cartridge, known as the 7-R among silhouette shooters.

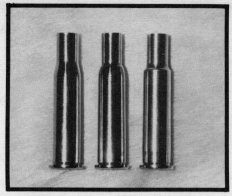

(Above) Steps to form 7-R (from left): a standard .30-30 Winchester case; necked down to 7mm with shoulder point established. Third case has been fire-formed to the 7-R. (Left) Cartridges (from left): 7mm IHMSA International, 7mm International Rimmed (7-R), 7-R on .225 Winchester case and 7mm/.223, now renamed as the 7mm T/C round.

TABLE A

T/C Super 14 Barrel Chambered In 7-R Unlimited

Test	Barrel	Case	Power Charge	Velocity, fps	Standard Deviation, fps
140 gr. Sierra Spitzer #1919, Remington #9½, C.O.A.L = 2.850", T=45°F					
5	14"	WW	33.0 Gr Win-748	2035	15
6	14"	WW	34.0 Gr Win-748	2114	6
7	14"	WW	35.0 Gr Win-748	2159	4
8	14"	WW	36.0 Gr Win-748	2225	14
13	14"	WW	29.0 Gr H4895	1994	38
14	14"	WW	30.0 Gr H4895	2044	21
15	14"	WW	31.0 Gr H4895	2118	8
16	14"	WW	32.0 Gr H4895	2190	12
154 Gr. Hornady Spire Point #2930, Remington #9½, C.O.A.L., =2.860", T=50°F					
22	14"	WW	31.0 Gr Win-748	1845	15
23	14"	WW	32.0 Gr Win-748	1896	9
24	14"	WW	32.5 Gr Win-748	1944	9
25	14"	WW	33.0 Gr Win-748	1977	9
26	14"	WW	34.0 Gr Win-748	2057	13
32	14"	WW	26.0 Gr H4895	1747	27
33	14"	WW	27.0 Gr H4895	1819	30
34	14"	WW	28.0 Gr H4895	1884	41
35	14"	WW	29.0 Gr H4895	1923	15
36	14"	WW	30.0 Gr H4895	1995	36
41	14"	WW	35.0 Gr Win-760	1921	14
42	14"	WW	36.0 Gr Win-760	1993	15
43	14"	WW	37.0 Gr Win-760	2026	9
44	14"	WW	38.0 Gr Win-760	2086	9
45	14"	WW	27.0 Gr IMR4320	1636	32
46	14"	WW	28.0 Gr IMR4320	1726	45
47	14"	WW	29.0 Gr IMR4320	1831	40
48	14"	WW	31.0 Gr IMR4320	1859	18
162 Gr. Hornady BTSP #2845, Remington #9½, C.O.A.L. = 2.900", T = 45°F					
53	14"	WW	28.0 Gr Win-748	1706	27
54	14"	WW	29.9 Gr Win-748	1750	15
55	14"	WW	30.0 Gr Win-748	1831	8
56	14"	WW	31.0 Gr Win-748	1901	17
57	14"	WW	32.0 Gr Win-748	1970	21
62	14"	WW	32.0 Gr Win-760	1754	13
63	14"	WW	33.0 Gr Win-760	1815	12
64	14"	WW	34.0 Gr Win-760	1851	8
65	14"	WW	35.0 Gr Win-760	1925	13
66	14"	WW	36.0 Gr Win-760	1982	13

C.O.A.L. = Cartridge overall length.

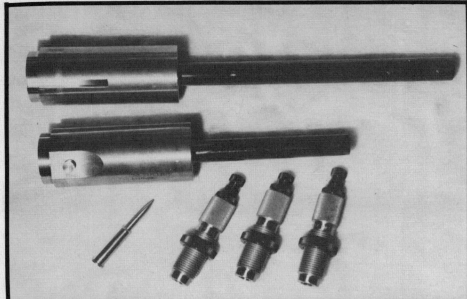

These special pressure barrels are used to establish maximum CUP ratings of 7-R cases. The .30-30 brass maxed at 54,000 CUP. Dies are custom-made 7-R by Redding.

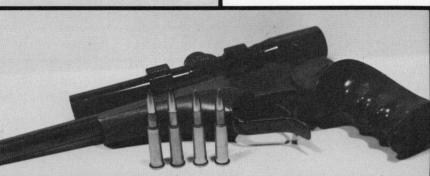

This scope-mounted T/C Contender was used with its 10-inch barrel to test load data for these 7-R cartridges.

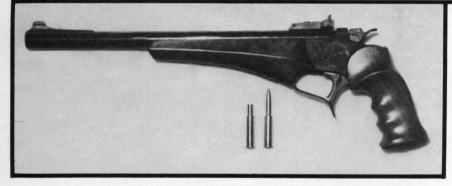

Empty and loaded 7-R cases from .375 Winchester brass are shown with the Thompson/Center Super 14 used in test.

The idea I had in mind in developing this series was to produce cartridges for the single-shot production handguns of the break-open or falling-block design which would handle and extract rimmed cases better than the rimless types.

No great stroke of ballistic genius was needed for this, nor was it needed for any of my other cartridge developments; all used existing cases as parents in one way or another.

Starting with the .30-30 Winchester, I simple necked it down to versions of 6.5mm, 7mm and .30, retaining the same body length and thirty-eight-degree shoulder angle of my IHMSA International unlimited series.

As in other instances, most of my original testing was concentrated on my favorite caliber, 7mm. In 1982, when it came time to release this series, I had pressure barrels made up for Hornady's testing lab. Ballistician Mike Wright had agreed to run the special lab tests in my ten-inch and fourteen-inch pressure barrels. In the meantime, for ease of identification, I dubbed the cartridge simply as the 7-R from its full name of 7mm International Rimmed.

In the 1975-1976 period, there was only one category in the new silhouette game; open competition. There was no differentiation between production and unlimited guns. You could shoot anything that reasonably could be considered a handgun of any caliber and any modifications you wanted. Also, there was no overhang rule in these early days. Rams were set full-foot for handgun competition, the same as they were for rifle competition. Thus, my

TABLE 1

Table lists load data for 7-R in T/C Super 14 barrel rechambered from 7mm T/C. Comparison of performance using brass converted from .375 Winchester is made with rounds using .30-30 brass.

Thompson/Center Contender 14" 7-International Rimmed Converted from 7mm T/CU

Bullet: Hornady 7mm 154 gr. SP No. 2830
Primer: CCI No. 200 Large Rifle Primer
Chronograph: Oehler Model 33
Temperature: 55 Degrees

LOAD	IMR(.375 Brass) Muzzle Velocity	7-R (.30-30 Brass) Muzzle Velocity
28.0 gr. IMR4895	1663	1620
29.0 gr. IMR4895	1773	1677
30.0 gr. IMR4895	1834	1733
31.0 gr. IMR4895	1914	1947
32.0 gr. IMR4895	2038	2025 Max
32.5 gr. IMR4895	2176	–
33.0 gr. IMR4895	2191	–
25.0 gr. H4198	1898	–
26.0 gr. H4198	1920	1819
27.0 gr. H4198	1997	1886
28.0 gr. H4198	2095	1975 Max
28.5 gr. H4198	2108	–
29.0 gr. H4198	2164 Warm	–
29.5 gr. H4198	2212 Too Hot	–
26.0 gr. H322	1836	1736
27.0 gr. H322	1914	1836
28.0 gr. H322	1961	1847
29.0 gr. H322	2021	2022
30.0 gr. H322	2112 Warm	2024
28.0 gr. IMR3031	1784	1837
29.0 gr. IMR3031	1883	1864
30.0 gr. IMR3031	1964	1962
31.0 gr. IMR3031	2133 Too Hot	1996 Max
22.0 gr. MP5744	1824	1750
22.5 gr. MP5744	1859	1809
23.0 gr. MP5744	1859	1865
23.5 gr. MP5744	1921	1895
24.0 gr. MP5744	1952	1922
24.5 gr. MP5744	2025	1954
25.0 gr. MP5744	2089 Warm	1999
21.5 gr. Win-680	1837	1762
22.0 gr. Win-680	1851	1796
22.5 gr. Win-680	1865	1861 Warm
23.0 gr. Win-680	1904	1908 Hot
23.5 gr. Win-680	1947	–
24.0 gr. Win-680	2011	–
24.5 gr. Win-680	1992	–
26.0 gr. RE-7	1950	1868
26.5 gr. RE-7	1979	1948
27.0 gr. RE-7	2020	1936
27.5 gr. RE-7	2054	1944
28.0 gr. RE-7	2090	2015
28.0 gr. RE-7	2178 Too Hot	2047
28.0 gr. BLC-2	1745	1700
28.5 gr. BLC-2	1757	1726
29.0 gr. BLC-2	1805	1730
29.5 gr. BLC-2	1812	1751
30.0 gr. BLC-2	1807	1769
30.5 gr. BLC-2	1892	1799
31.0 gr. BLC-2	1914	1810
31.5 gr. BLC-2	1958	1906
32.0 gr. BLC-2	1999	1909

These three pistols were used in the author's pressure tests of 7-R cartridges. From top are the Super 14 Contender with Pachmayr grip, Wichita's silhouette pistol and a scope-sighted 10-inch T/C.

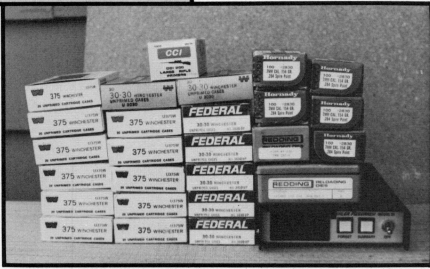

Components used in special tests of 7-R included .375 Winchester brass, .30-30 brass, assortment of bullets, Redding custom dies and chronograph made by Oehler.

A wide variety of bullets, brass and primers were needed to conduct the extensive loading tests on 7-R wildcat.

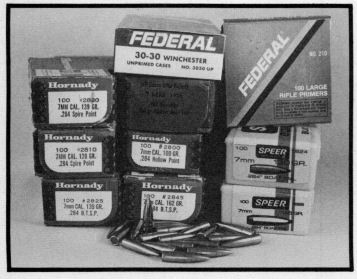

first consideration was to develop handgun silhouette cartridges powerful enough to knock down the hard-set rams consistently.

At first, I worked with a version of the 7-R case with the neck cut down to the same overall length of the 7mm IHMSA International, but for two specific reasons, I decided to retain the full 2.040-inch length of the .30-30 case.

Why? First, because the long neck would give better support and alignment for the long 160-175-grain 7mm bullets that were being used by silhouetters. Second, and more important, my entire philosophy was to design a high-performance 7mm production cartridge with the minimum possible amount of brass work involved. Anyone who has gone through the tiring, brass-wrestling chore of forming, trimming and cutting .30-30 cases down to make something like the .30 Herrett cases, or the nightmare of the endless struggle of making 1.5-inch BR brass from the full length .308 version, or even the semi-hassle of the expanding, neck-splitting chore of making 7mm TC cases from .223 brass knows what I'm talking about. There are a few purists out there who actually *like* to make such brass, but by far the vast majority of silhouette shooters don't enjoy it at all.

Forming the 7-R brass from common .30-30 brass is as

TABLE 2

Table 2 offers the same comparison of .375 Winchester brass versus .30-30 brass, when fired in the Wichita silhouette pistol.

Wichita 10½" 7-International Rimmed

Bullet: Hornady 7mm 154 gr. SP No. 2830
Primer: CCI No. 200 Large Rifle Primer
Chronograph: Oehler Model 33
Temperature: 55 Degrees

All loads very uniform in Witchita. No. primer problems using .30-30 brass. All fired cases fall easily from chamber.

Load	7-R (.375 Brass) Muzzle Velocity	7-R (.30-30 Brass) Muzzle Velocity
28.0 gr. IMR4895	1609	1581
29.0 gr. IMR4895	1746	1638
30.0 gr. IMR4895	1797	1735
31.1 gr. IMR4895	1862	1807
32.0 gr. IMR4895	1963	1891
32.5 gr. IMR4895	2022 Warm	2002
33.0 gr. IMR4895	2118 Too Hot	2013
25.0 gr. H4198	1788	1794
26.0 gr. H4198	1864 Max	1834
27.0 gr. H4198	1962 Hot	1967 Warm
28.0 gr. H4198	2001 Too Hot	2034 Max
26.0 gr. H322	1784	1817
27.0 gr. H322	1846	1823
28.0 gr. H322	1874 Max	1844
29.0 gr. H322	1960 Hot	1947
30.0 gr. H322	2026 Too Hot	2001 Hot
28.0 gr. IMR3031	1663	1622
29.0 gr. IMR3031	1757	1767
30.0 gr. IMR3031	1808 Max	1812
31.0 gr. IMR3031	1971 Too Hot	1851
22.0 gr. MP5744	1746	1764
22.5 gr. MP5744	1779	1804
23.0 gr. MP5744	1801	1821
23.5 gr. MP5744	1859	1886
24.0 gr. MP5744	1911 Max	1918
24.5 gr. MP5744	1971 Too Hot	1966
25.0 gr. MP5744	–	2002 Max
21.5 gr. Win-680	1827 Too Hot	1762
22.0 gr. Win-680	–	1796
22.5 gr. Win-680	–	1861 Warm
23.0 gr. Win-680	–	1873 Hot
26.0 gr. RE-7	1892	1786
26.5 gr. RE-7	1908 Too Hot	1844
27.0 gr. RE-7	–	1898
28.0 gr. RE-7	–	1873 Hot
28.0 gr. BLC-2	1593	1490
28.5 gr. BLC-2	1616	1583
29.0 gr. BLC-2	1648	1579
29.5 gr. BLC-2	1635	1615
30.0 gr. BLC-2	1747	1616
30.5 gr. BLC-2	1805	1679
31.0 gr. BLC-2	1814	1711
31.5 gr. BLC-2	1804	1734
32.0 gr. BLC-2	1915	1800

No primer cratering problems with any of the above loads using BLC-2

Erratic velocities using IMR3031 in all loads.

Loads marked hot: Primer slightly cratered
Loads marked too hot: Primers cratered, flowing back into firing pin hole. DO NOT USE!

METALLIC SILHOUETTE SHOOTING

From left: .375 Winchester virgin brass; case necked to .30 caliber as first step in conversion; necked to 7-R; Hornady 154-grain bullet; a bullet loaded in the case. At right is a case that has been fire-formed.

Accuracy of the 7-R loadings is shown by the bare-metal grouping near the center of the silhouette.

simple as ordinary loading, and that's the way I intended it to be. All that is required is one light stroke through the 7-R full-length die to neck the case to 7mm and establish the junction of the neck and shoulder. At this point, all that is necessary is to prime the case, put the powder charge in, seat the bullet in the ordinary reloading procedure and it is ready to fire. The round shoulder is the easiest part of all. On a rimmed case, the headspace is taken up on the rim, not the shoulder. Simply fire the round the first time for practice with a standard load and the case comes out of your gun perfectly fire-formed to the chamber.

With full charges, the 7-R turned out to be a potent production cartridge. So much so that a couple of the handgun makers were worried about the liability potential of a non-SAAMI created cartridge, even though the IHMSA technical committee approved it.

Other manufacturers, such as the M.O.A. Corporation, builders of the falling-block Maximum, Wichita, Competition Arms, and others with single-shot pistols having extremely strong actions, readily accepted the 7-R and chambered for it. Super 14 Thompson/Center barrels in 7mm T/C were rechambered to the 7-R and found ready acceptance by silhouette shooters seeking a modestly priced unlimited silhouette pistol.

The Contender, with a Super 14 barrel in 7-R, has been quite successful against the bolt guns in most of the lower classes of unlimited competition.

One minor problem was the old (circa 1895) .30-30 brass which was marginal in strength with the maximum silhouette loadings cranked out by silhouetters striving for ever more velocity, flatter trajectory and maximum knockdown power against the heavy rams. The guns being used were strong enough, and the old .30-30 brass worked fine with moderate loads — the 7-R case has about twenty-five percent more capacity than, for example, the 7mm/.223 case — but pushed to its limit of 38,000 CUP and beyond, the .30-30 brass was strained badly.

With this in mind, the next step was to go to the previously mentioned .375 Winchester brass which is thicker, tougher and has a pressure rating of 15,000 CUP more than .30-30 brass.

The accompanying load data tables cover the 7-R in both the .30-30 versions and the .375 versions for the Wichita silhouette pistol and the T/C Super 14 barrel chambered in 7-R.

Table A covers loads that utilize standard .30-30 Winchester-Western cases formed to 7mm International Rimmed (7-R) specifications, as described.

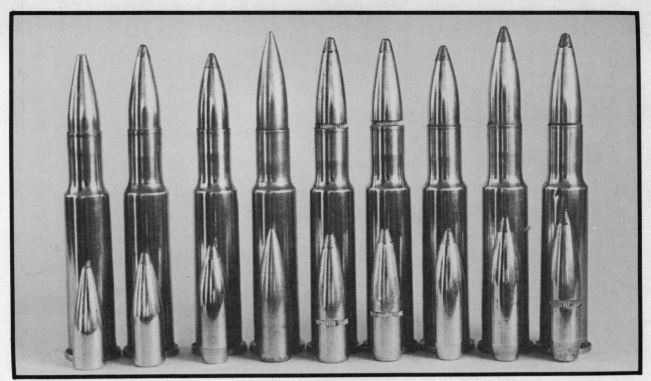

Bullets used in the extensive 7-R tests are (from left): 100-grain Hornady HP; 120-grain Hornady SP; 130-grain Speer BTSP; 139-grain military FMJ; 139-grain Hornady SP; 139-grain BTSP from Hornady; 145-grain Sierra BTSP; 160-grain Sierra SPT; and Hornady's 162-grain BTSP, which is the heaviest built of the group subjected to tests.

TABLE 3

Table 3 covers recommended top loads for the Super-14 Contender in 7-R and the Wichita silhouette pistol in 7-R.

Recommended Top Loads For the 7-R T/C 14" Using Hornady 154 gr. Sp

Power	Using .375 Brass	Using .30-30 Brass
IMR4895	32.5 grs. at 2176 fps	31.0 grs. at 1947 fps.
H4198	28.0 grs. at 2095 fps	26.0 grs. at 1819 fps.
H322	29.0 grs. at 2021 fps	28.0 grs. at 1847 fps.
IMR3031	30.0 grs. at 1964 fps	29.0 grs. at 1864 fps
MP5744	24.5 grs. at 2025 fpr	23.5 grs. at 1895 fps.
Win-680	24.0 grs. at 2011 fps	22.0 grs. at 1796 fps.
RE-7	28.0 grs. at 2090 fps	26.5 grs. at 1948 fps.
BLC-2	32.0 at 1999 fps	31.0 grs. at 1810 fps.

None of the above loads should be taken for granted. Always start low and work up carefully!

Recommended Top Loads For The Wichita 10½" 7-R Using Hornady 154 gr. Sp.

Powder	Using .375 Brass	Using .30-30 Brass
IMR4895	32.0 grs. at 1963 fps.	32.5 grs. at 2002 fps.
H4198	26.0 grs. at 1864 fps.	27.0 grs. at 1967 fps.
H322	28.0 grs. at 1874 fps.	29.0 grs. at 1947 fps.

IMR3031-Velocities erractic in Wichita-Not Recommended!

MP5744	24.0 grs. at 1911 fps.	24.5 grs. at 1966 fps.

Win 680-Pressures build too fast, not recommended

RE-7	26.0 grs. at 1892 fps.	27.0 grs. at 1898 fps.
BLC-2	32.0 grs. at 1915 fps	32.0 grs. at 1800 fps.

None of the above loads should be taken for granted. Always start low and work up carefully. Pressure builds faster in 7-R brass made of .375 brass than it does in 7-R brass made from .30-30 brass. Sharp recoil of the Wichita with loads over 1800 fps will cause most shooters to load at 1900 fps or lower.

Silhouette Loads For The Thompson-Center Contender Cover The Entire Range!

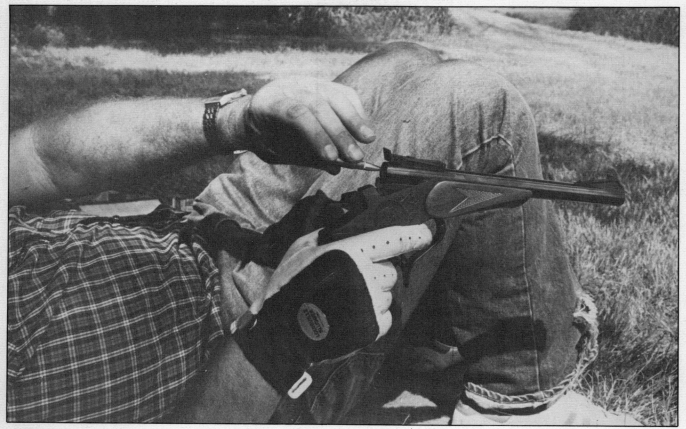

Competitor loads a .357 Herrett wildcat cartridge into the 10-inch bull-barrel Contender single-shot pistol. The first 40x40 score with a production handgun was fired in an officially sanctioned match with this round.

OVER THE past ten years, the Thompson-Center *Contender* has been one of the most versatile single-shot pistols available for the handgun metallic silhouette game.

Introduced in 1967, the Contender first came with light barrels chambered for a few of the common pistol cartridges. It quickly gained acceptance by target shooters and handgun hunters.

In 1975, when the first handgun silhouette championships were held, there was a single Contender, chambered in .44 magnum with a light barrel. A year later, at the second handgun silhouette championships held in El Paso, Texas, several Contenders with custom heavy barrels were introduced in competition.

From the beginning of the sport, Warren Center was extremely interested in the new silhouette game and was quick to listen to ideas and suggestions from silhouette shooters.

In late 1975 and early 1976, I had done some all-out testing with some of my Contenders, using special fifteen- and sixteen-inch barrels I had chambered and installed. As a result of correspondence and telephone calls with Warren Center, urging him to provide the long, heavy barrels as a standard factory item, the Super 14-inch bull barrels were introduced in the spring of 1977. Both the heavy ten-inch and the Super 14 bull barrels are direct byproducts of the silhouette game.

Back in 1972, three years before the handgun silhouette game got under way, Steve Herrett of Twin Falls, Idaho, came up with a .30-caliber wildcat hunting cartridge for the Contender and hung his name on it as the .30 Herrett. It was made from the .30-30 Winchester case by reducing its length from 2.03 inches to 1.61 inches.

In 1973, Thompson-Center offered Contenders chambered for this round. Being superior in performance to cartridges like the .30 Carbine and the .357 magnum, a fair amount of interest was generated in the ranks of handgun hunters.

Two years later, Thompson-Center came out with the .357 Herrett, also made from the .30-30 case, but this time cut to 1.75 inches.

Both of the Herrett cartridges were likely candidates for the silhouette game, and by 1977, both were being used steadily, especially the .30 Herrett.

The first perfect production gun 40X40 score ever recorded was fired in California by Bob Mijares with a .357

Herrett in a ten-inch bull barrel Contender on July 28, 1979. (The details are described in the chapter dealing with silhouette records.)

In spite of this record and good performance by the .30 Herrett, neither cartridge became too popular in the handgun silhouette game because of the difficulty in forming cases and the ensuing problems that went with it.

Normally, rimmed cases like the .30-30 are headspaced on the rim. However, due to form dies being manufactured improperly — and lack of technical understanding by new silhouette shooters — a host of problems were encountered. Unless precisely formed and properly headspaced, misfires, sub-par accuracy and short case life plagued the beginners.

More important, as silhouette handgunning went into high gear, was the appearance of better, more potent and more effective cartridges that were easier to form and load. After a brief reign near the top, both of the Herrett cartridges were pretty well replaced by the 7mm/.223 and several others. To be sure, both of the Herretts still are used for silhouette competition today and reliable load data has been developed.

While handgun hunters generally prefer lighter bullets, silhouetters choose the heavy bullets every time. The data that follows covers bullets from 100 to 150 grains for the .30 Herrett.

There will be a few Doubting Thomases around who will snort with disdain over what they will consider the "sissy" loads presented in these tables. My own contention is that hand-numbing, big boom, "dynamite" loads seldom are accurate, even if the pistol stays in one piece after firing them. Accuracy is more important than ultra velocity "show-off." Safety is more important than gun-busting "earthquake" loads. What is presented here is a combination of safe, near maximum (in many instances) and accurate loadings for the handgun metallic silhouette sport.

Special note: For those interested in a high pressure, high performance case for the .30 Herrett, the .375 Super Mag Winchester case cut down to 1.600 — the length of the .30 Herrett case — is ideal. It has a CUP rating of 53,000 against the 38,000 rating of the .30-30 case. A special Redding die forms the neck down to .30 caliber and establishes the shoulder. A second pass through the .30 Herrett full-length die does the rest.

.30 Herrett

CARTRIDGE: .30 Herrett
GUN: T/C Contender
BARREL AND LENGTH: Factory 10-inch and 14-inch bull barrel
TWIST: 1:10
PRIMER: Federal 210
CASE: Winchester .30-30 formed to .30 Herrett
BULLET: see below

These tests are based on ten-shot groups fired at fifty meters from sandbag-rest position.

POWDER	WEIGHT IN GRAINS	AVERAGE MUZZLE VELOCITY FPS 10" BBL	AVERAGE MUZZLE VELOCITY FPS 14" BBL	REMARKS
SPEER 110-gr. RN				
H-4227	24.5	2342	2520	accurate
H-4227	24.0	2304	2488	accurate
2400	23.5	2498	2560	max
WIN-296	23.0	2407	2543	max
WIN-296	22.5	2315	2568	very accurate
IMR-4227	25.2	2354	2542	very accurate
SIERRA 125 GR. SPITZER				
IMR-4227	24.2	2240	2360	accurate
HORNADY 130 GR. SPIRE-POINT				
WIN-296	26.6	2068	2243	accurate
SR4759	22.5	2015	2320	
H-4227	22.5	2107	2268	accurate
WIN-680	25.0	2165	2293	
IMR-4227	25.0	2380	2497	max
IMR-4198	27.5	2215	2353	accurate
SPEER 150 GR. SPITZER				
WIN-296	21.6	2003	2107	
H-4227	21.5	1917	2043	
WIN-680	22.0	1933	2067	
IMR-4227	21.5	1906	2037	
IMR-4198	25.5	2009	2102	

Note: All load data and information in this book is the result of safe and careful testing by the author and other contributors submitting the material contained herein. Since neither the author, DBI Books, Inc., nor any of the contributors has any control over the components, equipment and techniques used with this published information, no liability or responsibility for any injury or damage that occurs is either implied or assumed.

The late Elmer Keith (right) discusses development of cartridges with the author. Although Keith never was a serious silhouette competitor, he had a great deal to do with introducing such loads as the .357, .44 magnums.

During 1979 and 1980, several important improvements were made in the Contender by Warren Center as a result of the handgun silhouette game. It was no accident that the Contender was evolving rapidly into a precision shooting machine.

For the first couple of years of the sport, production single-shots were classed in the same category with revolvers, but it wasn't long before that would be changed by the superior performance of the Contender. At the same time, a sort of do-nothing apathy prevailed among revolver makers. They saw their products as short-range arms that few, if any shooters, used for long-range shooting. They saw no reason to make improvements or provide better sights. By the end of 1980, the Contender totally dominated the production category to the point that IHMSA created a separate revolver category.

Over and over, Warren Center has continued to acknowledge his gratitude to IHMSA competitors for consuming huge quantities of ammunition and thereby exposing some engineering flaws in the gun as it was designed originally.

Present Contenders have the best lockup ever and excellent reliability. Here is a partial list of improvements:

BOLT TABLE: The recess below the receiver face against which the spring-loaded bolt locks is the bolt table. The angle of the bolt table was changed in 1979 to match the engagement surface of the bolt more closely. The angles of the bolt and bolt table cannot be parallel or the action would seize and be impossible to open.

SPLIT BOLT: A new split bolt was incorporated to facilitate opening the action with its superior lockup, and to permit the bolt to follow the bolt table more securely. The bolt also was redimensioned to further intensify lockup.

UNDERLUG: The portion of the underlug directly below the bolt was made heavier and given a new heat treatment to provide the bolt with greater support at the moment of firing.

Contrary to the thoughts of a few individuals who believe Contender accuracy centers on the hinge pin, exhaustive testing show it emanates from sound lockup.

WATER TABLE: As with break-open shotguns, the receiver ways, which support the chamber section of the barrel, are called the water table. The water table, where it joins the receiver face, was beefed up to prevent the possibility of receiver-flex in this area.

LOCKWORK: Various subtle changes were introduced to the lockwork to sophisticate timing.

FURNITURE: New finger-groove stocks and a longer forend were supplied by Steve Herrett. These, in turn, would be replaced on 1987 Contenders with what is called the "Competitor" grip — wood backed with a rubber cushion that several handgun makers are adopting. Also included in 1987 was a new slimmer forend.

BARRELS: The biggest option offered by Thompson-Center is the wide array of different barrels and chamberings. In the IHMSA game, competition is with the ever-popular T/C bull barrels.

SIGHTS: More than any other handgun manufacturer, Thompson-Center, again with Warren Center's expertise and design genius holding sway, have led the way in improved sights. By 1980, a complete new and improved rear sight was available. Early 1987 saw the introduction of T/C Ultimate sights as accessory items, both front and rear.

The Ultimate sight readily fits any existing Contender, ten-inch or Super 14. The all-steel assembly allows the shooter to select any of four different notch widths — .060, .080, .100 or .120-inch — simply by rotating the notch selector. A wide elevation screw offers positive click adjustment at thirty per revolution, each click being the equivalent of one-half inch at one hundred meters. The Ultimate front sight also is all-steel. The shooter may select any one of four different blade widths the same as the rear sight widths simply by rotating the blade selector.

Development and product refinement continues at Thompson-Center. Warren Center, although virtually totally retired, still keeps his hands in and listens to silhouette shooters. In addition, there is a fine crew at Thompson-Center to provide ideas and help in carrying them out. More improvements are promised.

While never considered as top performer in silhouette, the old .35 Remington is an effective cartridge and no treatise on silhouette load data would be complete without it.

.35 Remington

CARTRIDGE: .35 Remington
GUN: T/C Contender
BARREL AND LENGTH: Factory 14-inch bull barrel
TWIST: 1:14
PRIMER: Federal 210
CASE: Winchester
BULLET: see below

These tests are based on ten-shot groups fired at fifty meters from sandbag rest position.

BULLET	POWDER	WEIGHT IN GRAINS	AVERAGE MUZZLE VELOCITY FPS	REMARKS
180-gr. Speer TMJ	H-414	45.0	1628	start
180-gr. Speer TMJ	H-414	46.5	1741	max
180-gr. Speer TMJ	H-322	39.5	1993	start
180-gr. Speer TMJ	H-322	42.1	2227	max
180-gr. Speer TMJ	IMR-4895	38.2	1793	start
180-gr. Speer TMJ	IMR-4895	40.0	1893	max
180-gr. Speer TMJ	IMR-4198	30.2	1847	accurate
200-gr. Hornady RM	WW748	39.5	1704	start
200-gr. Hornady RM	WW748	41.5	1803	max
200-gr. Hornady RM	IMR-4895	36.4	1662	start
200-gr. Hornady RM	IMR-4895	38.1	1787	max
200-gr. Hornady RM	IMR-4198	26.5	1583	start
200-gr. Hornady RM	IMR-4198	28.5	1790	max
200-gr. Hornady RM	RE-7	26.2	1532	start
200-gr. Hornady RM	RE-7	28.2	1621	accurate
220-gr. Speer FN	H-4895	33.4	1527	start
220-gr. Speer FN	H-4895	35.4	1607	accurate
220-gr. Speer FN	WW748	33.2	1448	start
220-gr. Speer FN	WW748	35.2	1565	max
220-gr. Speer FN	RE-7	23.0	1273	start
220-gr. Speer FN	RE-7	24.5	1415	max
220-gr. Speer FN	H-335	32.0	1523	max

Note: All load data and information in this book is the result of safe and careful testing by the author and other contributors submitting the material contained herein. Since neither the author, DBI Books, Inc., nor any of the contributors has any control over the components, equipment and techniques used with this published information, no liability or responsibility for any injury or damage that occurs is either implied or assumed.

.30-30 WINCHESTER

The .30-30 Winchester cartridge was created in 1894 and first marketed in 1895 for the Model 94 lever-action rifle.

Nobody in his right mind ever would have dreamed this old dog would become a potent pistol cartridge eighty-five years later for handgun metallic silhouette competition, nor that dozens of wildcat silhouette cartridges would be based on it.

Even in its original configuration, it became a top performer, second only to a few of the high-performance 7mm silhouette rounds. At the IHMSA Internationals of 1982, Richard Folz of Alaska won the title of international production gun champion with a standard ten-inch bull barrel Contender chambered in .30-30. Folz shot a perfect 80x80 score, then won the shootoff to take top honors.

Thompson-Center was the first handgun manufacturer to commercially chamber a pistol for the standard factory .30-30 round. Eventually other single-shot pistol makers would follow suit.

In a game of high pressure cartridges and heavy bullets, there are some drawbacks to the .30-30. For one, its CUP rating — copper units of pressure — of 38,000, while more than adequate for the old, low pressure lever-action rifles, the brass is barely strong strong enough for some of the high-performance silhouette cartridges that have been made from it.

During my own experimental ballistic developments, I found the standard .30-30 case marginal for heavy-duty silhouette work. Consequently, I collaborated with Richard Beebe of Redding to produce a special one-stage forming die that will convert the newer .375 Winchester rifle brass with a CUP rating of 53,000 to perfectly formed .30-30 brass with one simple pass through the die.

I have not explored the upper limits of high performance to be had out of this brass in .30 caliber, as I have with the top-ranked silhouette caliber of 7mm. Suffice to say that the maximum .30-30 loadings in the following tables can be increased somewhat without affecting accuracy *by using reformed .375 Winchester rifle brass.*

Any shooter using .375 Winchester brass reformed to .30-30 in the manner described should proceed with caution by raising the listed power charges a half-grain at a time, watching carefully for excessive pressure signs on the primer and for chamber binding. That's the place to

.30-30 Winchester

CARTRIDGE: .30-30 Winchester
GUN: T/C Contender
BARREL AND LENGTH: Factory 10-inch and 14-inch bull barrel
TWIST: 1:10
PRIMER: CCI 250
CASE: Federal
BULLET: see below

These tests are based on ten-shot groups fired at fifty meters from sandbag-rest position.

BULLET	POWDER	WEIGHT IN GRAINS	AVERAGE MUZZLE VELOCITY FPS 10" BBL	AVERAGE MUZZLE VELOCITY FPS 14" BBL
110-gr. Speer SP	WW296	18.0	1782	1923
110-gr. Speer SP	IMR-4227	18.5	1741	1903
110-gr. Speer SP	WW680	20.2	1846	1890
110-gr. Speer SP	RE-7	26.2	1937	2045
110-gr. Speer SP	IMR-3031	32.0	1863	2012
130-gr. Hornady SP	WW296	18.0	1724	1873
130-gr. Hornady SP	IMR-4227	18.2	1652	1804
130-gr. Hornady SP	WW680	19.0	1753	1902
130-gr. Hornady SP	RE-7	25.0	1829	1973
130-gr. Hornady SP	H-4198	27.0	2083	2198 max
150-Speer Spitzer	2400	16.5	1544	1692
150-Speer Spitzer	WW296	18.0	1523	1674
150-Speer Spitzer	H-4895	33.0	1824	1981 max
150-Speer Spitzer	H-4198	26.2	1893	2032 max
150-Speer Spitzer	H-335	33.1	1822	1978 max
165-gr. Hornady SP	2400	15.0	1373	1520
165-gr. Hornady SP	WW680	19.2	1538	1684
165-gr. Hornady SP	RE-7	24.0	1740	1992
165-gr. Hornady SP	H-335	32.0	1820	1968
165-gr. Hornady SP	H-4895	30.0	1729	1874
165-gr. Hornady SP	H-4198	26.0	1765	1898
165-gr. Hornady SP	H-322	29.0	1783	1927

Note: All load data and information in this book is the result of safe and careful testing by the author and other contributors submitting the material contained herein. Since neither the author, DBI Books, Inc., nor any of the contributors has any control over the components, equipment and techniques used with this published information, no liability or responsibility for any injury or damage that occurs is either implied or assumed.

stop and back off a half-grain or so until the case extracts easily.

.357 MAGNUM

While originally created as a revolver cartridge, the old .357 magnum rimmed case was one of the first rounds latched onto by every manufacturer of single-shot pistols. It is widely popular, fairly safe and brass is available worldwide.

As the silhouette game gained momentum, both the .357 magnum and the .44 magnum in revolvers AND single-shots were the first calibers with which most shooters started. The big drawback, at first, was insufficient bullet weight. The slow-moving 158-grain .357 bullets just wouldn't take down the heavy rams reliably.

I hammered long, hard and repeatedly on every bullet-maker in the country during the 1976-1978 period to get them to make heavy-jacketed .357 bullets. In the meantime, my own experiments were carried out with .358 rifle bullets such as the 180-grain Speer flat-nose, and the 200-grain Remington, Hornady and Sierra bullets. Negotiations with Bob Hayden of Sierra, in those early days, resulted in some prototype 170-grain and 200-grain full metal jacketed .357 bullets.

No matter what I tried, the old .357 magnum case, circa 1935, had met its match against the steel silhouette rams and results were marginal until we adopted the ram overhang rule. This allowed the rams to be set on the stands with the rear edge of the feet overhanging the back edge of the stand; this required less striking force to topple them over. This rule change revived the old .357 magnum for a couple more years, until the .357 Super Mag made its debut. After that, the .357 magnum faded out rather quickly, with only a few women shooters and old-timers left to play with it along a cadre of shooters in the lower classes.

Then, in 1986, IMHSA adopted the field pistol course of fire using half-size silhouette targets at half distances: 25, 50, 75 and 100 yards or meters. Once again, the venerable old .357 magnum made a comeback. Everybody has a .357 magnum revolver or single-shot in his gun room and all one had to do was wipe off the dust and bring it out to use in the new field pistol game.

The load data listed is for the heavier bullets and loads used in the T/C Contender for the full-size silhouettes at fifty to two hundred meters.

.357 Magnum

CARTRIDGE: .357 Magnum
GUN: T/C Contender
BARREL AND LENGTH: Factory 10-inch
TWIST: 1:14
PRIMER: Federal
CASE: Federal
BULLET: Listed below

These tests are based on ten-shot groups fired at fifty meters from sandbag-rest position.

BULLET	POWDER	WEIGHT IN GRAINS	AVERAGE MUZZLE VELOCITY FPS	REMARKS
158-gr. Sierra	H-4227	14.0	1463	
158-gr. Sierra	H-4227	15.5	1567	
158-gr. Sierra	H-110	15.2	1555	accurate
158-gr. Sierra	H-110	16.1	1624	
170-gr. Sierra	H-4227	13.5	1256	
170-gr. Sierra	H-4227	14.1	1285	
170-gr. Sierra	H-110	14.5	1347	
170-gr. Sierra	H-110	15.1	1398	
180-gr. Speer	H-4227	12.2	1167	
180-gr. Speer	H-4227	13.6	1273	
180-gr. Speer	H-110	13.2	1246	
180-gr. Speer	H-110	14.1	1291	accurate
180-gr. Speer	WW680	16.0	1540	
180-gr. Speer	WW296	15.5	1520	
180-gr. Speer	2400	13.5	1422	
180-gr. Speer	IMR-4227	15.6	1418	
200-gr. Speer	H-110	14.5	1397	
200-gr. Speer	WW296	14.0	1376	
200-gr. Speer	2400	12.1	1336	accurate
200-gr. Speer	IMR-4227	13.3	1225	
200-gr. Speer	AA #9	12.6	1350	
200-gr. Speer	WW680	14.0	1352	

Note: All load data and information in this book is the result of safe and careful testing by the author and other contributors submitting the material contained herein. Since neither the author, DBI Books, Inc., nor any of the contributors has any control over the components, equipment and techniques used with this published information, no liability or responsibility for any injury or damage that occurs is either implied or assumed.

THE .357 SUPER MAG

The .357 Super Mag cartridge, developed by the author, has enjoyed phenomenal success in revolver silhouette competition, for which it was designed. The story of its development, as well as revolver load data, is detailed in seperate chapters.

It also has been successful as a single-shot cartridge, particularly in the Contender, and is capable of astounding accuracy.

Written off early by some gun writers, the .357 Super Mag has proved to have the combined qualities of excellent accuracy and relatively low recoil. It is one cartridge that not only is available for all three forms of competition — revolver, production and unlimited — but it is also possible to come up with one load that works in all three classes of competition. It gives fifty-meter ten-shot groups of less than one-inch in ten-inch and fourteen-inch T/C bull barrels.

The best bullets available for the .357 Super Mag are the 180-and 200-grain FMJs with the 200-grain Speer FMJ probably the best all-around choice. The best powders proved to WIN-296, WIN-680 and H4227 for the test results shown here.

Target that is a spring-loaded pop-up type was used to test the Super 14 Contender in .44 magnum. Results of the tests are reflected on splashes on chicken target.

.357 Super Mag/.357 Maximum

CARTRIDGE: .357 Super Mag (Maximum)
GUN: T/C Contender
BARREL AND LENGTH: Factory 10" and 14" bull barrel
TWIST: 1:14
PRIMER: Federal 205 M
CASE: Federal
BULLET: see below

These tests are based on ten-shot groups fired at fifty meters from sandbag-rest position.

BULLET	POWDER	WEIGHT IN GRAINS	AVERAGE MUZZLE VELOCITY FPS 10" BBL	AVERAGE MUZZLE VELOCITY FPS 14" BBL
158-gr. Hornady JHP	WW296	26.0	2092	2187
170-gr. Sierra FMJ	H-110	23.0	1804	1954
170-gr. Sierra FMJ	WW296	21.5	1843	1962
170-gr. Sierra FMJ	WW296	24.0	1948	2082
170-gr. Sierra FMJ	WW296	24.8	1957	2126
170-gr. Sierra FMJ	H-110	25.0	1940	2083
180-gr. Speer FP	WW296	17.0	1540	1601
180-gr. Speer FP	WW296	18.0	1588	1654
180-gr. Speer FP	WW296	25.7	1982	2148
180-gr. Hornady FMJ	WW680	23.0	1617	1712
180-gr. Hornady FMJ	WW680	24.0	1753	1836
180-gr. Hornady FMJ	H-4227	21.0	1563	1627
180-gr. Hornady FMJ	H-427	20.0	1614	1704
200-gr. Speer FMJ	WW680	21.0	1510	1587
200-gr. Speer FMJ	H-4227	20.0	1501	1554
200-gr. Speer FMJ	H-4198	23.0	1403	1476
200-gr. Speer FMJ	H-4198	24.0	1463	1542
200-gr. Sierra RN	WW680	24.1	1643	1748
200-gr. Sierra RN	WW680	25.2	1697	1793
200-gr. Sierra RN	H-4198	24.1	1366	1417
200-gr. Sierra RN	H-4198	25.1	1493	1607

Note: All load data and information in this book is the result of safe and careful testing by the author and other contributors submitting the material contained herein. Since neither the author, DBI Books, Inc., nor any of the contributors has any control over the components, equipment and techniques used with this published information, no liability or responsibility for any injury or damage that occurs is either implied or assumed.

.41 MAGNUM

For reasons that probably never will be properly explained, the .41 magnum is one of those handgun cartridges that never caught on in a big way, either in the overall world of handgunning or in the silhouette game.

The late Elmer Keith, the late Skeeter Skelton and dozens of others have lauded the .41 magnum in various degrees as a great hunting round, the answer to law enforcement and so on. Actually, it is a perfectly good cartridge, but as mentioned, it just never caught on in a big way. Not enough horsepower to significantly outshine the .357 magnum and no way to catch up with the .44 magnum.

The caliber first entered the scene in 1877, when Colt introduced it for their double-action Lightning model as the .41 Long Colt. Later, it was used in the Single-Action Army, Army Special, New Army, New Navy and the Bisley. There also was a .41 Short Colt.

In its early days, it was quite popular. I remember a long-ago day in 1938, working in a gas station on highway 66 near the Arizona-California border, when I traded ten gallons of gasoline for a Colt .41 Army Special revolver with a five-inch barrel to an Oklahoman on his way to Bakersfield. With gas selling at twenty-two cents a gallon — it was nine cents a gallon in Los Angeles — I figured it was a good buy. I enjoyed a lot of fun plinking with that old gun. It still resides in my collection.

Like other calibers, the .41 remained somewhat dormant until resurrected in 1963, given a face-lift and introduced by Smith & Wesson in June 1964 in their Model 57 revolver. The same old trick of lengthening the case had been pulled, this time by a mere fifteen thousandths of an inch. Actually, to give give proper credit, the new .41 magnum case was improved in several important aspects. First, the bullet diameter was increased to a true .410 from the .386 diameter of the .41 Colt version. The neck diameter was .431 versus the original .405 and the rim was .488 diameter as opposed to .430 for the .41 Colt.

However, even this obvious upgrading and rejuvenation of the old .41 Long Colt still did not catch on in a popular way, and it has been rumored for several years that Smith & Wesson is on the verge of dropping their Model 57 from the lineup. It still was listed in their 1988 catalog, however.

As silhouette history goes, there was a single .41 Smith & Wesson magnum entered in the first silhouette championships of 1975, and a couple in the 1976 championships.

Thompson-Center got into the act by offering the .41 magnum as a chambering for their Contender for a number of years and, in the early days of silhouette competition, this caliber appeared as an occasional winner. However, its slowly declining popularity and lack of sales finally convinced Thompson-Center to drop the .41 magnum from their catalog.

The data presented here is for silhouette shooting with the .41 Contender using ten- and fourteen-inch bull barrels.

.41 Magnum

CARTRIDGE: .41 Magnum
GUN: T/C Contender
BARREL AND LENGTH: 10" + 14" factory bull barrels
TWIST: 1:20
PRIMER: Federal 210 large pistol
CASE: Winchester
BULLET: see below

These tests are based on ten-shot groups fired at fifty meters from sandbag-rest position.

BULLET	POWDER	WEIGHT IN GRAINS	AVERAGE MUZZLE VELOCITY FPS 10" BBL	AVERAGE MUZZLE VELOCITY FPS 14" BBL
200-gr. Speer JHP	IMR-4227	20.5	1386	1443
200-gr. Speer JHP	Blue Dot	15.5	1537	1591 max
200-gr. Speer JHP	Unique	10.5	1415	1448 accurate
200-gr. Speer JHP	2400	15.2	1508	1567
200-gr. Speer JHP	WW296	20.0	1515	1577
210-gr. Sierra JHC	Blue Dot	14.2	1473	1546
210-gr. Sierra JHC	Unique	11.0	1437	1451
210-gr. Sierra JHC	2400	20.2	1515	1623
210-gr. Sierra JHC	IMR-4227	21.0	1408	1482
220-gr. Sierra SP	2400	17.5	1337	1368
220-gr. Sierra SP	IMR-4227	19.8	1310	1358
220-gr. Sierra SP	Blue Dot	14.3	1429	1462
220-gr. Sierra SP	Unique	10.0	1281	1337

Note: All load data and information in this book is the result of safe and careful testing by the author and other contributors submitting the material contained herein. Since neither the author, DBI Books, Inc., nor any of the contributors has any control over the components, equipment and techniques used with this published information, no liability or responsibility for any injury or damage that occurs is either implied or assumed.

.44 MAGNUM

One of the beloved straight-wall pistol cartridges, the .44 magnum has stayed in the silhouette game from day one. Although finally outclassed by the superior ballistics and accuracy of the .357 Super Mag, the .44 magnum is still going strong and is still a big winner in the revolver classes on silhouette ranges across the country. Enough has been written about this cartridge during the past thirty-three years since its introduction in 1955 that it would be tedious to repeat it here.

My own ballistic experiments with the .44 magnum were limited specifically to silhouette applications. Two things were involved. The first was trying to convince the bullet industry we needed heavier bullets with thicker jackets. Secondly, my efforts were directed at the revolver makers, trying to get them to build stronger, more rugged guns for the silhouette game; guns that would stay together during the rigorous ordeal of silhouette competition.

All but one of the bulletmakers were responsive to my request for experimental .44 bullets. I also ran some 300-grain and 350-grain .45 caliber bullets through a special .44 swaging die and came up with some heavy .44 magnum bullets otherwise unavailable in those days. The results were both interesting and gratifying.

In retrospect, no stroke of ballistic genius was needed in working up powder-bullet combinations for the .44 magnum. We already had what we needed. Any bullet over 200 grains with sufficient velocity would knock down the heavy steel rams. In simple terms, the mass and momentum of a 200-grain-plus chunk of lead, jacketed or not, and its remaining energy — what I've always called *impact* energy in silhouette jargon — was enough to get the job done.

Given this, the only real problem was accuracy — to get the bullet there and impact it on the silhouette target. In short, hit 'em and you've got 'em.

The .44 magnum is far more popular in the silhouette game as a revolver cartridge and seldom is used these days in single-shot pistols. Nevertheless, load data has been developed for the Thompson-Center and is presented herewith, both for ten-inch and fourteen-inch bull barrels.

.44 Magnum

CARTRIDGE: .44 Magnum
GUN: T/C Contender
BARREL AND LENGTH: 10-inch and 14-inch factory bull barrels
TWIST: 1:22
PRIMER: Federal 210
CASE: see below

These tests are based on ten-shot groups fired at fifty meters from sandbag-rest position.

BULLET	POWDER	WEIGHT IN GRAINS	AVERAGE MUZZLE VELOCITY FPS 10" BBL	AVERAGE MUZZLE VELOCITY FPS 14" BBL
180-gr. Sierra JHC	BLue Dot	20.3	1776	1833
180-gr. Sierra JHC	Unique	13.6	1631	1682
180-gr. Sierra JHC	2400	25.4	1678	1771
180-gr. Sierra JHC	IMR-4227	27.0	1635	1743
180-gr. Sierra JHC	H-110	32.0	1983	2120 accurate
200-gr. Speer JHP	Blue Dot	18.8	1610	1697
200-gr. Speer JHP	Unique	13.0	1501	1573
200-gr. Speer JHP	2400	23.5	1560	1648 accurate
200-Speer JHP	IMR-4227	26.5	1635	1714
200-gr. Speer JHP	H-110	30.0	1847	1992
200-gr. Speer JHP	WW296	28.4	1740	1883
240-gr. Hornady FMJ	BLue Dot	16.8	1451	1542
240-gr. Hornady FMJ	Unique	12.2	1354	1415
240-gr. Hornady FMJ	2400	21.1	1424	1480 accurate
240-gr. Hornady FMJ	IMR-4227	23.2	1418	1509
240-gr. Hornady FMJ	WW296	22.8	1475	1571
265-gr. Hornady FP	Blue Dot	16.0	1374	1402
265-gr. Hornady FP	Unique	11.5	1250	1317
265-gr. Hornady FP	2400	20.5	1388	1421
265-gr. Hornady FP	IMR-4227	22.2	1377	1396
265-gr. Hornady FP	WW296	22.1	1465	1503 accurate

Note: All load data and information in this book is the result of safe and careful testing by the author and other contributors submitting the material contained herein. Since neither the author, DBI Books, Inc., nor any of the contributors has any control over the components, equipment and techniques used with this published information, no liability or responsibility for any injury or damage that occurs is either implied or assumed.

.45 WINCHESTER MAGNUM

The .45 Win Mag originally was developed for the Wildey semi-auto, gas-operated pistol in 1978-79. The same old stunt of getting more horsepower was used by the process of lengthening the .45 ACP case an extra .300 thousands from .898 to 1.198.

Actually, it is a fine cartridge with a good potential and, had it been brought out twenty or thirty years ago, it would have created a sensation in the firearms world.

There are claims that the .45 Win Mag and the Wildey originally were developed for hunting and the silhouette game. If so, it is a total mystery to me, as the Wildey never was officially submitted to IMHSA for approval by the rules committee.

At the first Shot Show ever held — 1979 in St. Louis — Wildey had a booth and we talked for a half-hour and looked over the prototype guns on display. The main problem was that the big pistol was over the maximum legal weight for IHMSA competition, except in the short-barrel version which would be of no interest to silhouette shooters. Another problem was that — like the Auto Mag — the Wildey went through a series of financial problems so that,

Split case of this .41 magnum was caused by overloading. As age and lot number of powders can cause a variance, it is best to start loads at 10 percent under the published data for the sake of shooter safety.

when the gun finally was produced in limited numbers, it had a price tag over $1000. This disqualifies it under IHMSA's production gun rule that puts a retail price limit of $675 on any pistol approved for competition in the production gun categories.

The silhouette load data presented here is for the ten-inch and fourteen-inch Contender bull barrels.

.45 Winchester Magnum

CARTRIDGE: .45 Winchester Magnum
GUN: T/C Contender
BARREL AND LENGTH: Factory 10-inch bull barrel and 14-inch
TWIST: 1:16
PRIMER: Federal 210
CASE: Winchester
BULLET: see below

These tests are based on ten-shot groups fired at fifty meters from sandbag-rest position.

BULLET	POWDER	WEIGHT IN GRAINS	AVERAGE MUZZLE VELOCITY FPS 10-inch	AVERAGE MUZZLE VELOCITY FPS 14-inch
185-gr. Sierra JHP	WW296	30.4	1926	1958
185-gr. Sierra JHP	2400	28.6	1873	1937
185-gr. Sierra JHP	H-110	29.2	1809	1878 accurate
185-gr. Sierra JHP	Blue Dot	21.3	1852	1967
200-gr. Speer JHP	WW296	30.0	1840	1951
200-gr. Speer JHP	2400	22.3	1516	1583 accurate
200-gr. Speer JHP	H-110	27.4	1657	1734
200-gr. Speer JHP	Blue Dot	19.1	1750	1783
230-gr. Hornady FMJ	WW296	28.2	1720	1814
230-gr. Hornady FMJ	2400	22.0	1473	1547 accurate
230-gr. Hornady FMJ	Unique	13.0	1457	1489
230-gr. Hornady FMJ	Blue Dot	18.2	1563	1622
250-gr. Hornady JHP	WW296	23.0	1502	1548 accurate
250-gr. Hornady JHP	IMR-4227	24.5	1515	1593
240-gr. Hornady JHP	2400	20.2	1403	1441
250-gr. Hornady JHP	HS-7	17.0	1410	1438 accurate
260-gr. Speer JHP	H-4227	22.0	1354	1367
260-gr. Speer JHP	H-110	22.2	1374	1398
260-gr. Speer JHP	HS-7	15.2	1241	1268
260-gr. Speer JHP	2400	21.1	1443	1479
260-gr. Speer JHP	IMR-4227	24.0	1384	1416
260-gr. Speer JHP	WW296	26.5	1593	1622

Note: All load data and information in this book is the result of safe and careful testing by the author and other contributors submitting the material contained herein. Since neither the author, DBI Books, Inc., nor any of the contributors has any control over the components, equipment and techniques used with this published information, no liability or responsibility for any injury or damage that occurs is either implied or assumed.

THE .45 LONG COLT

The .45 Long Colt is another caliber that never really caught on in silhouette competition, although it was used in the early days of the game, mostly as a revolver cartridge. It was another caliber that Thompson-Center chambered for a few years in their ten-inch bull barrel.

As the silhouette game progressed, one positive conclusion was established. In the beginning, the theory was simple: To knock down the heavy steel rams, use the biggest and — by assumption — the most powerful handgun you could get your hands on. Had any manufacturer chambered handguns for .50, .60 or even .70 or .80 caliber, some of the early silhouette shooters would have wanted them.

The prevailing idea — at least, for a short time — was to hit the steel rams with the biggest chunk of lead you could fire out of a pistol and hope for the best.

I am one of the few who saw it differently. It was obvious to me, at that very first 1975 silhouette championship, that the answer to shooting silhouettes successfully was with

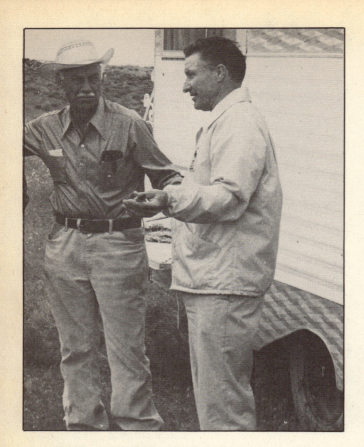

The late Steve Herrett (left) developed the .30 and .357 wildcat cartridges that bear his name. They originally were developed for hunting, but found rapid favor among silhouette shooters. (Below) David Bradshaw closes the action on a Contender chambered for the .45 Winchester mag. Though accurate, the cartridge never became too popular.

smaller calibers in the 7mm-.30 caliber range. For revolvers, I favored a maximum of .44 magnum, preferably a more potent .357 caliber. This was the motivation that led me to dig out my old .357 long case cartridges from African safari days of the early 1950s.

After ten years of intense silhouette competition, the proof is plain to see. The smaller caliber bottleneck cartridges with their higher velocities, better accuracy and better knock-down ballistics have dominated the sport.

It may ruffle some feathers when I state that the past five years of the game have made it obvious that the .357 Super Mag, with its accuracy and superior long range ballistics, is the premier revolver cartridge for silhouette. Within another ten years, unless some miracle gun/cartridge combination comes along, the .357 Super Mag will reign supreme.

And yes, the old and beloved .44 magnum will still be around. But in the demanding game of handgun metallic silhouette, the .44 magnum already has been eclipsed by the high performance .357 Super Mag. In years to come, my flat prediction is that the .44 magnum will fade slowly to near obsolescence in the silhouette game, at least in the ranks of the top competitors and champions. And as long as there are T/C Contenders out there chambered for the .45 Long Colt, some of them will be used in the silhouette game.

Competitor utilizes the spraddle-leg standing position as he levels his Contender on target. This significant pistol has been the top winner in standing competition.

.45 Long Colt

CARTRIDGE: .45 Long Colt
GUN: T/C Contender
BARREL AND LENGTH: Factory 10-inch bull barrel
TWIST: 1:24
PRIMER: Federal 210 large pistol
CASE: Winchester
BULLET: see below

These tests are based on ten-shot groups fired at fifty meters from sandbag-rest position.

BULLET	POWDER	WEIGHT IN GRAINS	AVERAGE MUZZLE VELOCITY FPS	REMARKS
200-gr. Speer JHP	H-4227	24.0	1373	
200-gr. Speer JHP	2400	21.5	1368	accurate
200-gr. Speer JHP	H-110	25.2	1407	
200-gr. Speer JHP	Blue Dot	16.0	1323	
240-gr. Sierra JHP	IMR-4227	25.0	1430	
240-gr. Sierra JHP	2400	23.2	1473	
240-gr. Sierra JHP	Unique	12.5	1356	accurate
240-gr. Sierra JHP	Blue Dot	14.5	1206	
240-gr. Sierra JHP	H-110	22.0	1260	
250-gr. Hornady JHP	IMR-4227	24.0	1364	accurate
250-gr. Hornady JHP	2400	22.2	1429	
250-gr. Hornady JHP	Blue Dot	14.8	1187	
250-gr. Hornady JHP	H-110	22.2	1263	
260-gr. Speer JHP	H-4227	20.1	1165	
260-gr. Speer JHP	H-110	21.0	1176	
260-gr. Speer JHP	Unique	10.0	1143	
260-gr. Speer JHP	HS-6	13.2	1160	
260-gr. Speer JHP	HS-7	14.6	1168	

Note: All load data and information in this book is the result of safe and careful testing by the author and other contributors submitting the material contained herein. Since neither the author, DBI Books, Inc., nor any of the contributors has any control over the components, equipment and techniques used with this published information, no liability or responsibility for any injury or damage that occurs is either implied or assumed.

Competitor levels down on javelina targets at 100 meters with a .357 magnum Ruger Blackhawk six-gun.

SILHOUETTE SIX-GUNS & LOADS

CHAPTER 11

...Or A History Of The Revolver In The Silhouette Sport

FROM THE day Samuel Colt sold his first pistol with a rotating cylinder, men have been fascinated with the revolver. Nothing can ever equal the romance and legend of the old West, where the single-action Colt reigned supreme.

It really didn't matter that six-guns had fixed sights or sometimes no sights at all. They were built for close-range shooting. Anything much beyond fifty feet was for rifles.

As the years went by, the revolver was improved and the double-action came into being. There were a few changes in the single-action, but not many. Men liked them the way they were and the basic design has remained about the same for well over a hundred years. And when Colt's patents ran out, there were lots of imitators ready for a piece of the action. They didn't change the design, either.

When the handgun metallic silhouette game came along, it was only natural that revolvers would be used. In fact, a brief resume of the early silhouette match statistics show that revolvers dominated the competition.

At the first-ever shoot in 1975, of the forty-six handguns listed, thirty of them were revolvers. Fourteen were Smith & Wessons, nine were Rugers and seven were Colts. The ratio was about the same at the 1976 championships at El Paso, Texas.

At IHMSA's first sanctioned match in January, 1977, there were five categories of competition. Of the first four finishers in each category — for a total of twenty trophy winners — sixteen were using revolvers.

However, it wasn't long before the superior accuracy, ballistics and performance of single-shot pistols began to outclass the wheelguns. Within two years, you could hardly find a revolver in the production category winner's circle.

But tradition, romance and history die hard. Silhouetters refused to lay down their revolvers. The entire matter was resolved to the satisfaction of all concerned when we established a separate revolver category in the fall of 1980.

Silhouette is a woman's game, too. Edna Huff won IHMSA Women's International production gun championship using Model 29 Smith & Wesson .44 magnum, light loads.

In her Pennsylvania home, Edna Huff checks out some of the trophies she has won in handgun silhouette contests.

METALLIC SILHOUETTE SHOOTING

This shooter uses what he calls an Elmer Keith position during match. The revolver he is shooting is the Smith & Wesson Model 27 .357 magnum.

Bullets for silhouettes (from left) are: Speer .357 180-grain FMJ, the Hornady .38 200-grain RN, Hornady .358 200-grain SP, Sierra .44 220-grain Silhouette, Hornady .44 240-grain JTC-Sil, Sierra's 220-grain JCL and Hornady .375 220-grain FP.

Shooter with S&W Model 27 in .357 magnum fires from the front-facing prone position, popular in early contests.

Another important thing came out of this decision — stimulation for a few of the revolver makers to improve their products in significant ways after an age of near stagnation.

I don't think Dan Wesson, for example, was thinking of silhouettes when they originated their decision to come out with a big frame .44 magnum revolver. Nevertheless, they were quick to see the sales potential in the game, and equally quick to listen to knowledgeable silhouette shooters. The net result was pleasing to everyone.

The data in this chapter will cover the history and refinement of various revolvers for the silhouette sport and load data to go with it.

The .357 magnum and .44 magnums were, of course, already on the scene when the silhouette game came to town. Silhouette shooters learned from the very beginning that the .357 magnum was marginal, at best, and some of them switched over the .44 magnum.

However, after six months of intense competition around the country, as the silhouette game spread like wildfire, a very serious problem cropped up that could have crippled the new sport before it really got into high gear.

In short, bullets from existing revolvers in any caliber were not consistently knocking down the heavy steel rams that were set full foot on their stands.

In desperate attempts to get more knockdown power out of their revolvers, many shooters brewed up severe overloads. I called them "dynamite loads" or "earthquake loads." They became the order of the day at every match.

While single-shot pistols could better handle such severe overloading, revolvers could not. By virtue of design, the revolver is the weakest of the handguns. Revolvers began to shoot loose, shave lead and come apart at the seams. It was a miracle that no one was seriously injured in those early months of 1977.

The new game quickly came to a crisis point and easily could have folded up as the result of a serious injury or death. Something had to be done immediately to alleviate this problem or we would have to pack it up. Firearms safety in the shooting sports is more important than anything else. The quickest way to alienate the revolver makers

David Bradshaw won the International revolver title the first year this match was held. His field testing has been instrumental in silhouette handgun upgrading.

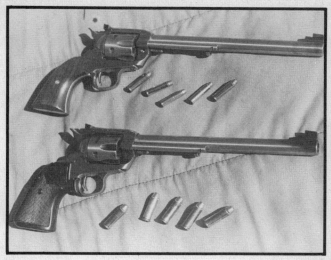

Interarms Silhouette Dragoons have become popular with shooters. Top gun is .357 magnum, with rounds loaded with Federal 180-grain JHP bullets. Other gun is the .44 magnum Dragoon. Bullets are Hornady 240-grain JTC.

Loaded in Federal .357 nickel cases, silhouette loads (from left) are: Federal 180-gr. JHP; Hornady 180-gr. JTC-Sil; Speer 180-gr. FMJ; .38 Special case trimmed to 1.020 inches with Hornady 200-grain RN .358 bullet. At right, load carries 200-gr. Hornady spire point.

and lose their support would be to abuse their products. Even then, the anti-gun forces were focusing on handguns as their first target. And for the manufacturers, the spectre of liability was just around the corner. We didn't need any of it in the new silhouette sport.

During three days of frenzied activity and testing over the July Fourth weekend of 1977, we arrived at a solution. With approval of the association's executive officers, they implemented the directive immediately. The directive reads as follows:

Directive 5, July 11, 1977.

The ram target may be mounted on its stand with three-quarters to one inch of the rear of its feet overhanging the stand.

Along with the directive went this explanation:

As you all know, the bulk of our shooters are using stock .357 and .44 magnum production guns and even with "hot" handloads are experiencing trouble knocking down the standard rifle ram silhouette. We have had reports of several .44 magnums blowing up by the use of overloads in an attempt to knock the rams down consistently.

Even then there was confusion over what the new ruling meant and there were protests from a few big-bore disciples who felt we were turning the sport into a "sissy" game by making it easier to knock the rams down.

We had to follow up the directive with an editorial explaining the matter to the entire membership in detail. The points expressed in the editorial are just as valid today as they were in 1977, and reprinted below:

When handgun silhouette shooting came onto the scene, it was a natural thing to utilize the already existing rifle targets at shorter ranges. The reasons were obvious: Standardization meant that rifle shooters could use the targets one weekend and handgunners the next weekend without the expense of designing a whole new set of targets of different dimensions and sizes just for handgun shooting.

This theory has, in fact, worked out quite well overall.

Forster trimmer is used to trim Federal .38 Special brass to 1.202 inches for loading with either Hornady 200-grain spire-point or round-nose silhouette bullets.

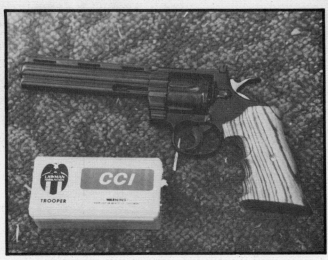

Colt Python in .357 magnum is considered one of the best in that caliber, but the author feels manufacturer lost an opportunity by not making the gun in .44 magnum.

From left: Standard .357 magnum round with 180-grain FMJ bullet; .357 Super Mag case with the same bullet; round on right is loaded with the 180-grain SP bullet.

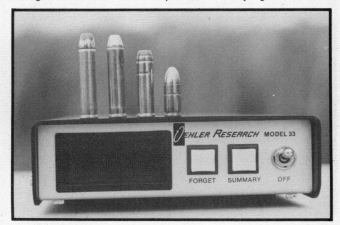

From left: .357 Super Mag case loaded with 158-grain JHP; same case with Hornady 200-grain FMJ; standard .357 magnum with 125-grain JHP; standard factory 9mm at right for the sake of comparison of varying size.

A number of rifle and pistol clubs share the same targets and use the same range. With the handgun stands placed at shorter distances and more or less at ground level, there is no interference to the rifle shooters when they reset the targets at their longer ranges.

However, with the experience of many matches to go by, there is one small but very important matter regarding the rams and involving a unique kind of safety that must be resolved.

The standard dimensions for the ram's feet are four inches wide by five inches long and it is the width we are concerned with.

Before proceeding, let it be mentioned that the other three types of targets — the chickens, javelinas and turkeys — can be knocked down consistently with a good hit by virtually any bullet from any cartridge and handgun.

The combination of the heavy steel ram at about fifty pounds, with the full width of the feet on the stand, plus the fact that at two hundred meters, bullets from most handguns are rapidly losing their effectiveness, a good many rams remain standing even after a solid hit.

And here we come to the matter of safety. Any shooter hitting, say, five out of ten rams and knocking down only one, is going to react in a predictable way. In an effort to deliver more energy and, presumably, more knockdown power against the rams, he will use the only method he knows which is to use heavier bullets when, where and however he can and cram in more powder to step up velocities.

Better results have been achieved, but if you have been on the firing line as I have and felt the concussion of what I call "earthquake" and "dynamite" loads, you would readily understand that the outer limits of safety also have been achieved and, indeed, exeeded in many cases. While acting as line referee, I have seen a number of revolvers with frames warped to the point where the cylin-

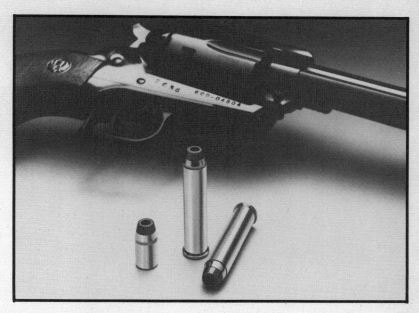

Federal .357 Super Mag ammo with a unique 180-grain hollow-point bullet was tested in Ruger Maximum revolver. The latter, however, was dropped soon after introduction.

At top is the stainless steel .357 Super Mag Seville silhouette or hunting model, while Ruger Maximum is beneath. The longer cylinder of the Seville ensured its success.

der would hardly turn. Several were locked. I have picked up the fractured bolt head and assorted pieces from other guns.

So far, no one has been hurt that I know of, other than by slight wounds inflicted by lead shavings. But if this rush for ever more powerful loads to knock down the rams continues, I am apprehensive that someone will, indeed, get hurt when a gun comes apart, possibly injuring other shooters on the line as well as coaches and spectators. The anti-gun media would love every gory detail of it.

In spite of this, opinions have been expressed in some areas that the whole idea of the game is to make it as tough as possible to knock down targets, especially the rams. Weighed against the inherent dangers expressed above, this is not a wise position.

At one major western match, many of the rams were set with the full width of the feet well forward of the rear edge of the stands. Solid hits even from unlimited guns in full-length .308 and .358 calibers failed to take them down. A number of production gun competitors hit as many as seven or eight without knocking a single one down. You should have heard the comments about what each shooter was going to do before the next match in order to down the rams. All of the comments involved more powder, heavier bullets and hotter overloads.

A large majority of production gun shooters are using .357 magnums. IHMSA takes the position that a solid body hit on the upper half of the ram with a commercial .357 load should entitle the shooter to a score point, i.e. the ram should topple off the stand.

There is one rather simple way to achieve or improve this possibility, one which IHMSA endorses in the name of preventive safety. By overhanging both feet of the rams about an inch beyond the rear of the stand or rail, a topple effect is produced and any good hit will take him off. A good suggestion is to use stands or pads that are only

At left is round loaded with 180-grain bullet, with 24 grains of H4227 powder in a Remington cartridge case. At right is a handloaded 200-grain Speer .357 FMJ, with 22 grains of IMR 4198. David Bradshaw used latter combination for 40x40 in his .357 Super Mag revolver.

In comparison of cylinder lengths, the blued Ruger .357 Maximum is 1.935 inches, while the Seville cylinder measures 2.075, a most important eighth of an inch!

Author contends, based upon wide testing, that the .357 Super Mag Dan Wesson has superior engineering, design.

three inches wide and set the rams so that the front edge of the feet are flush with the front edge of the three-inch-wide stand, thus leaving a one-inch overhang at the rear edge. Or, if the stands are wider, simply take care to set the bank of rams with the same overhang for each, using, say, a trigger scale to hook on top of the back and establish the same pull-over weight for each; about two pounds pull or less. Then take the can of flat black spray paint used to paint out the bullet splashes and spray around the feet of each ram while in place and instruct the target setters to put the rams in this same place each time where the feet have been outlined by the paint.

This is a far better solution, particularly from the standpoint of safety, than letting shooters become involved in a race for ever more potent overloads with the potential deadly consequences thereof. Once the shooters know they can knock the rams off without resorting to the super-dynamite overloads, then the chances of injury from a gun coming apart will be virtually nil.

The overhang rule, as it was called, breathed new life into the old .357 magnum, although it still was a marginal cartridge at best. It was the creation of a separate revolver category in 1980, as previously mentioned, that brought the six-gun into its own.

After that, development and introduction of the .357 Super Mag cartridge closed the gap between performance of the revolver and the single-shots. Nevertheless, the decision was made to continue the revolver and single-shot competition as separate categories.

Finally, there was the willingness of three revolver manufacturers to take a chance on building a long-cylinder gun

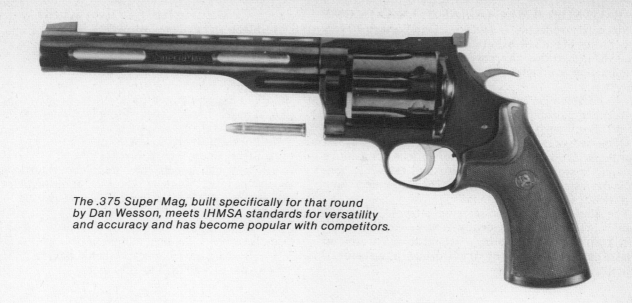

The .375 Super Mag, built specifically for that round by Dan Wesson, meets IHMSA standards for versatility and accuracy and has become popular with competitors.

Edd Page, IHMSA public relations director, finally won a trophy at Internationals with .41 mag Ruger Blackhawk.

Oregonian Larry Perry displays group shot with a Dan Wesson .375 Super Mag at 210 yards. Group that is circled has been submitted as world record group.

to take the new high-performance cartridge, something no revolver maker had been willing to do heretofore. One manufacturer failed in the attempt, and discontinued their long-cylinder design. The other two, Dan Wesson and United Sporting Arms, handled it right and their revolvers are big winners in the revolver category. The Dan Wesson is double-action; the USA Seville is a single-action.

So where are we now, after ten years of big-bore revolver competition?

The original .357 magnum, marginal at best, was partly what prompted me to dig out my old African hunting cartridges and refine the design to come up with the .357 Super Mag.

The old .357 magnum kept going for a few more years, until the .357 Super Mag entered the scene. The old .357 magnum faded out again, but made a comeback with the introduction of the IHMSA field pistol course of fire. It now has found its home. It is an excellent cartridge for the field pistol game.

Data is presented here for the major revolvers and calibers used for metallic silhouette, preceded by an explanation of each, starting with the .357 magnum. Since enough general load data for this caliber has been published over the past fifty-three years to fill a boxcar, the data presented here is limited specifically to silhouette shooting with heavier bullets.

THE .357 SUPER MAG (ALIAS .357 MAXIMUM)

Since its introduction in 1983, the Dan Wesson 40V8S Super Mag, in both blue and stainless steel, with the .357 Super Mag cartridge, has proved to be the most successful combination ever introduced in the silhouette revolver category.

This combination has won the IHMSA International revolver championship an unprecedented five years in a row, from 1983 through 1987, with perfect 80x80 scores.

Of the many revolvers available to silhouetters, why is it that the selection of a wheelgun for serious competitive shooting is so narrow? Is it advertising? Glowing, noncritical magazine write-ups? Style? The recommendation of a friend? Or is it performance?

The silhouette shooter in search of a revolver for competition in sanctioned silhouette matches — and by extension, a top revolver for hunting — would do well to draw up a list of desirable features by which to judge a gun before it is fired:

MECHANICAL CHECKLIST

1. Make and model of revolver.
2. Caliber.
3. Barrel length.
4. Action type (single or double action?).
5. Cylinder lock-up (stronger or weak — subject to unlock at the moment of fire?).
6. Trigger break (does it really submit to careful tuning?).
7. Lock time (fast or slow?).
8. Sight picture (sharp, black?).
9. Sight adjustments (are the clicks distinct, adjustments "snappy?" Is there .150-inch of distinct elevation adjustment, .100-inch distinct windage adjustment — from zero?).
10. Sight fit (is the rear sight slide tight or loose? Is the sight base firm in the sight mortise of the frame or loose?).
11. Barrel groove diameter (should be)
   a. .44 — .428 inch to .430 inch.

.357 Magnum

CARTRIDGE: .357 magnum
GUN: Dan Wesson .357 magnum
BARREL AND LENGTH: Factory 8-inch
PRIMER: CCI 550
CASE: Winchester
BULLET: see below

These tests are based on ten-shot groups fired at fifty meters from sandbag rest position.

BULLET	POWDER	WEIGHT IN GRAINS	AVERAGE MUZZLE VELOCITY FPS	REMARKS
180-gr. Speer TMJ	Win-680	14.4	1123	
180-gr. Speer TMJ	Win-296	13.8	1112	
180-gr. Speer TMJ	2400	12.0	1016	
180-gr. Speer TMJ	H-110	14.0	1104	
180-gr. Speer TMJ	IMR-4227	13.8	1022	
180-gr. Speer TMJ	800-X	10.5	1147	
180-gr. Speer TMJ	AA-9	12.9	1407	
180-gr. Speer TMJ	HS-6	9.4	1034	
200-gr. Speer TMJ	Win-296	14.3	1116	
200-gr. Speer TMJ	2400	12.2	1010	
200-gr. Speer TMJ	AA-9	12.8	1072	
200-gr. Speer TMJ	H-110	14.3	1093	
200-gr. Speer TMJ	800-X	9.7	1021	
200-gr. Speer TMJ	Win-680	14.2	1060	
200-gr. Speer TMJ	IMR-4227	13.6	1006	
200-gr. Speer TMJ	Blue Dot	9.6	985	

NOTE: This load data may be used in other comparable revolvers chambered for the .357 magnum cartridge although results may vary widely due to barrel length, cylinder gap, cylinder exit holes, forcing cone shape and other variables.

CAUTION: When using Smith & Wesson revolvers, start with fifteen percent lighter powder charge for all listed loads.

Note: All load data and information in this book is the result of safe and careful testing by the author and other contributors submitting the material contained herein. Since neither the author, DBI Books, Inc., nor any of the contributors has any control over the components, equipment and techniques used with this published information, no liability or responsibility for any injury or damage that occurs is either implied or assumed.

Joe Wright, a member of the IHMSA technical staff, tests .41 magnum Seville six-gun using Creedmoor position.

    b. .41 — .406 inch to .410 inch.
    c. .357 — .355 inch to .357 inch.
(Excessive groove diameter is death on accuracy.)
12. Chamber exit hole diameter (should be)
    a. .44 — .432 inch maximum.
    b. .41 — .412 inch maximum.
    c. .357 — .359 inch maximum.

(Note: exit holes of exact bullet diameter to .001 inch over are best.)
13. Cylinder gap (prefer .001 inch to .003 inch; .006 inch is maximum.)
14. Grip (is it comfortable? Are good — namely Pachmayr — accessory stocks available? Will the gun make the weight limit with the accessory stock?).
15. Factory service (is it fast, inexpensive, reliable? Or is it slow and costly?).
16. Has the revolver a reputation for durability or breakage?

Your mechanical checklist cannot be completed without arming yourself with — and knowing how to use — a dial

.357 Super Mag, Alias The .357 Maximum

CARTRIDGE: .357 Super Mag, alias .357 Maximum
GUN: Dan Wesson 40V8S .357 Super Mag
BARREL AND LENGTH: Factory 8-inch
PRIMER: Federal 205M
CASE: Federal IHMSA
BULLET: see below

These tests are based on ten-shot groups fired at fifty meters from sandbag rest position.

BULLET	POWDER	WEIGHT IN GRAINS	AVERAGE MUZZLE VELOCITY FPS	REMARKS
180-gr. Sierra FPJ	H-4227	19.0	1320	
180-gr. Sierra FPJ	H-4227	19.5	1368	
180-gr. Sierra FPJ	H-4227	20.0	1423	
180-gr. Sierra FPJ	AA-9	17.0	1346	
180-gr. Sierra FPJ	AA-9	18.0	1388	
180-gr. Sierra FPJ	H-110	18.1	1286	
180-gr. Sierra FPJ	H-110	19.0	1348	accurate
180-gr. Sierra FPJ	H-110	19.5	1364	
180-gr. Sierra FPJ	H-110	20.0	1402	
200-gr. Speer FMJ	IMR-4227	19.8	1331	
200-gr. Speer FMJ	IMR-4227	21.0	1374	
200-gr. Speer FMJ	IMR-4198	21.0	1160	
200-gr. Speer FMJ	IMR-4198	22.0	1259	very accurate
200-gr. Speer FMJ	IMR-4198	22.5	1296	
200-gr. Speer FMJ	AA-5744	21.6	1325	
200-gr. Speer FMJ	AA-5744	21.6	1394	
200-gr. Speer FMJ	H-110	16.0	1046	
200-gr. Speer FMJ	H-110	17.0	1117	
200-gr. Speer FMJ	H-110	18.0	1156	
200-gr. Speer FMJ	H-110	20.0	1342*	maximum

Note: All load data and information in this book is the result of safe and careful testing by the author and other contributors submitting the material contained herein. Since neither the author, DBI Books, Inc., nor any of the contributors has any control over the components, equipment and techniques used with this published information, no liability or responsibility for any injury or damage that occurs is either implied or assumed.

METALLIC SILHOUETTE SHOOTING

vernier caliper. Remember, misreading a dial caliper will render the tool worse than useless; you might reject a gun that is dimensionally sound. Nevertheless, the knowledgeable silhouetter knows that problems of quality control afflict all too many firearms. (Smith & Wesson barrels are broached with five grooves, impossible to measure with a dial caliper. Fortunately, S&W barrels tend to be excellent.)

To the mechanical checklist we must add the performance checklist. Whereas the mechanical checklist is measurable, the performance checklist is largely subjective. Such things as whether you are more comfortable with a single-action or a double-action, whether one set of sights "looks" better than another — these criteria are influenced by personal perference. Personal preferences can be arrived at only through the application of marksmanship. Before we get into the performance checklist, let us weigh the Dan Wesson Model 40 Super Mag against the field:

MECHANICAL CHECKLIST

1. Dan Wesson Arms Model 40V8S Super Mag.
2. .357 Super Mag alias .357 Maximum.
3. Eight-inch vent silhouette barrel.
4. Double-action.
5. Cyinder lock-up: thumb-operated crane latch. Strong. Cylinder stop (bolt) offset from chamber centerline. Cylinder stop angled away from chamber for further offset. Author considers angle exaggerated. Some early DWA .44 cylinders were subject to open or counter-rotate under recoil. Problem basically cured. Author knows of no such occurrences with the M40 Super Mag.
6. Trigger break: Factory trigger breaks with perceptible creep at four pounds. May be tuned for a clean break

.357 Super Mag

CARTRIDGE: .357 Super Mag
GUN: Seville Stainless Silhouette
BARREL AND LENGTH: 10½-inch
PRIMER: Federal 205M
CASE: Federal IHMSA
BULLET: see below

These tests are based on ten-shot groups fired at fifty meters from sandbag rest position.

BULLET	POWDER	WEIGHT IN GRAINS	AVERAGE MUZZLE VELOCITY FPS	REMARKS
180-gr. Hornady FMJ	Win-680	21.0	1332	
180-gr. Hornady FMJ	Win-680	22.0	1426	
180-gr. Hornady FMJ	Win-680	22.5	1463	accurate
180-gr. Hornady FMJ	Win-680	23.0	1547*	* maximum
180-gr. Hornady FMJ	H-110	21.0	1564	
180-gr. Hornady FMJ	H-110	21.5	1572	accurate
180-gr. Hornady FMJ	H-110	22.0	1605*	* maximum
200-gr. Speer FMJ	Win-680	20.0	1283	
200-gr. Speer FMJ	Win-680	21.0	1372	
200-gr. Speer FMJ	Win-680	21.5	1448	accurate
200-gr. Speer FMJ	Win-680	22.0	1477	
200-gr. Speer FMJ	H-110	19.1	1370	
200-gr. Speer FMJ	H-110	20.0	1442	accurate
200-gr. Speer FMJ	H-110	21.0	1570	
200-gr. Hornady SP	H-4227	20.0	1535	
200-gr. Hornady SP	H-4227	20.5	1578	
200-gr. Hornady SP	H-4227	21.0	1632	
200-gr. Hornady SP	H-4227	21.5	1664	
200-gr. Hornady SP	H-4227	22.0	1702**	* compressed load too hot
200-gr. Hornady SP	Win-680	22.5	1480	
200-gr. Hornady SP	Win-680	23.0	1540	
200-gr. Hornady SP	Win-680	23.5	1592	

Note: All load data and information in this book is the result of safe and careful testing by the author and other contributors submitting the material contained herein. Since neither the author, DBI Books, Inc., nor any of the contributors has any control over the components, equipment and techniques used with this published information, no liability or responsibility for any injury or damage that occurs is either implied or assumed.

down to two pounds. Has adjustable stop. M40 (along with M44) may be tuned for lightest single-action break of any DA revolver, except Colt Python

7. Lock time: Faster than any single-action; a bit slower than a smaller-frame .357.

8. Sight picture: Sharp and black. Choice of patridge front sight width: .100 inch or .125 inch. Choice of rear sight width: .080 inch or .120 inch.

9. Sight adjustments. Detents located on underside of screw, thirteen clicks per revolution. Clicks should be in units of 4, i.e., 8, 12, 16. Screws vary in quality. Need for improvements at factory level. Total elevation adjustment .110 inch. Windage adjustment, .090 inch left of zero (center). Windage adjustment, .088 inch right of zero.

10. A barrel groove diameter measures .357 inch. Excellent. Broached; one turn in 18¾ inches. Original M40 barrels were button rifled 1:14. Air-gauged barrels revealed dimensional inconsistencies Whether the braoched 1:18¾ barrels properly stabilize Hornady and Sierra 200-grain round-nose bullets seems to have been settled in the affirmative. However, the 1:18¾-inch barrel is marginal at

This limited edition USA .44 magnum single-action with serial number IHMSA-01 has logo on side of gun's frame.

.375 Super Mag

CARTRIDGE: .357 Super Mag
GUN: Dan Wesson .375 Super Mag
BARREL AND LENGTH: 8-inch
PRIMER: CCI 350 Mag Pistol
CASE: Winchester
BULLET: 220-grain Hornady FP

These tests are based on ten-shot groups fired at fifty meters from sand-bag rest position.

BULLET	POWDER	WEIGHT IN GRAINS	AVERAGE MUZZLE VELOCITY FPS	REMARKS
220-gr. Hornady	H-110	20.2	1183	
220-gr. Hornady	H-110	21.2	1214	
220-gr. Hornady	H-110	22.2	1273	
220-gr. Hornady	H-110	23.0	1285	
220-gr. Hornady	Win-296	20.1	1123	
220-gr. Hornady	Win-296	21.1	1151	
220-gr. Hornady	Win-296	22.2	1217	
220-gr. Hornady	Win-296	24.2	1327	
220-gr. Hornady	H-4227	21.0	1222	
220-gr. Hornady	H-4227	22.0	1261	
220-gr. Hornady	H-4227	23.0	1320	
220-gr. Hornady	Win-680	24.0	1193	
220-gr. Hornady	Win-680	25.0	1274	
220-gr. Hornady	Win-680	26.0	1312	
220-gr. Hornady	Win-680	27.0	1368	
220-gr. Hornady	AA-9	17.0	1283	
220-gr. Hornady	AA-9	18.0	1352	
220-gr. Hornady	AA-5744	22.0	1402	
220-gr. Hornady	AA-5744	23.0	1439	
220-gr. Hornady	AA-5744	24.0	1483	

Note: All load data and information in this book is the result of safe and careful testing by the author and other contributors submitting the material contained herein. Since neither the author, DBI Books, Inc., nor any of the contributors has any control over the components, equipment and techniques used with this published information, no liability or responsibility for any injury or damage that occurs is either implied or assumed.

METALLIC SILHOUETTE SHOOTING

best with the excellent Hornady 200-grain spire-point .358 rifle slug. Quality of DWA barrels is second to none.

11. Chamber exit hole diameter measures .358 inch on all chambers. Excellent.

12. Cylinder gap: infinity. We recommend .004 inch or as tight as possible while maintaining free cylinder rotation. Due to the spring-loaded ball detent arrangement of the junction of the standing breech and cylinder ratchet, a certain amount of cylinder gap is necessary.

13. Grip: Traditional-style target stock supplied. This author prefers optional birdshead "combat" stock. Pachmayr stock features a short length of pull — desirable for competitors with small hands. Unfortunately, Pachmayr neoprene stock brings M40 over four-pound production gun limit.

14. Factory service: Rated excellent; fast, minimal cost (often none).

15. Reputation: M40 Super Mag has been on market for only a short while. Since it is built on an elongated M44 frame, we expect the service life of the revolver to be many thousands of rounds. Elevation screws of earliest production were over-hardened, tending to snap. Barrel nuts of same vintage were soft, tending to shear at the spanner grooves. These problems have been corrected.

Speer 240-grain .44 magnum FMJ bullets are popular in the silhouette game. Thicker, tougher jackets increase the effectiveness of bullets against the steel targets.

.375 Super Mag

CARTRIDGE: .375 Super Mag
GUN: USA Stainless Seville
BARREL AND LENGTH: 10½-inch
PRIMER: CCI 350 Mag Pistol
CASE: Winchester .375 Super Mag
BULLET: 220-gr. Hornady FP

These tests are based on ten-shot groups fired at fifty meters from sandbag rest position.

BULLET	POWDER	WEIGHT IN GRAINS	AVERAGE MUZZLE VELOCITY FPS	REMARKS
220-gr. Hornady FP	IMR-4227	22.5	1576	
220-gr. Hornady FP	IMR-4227	23.0	1618	accurate
220-gr. Hornady FP	IMR-4227	23.5	1639	maximum
220-gr. Hornady FP	Win-296	22.5	1603	accurate
220-gr. Hornady FP	Win-296	23.5	1611	
220-gr. Hornady FP	Win-296	24.0	1635	
220-gr. Hornady FP	Win-296	24.5	1671	maximum
220-gr. Hornady FP	H-110	24.5	1650	accurate
220-gr. Hornady FP	H-110	25.0	1672	
220-gr. Hornady FP	H-110	25.5	1676	
220-gr. Hornady FP	H-110	26.0	1709	maximum
220-gr. Hornady FP	Win-680	26.0	1625	
220-gr. Hornady FP	Win-680	26.5	1649	
220-gr. Hornady FP	Win-680	27.0	1692	max
220-gr. Hornady FP	2400	20.5	1603	best accuracy
220-gr. Hornady FP	2400	21.0	1634	
220-gr. Hornady FP	2400	21.5	1688	maximum
220-gr. Hornady FP	AA-9	18.5	1578	
220-gr. Hornady FP	AA-9	19.0	1558	
220-gr. Hornady FP	AA-9	19.5	1557	accurate
220-gr. Hornady FP	AA-9	20.0	1575	maximum

Note: All data and information in this book is the result of safe and careful testing by the author and other contributors submitting the material contained herein. Since neither the author, DBI Books, Inc., nor any of the contributors has any control over the components, equipment and techniques used with this published information, no liability or responsibility for any injury or damage that occurs is either implied or assumed.

This group was fired by Bradshaw with Smith & Wesson Model 29 .44 magnum. A scope was used in tests as an aid in testing the accuracy.

Against the mechanical checklist, the Dan Wesson Super Mag sugars off as one of the best revolvers for silhouette. Moving over to the performance checklist, we are almost certain to find our Model 40 in need of a trigger tune. For the purpose of rudimentary testing, a clean-breaking four-pound trigger is acceptable. However, "grunge," "creep" and "rolloff" are wholly unacceptable.

To tune the trigger, remove the grip and cock the hammer (gun *obviously* has been unloaded first!). Carefully dry-fire revolver by pinching trigger against trigger guard. Observe creep. If take-up is apparent, cock hammer and, holding it rearward, secure compressed mainspring with screw provided. Now apply thumb pressure to "cocked" hammer and gently squeeze trigger to observe for creep.

Strip trigger assembly from frame per DWA instructions. Pin hammer to trigger guard module and once again cycle the assembly to observe for creep. Clip one coil from trigger rebound spring. Periodically check letoff in reassembled revolver! Be patient! You can take off, but you cannot put back!

If trigger rebounds — bounces forward — during hammer fall, single-action is unsafe! This rule applies to all single-action and double-action revolvers.

Caution: It is the responsibility of the shooter to make sure his or her gun is safe. Firearm safety is the responsibility of the person handling the firearm.

If you are not familiar with trigger tuning of your particular piece, leave the work to someone who is. With the trigger tuned, we are ready for the...

PERFORMANCE CHECKLIST

1. Carefully dry-fire revolver twenty-five times.
2. First two sighter shots at ten yards to be sure you are on the paper.
3. Sight in at twenty-five yards. Use six-inch bull or a chicken painted on cardboard.
4. Sight in at fifty meters. Preferred target is a chicken painted on cardboard. Use ammunition of known quality. Record load data and sight settings in notebook. Record date, location, time, light and wind conditions. Don't pretend you will remember all this: you won't!
5. Sight in at one hundred meters. Preferred target is a pig painted on cardboard. A ten- or twelve-inch bull will suffice. Note: A top IHMSA revolver is capable of five-shot, three-inch groups at one hundred meters. None of us can shoot that well all the time. A couple of five-inch groups will get us in the ballpark.
6. How does the gun feel? Is it comfortable to shoot? Is recoil light or heavy?
7. How do the sights look? Is the sight picture clean? The front sight should look blacker than the rear sight.
8. Does the gun recoil past the twelve O'clock position? If so, the problem is one or more of the following:
   a. Too much gun for the shooter.
   b. Incorrect position.
   c. Jellyfish grip.

Remember, the muzzle must be pointed downrange at all times while on the firing line.

9. Does the revolver shoot...better than, as well as, not as well as, your best shooting revolver?
10. Sight in at 150 and two hundred meters. Observe or have others observe ram knockdown. (This is more a func-

Hornady JTC/Sil is name given the 240-grain .44 caliber bullets developed for silhouette game.

Bullets included in tests are (from left): Federal 240-grain HP; Az Police Equipment 250-grain cast SWC; Ohio Shooters Supply 250-grain magnum cast SWC; Sierra 220-grain Silhouette; 240-grain HP; Speer 240-grain SP; and Hornady's 240-grain FMJ, a real heavyweight!

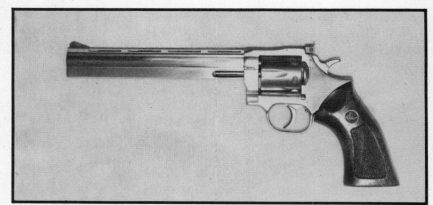

Dan Wesson 744 VH8 stainless model has been successful in silhouette. Gun was designed for this game.

tion of caliber, bullet weight and velocity, than of the gun itself.)

For a mild, but accurate load try: Hornady 200-grain RN .358 bullet; 21.0 grains Winchester 680, Federal 205M primer, Remington .357 Maximum case trimmed to 1.450 inch. Velocity, as chronographed on the Oehler Model 33, averages 1351 fps for six shots. Extreme spread is forty-three feet per second. Standard deviation sixteen feet per second. My first group at one hundred meters read 2.5 inches ES for five shots. Sight settings are: C-0, P-1, T-12, R-18.

Whatever stocks you choose, weigh the gun as you plan to shoot it; some DWA M44s crowd the four-pound limit. The possibility exists that a piece of extra-dense wood will bring your gun over. Waiting until a championship match to find out your gun is overweight may severely bend your mind.

DWA has struggled with a weight problem ever since introduction of the Model 44; the barrel and shroud assembly are heavy, the frame massive. We were even asked, in 1980, to modify our production gun rule. We refused. Shortly thereafter, DWA thanked us for not bowing to pressure; IHMSA had provoked needed refinement of the revolver.

When DWA decided to roll with the Super Mag, there was much activity directed at keeping the gun within four pounds. With the M44VH8 and M44V10 hugging the weight limit, how was the Model 40V8S Super Mag — with smaller holes drilled in it — possibly going to make weight? First the ten-inch barrel was scrapped. Then the eight-inch shroud of the M44 was whittled down, metal hogged from within, slots hogged along the sides, with most of the underlug hogged off as well.

Bob Domian of Dan Wesson designed a new rear sight. Upon testing and evaluating an early .44 DWA in 1980, we let Dan Wesson Arms know our opinion of that so-called adjustable sight, stating, "The M44 is a damn good revolver, but without match grade sights it will flounder."

The silhouette sights were purchased from an outside source. As silhouetters know too well, deliveries were slow and the supply never met demand. The new DWA silhouette sight is produced by Dan Wesson. It was introduced on the M40V8S. As production catches up, it will replace the existing rear sight on all Dan Wesson models.

The rear sight slide is flat and drafted slightly to reduce glare. Slides are available with either an .080- or .120-inch notch. Slides are easily interchanged by the owner.

Front sights are available in a selection of three heights, with a fourth to be added soon. Blades of .100 inch and .125 inch are offered. In addition, the standard DWA red, yellow and white insert ramps are available. The light inserts are the only way to fly for hunting during early morning and late afternoon.

Get hold of a can of International Harvester "Anti-Seize" compound or Permatex "Never Seize." These are viscous bronze-base grease-type lubricants designed for assembly of engine manifold fasteners and other threaded joints exposed to heat and high stress. Apply this lubricant to front and rear barrel threads. The barrel-tensioning nut will torque down with less imposed force on the spanner (barrel) nut. Disassembly will be easier.

Lubricate the elevation screw with Anti-Seize. Break-free and Tri-Flon also work fine. Lube the windage screw. Lube the action with molybdenum-disulphide or Break-Free. Lube the cylinder barrel or crane (yoke).

Check barrel nut tension following each match and practice session. Likewise the grip screw.

Do not disassemble the barrel from frame any more than necessary. Each time the barrel and shroud are removed — or the spanner nut loosened — the gun must be re-zeroed. That consumes ammunition. It may even necessitate changing to a different height front sight.

With demonstrably less recoil than the DWA M44 (which itself has less recoil than than any other .44 magnum), silhouette accuracy the equal of any revolver and better than most, a fast lock time and quality silhouette sights, the M40V8S Super Mag is a hands-down winner.

.357 SUPER MAG SEVILLE STAINLESS

The Seville is a precision, super-tight (.001½ to .002 cylinder gap) revolver of single-action design. It is the only single-action being currently manufactured to take the .357 Super Mag cartridge. Accuracy is superb, and it is a frequent winner at handgun metallic silhouette matches. Made by United Sporting Arms, it is available on special order through The Silhouette, Box 1509, Idaho Falls, ID 83403.

Shooter with 6-inch barrel Smith & Wesson Model 29 .44 magnum shoots from the forward-facing position, while his spotter uses binoculars to observe bullet strikes.

THE .375 SUPER MAG

After the introduction of the .45 Colt in 1873, it would be sixty-two years before a significantly more powerful

.41 Magnum

CARTRIDGE: .41 magnum
GUN: Ruger
BARREL AND LENGTH: 6½-inch
PRIMER: CCI 350 Mag Pistol
CASE: Winchester
BULLET: see below

These tests are based on ten-shot groups fired at fifty meters from sandbag rest position.

BULLET	POWDER	WEIGHT IN GRAINS	AVERAGE MUZZLE VELOCITY FPS	REMARKS
200-gr. Speer HP	H110	21.0	1326	
200-gr. Speer HP	AA-9	21.5	1372	
200-gr. Speer HP	2400	18.6	1391	
200-gr. Speer HP	IMR-4227	20.1	1264	accurate
200-gr. Speer HP	Win-296	22.1	1353	
200-gr. Speer HP	Unique	9.1	1193	
200-gr. Speer HP	Blue Dot	14.1	1352	
200-gr. Speer HP	HS-7	14.6	1337	
200-gr. Speer HP	800X	15.1	1301	
220-gr. Speer SP	H-110	20.2	1309	accurate
220-gr. Speer SP	Win-296	20.5	1312	
220-gr. Speer SP	2400	17.6	1301	
220-gr. Speer SP	HS-7	14.1	1284	
220-gr. Speer SP	Unique	8.5	1074	accurate
220-gr. Speer SP	HS-6	11.6	1203	
220-gr. Speer SP	Blue Dot	14.2	1314	

Note: All data and information in this book is the result of safe and careful testing by the author and other contributors submitting the material contained herein. Since neither the author, DBI Books, Inc., nor any of the contributors has any control over the components, equipment and techniques used with this published information, no liability or responsibility for any injury or damage that occurs is either implied or assumed.

revolver cartridge would come on the market. This was the .357 magnum of 1935. Twenty more years would pass before another solid improvement in handgun cartridges would enter the scene in 1955: the .44 magnum. Still another twenty years would pass before the high-performance .357 and .375 Super Mags would enter the scene, both developed specifically for the silhouette game. Both of these are part of a Super Mag series developed by the author with a length of 1.610, including a 7mm, .305, .357, .375, .414, .445, .505 and .610 Super Mags.

There have been, of course, rumors floating around about this or that .375-caliber revolver cartridge, usually in short versions. Apparently, none ever has enjoyed any commercial success until I gave Dan Wesson a good order for .375 Super Mags in 1983. The revolver is a duplicate of the DW .357 Super Mag, only chambered for the larger caliber. Its model name is the DW .375 V8S. It has since been a standard item in the DW line and is available to the public.

The load data presented here is primarily for silhouette competition, but also is good for handgun hunting.

United Sporting Arms of Arizona also chambered their single-action stainless steel Seville 10½-inch barrel silhouette model in .375 Super Mag. Performance has been excellent. The silhouette-hunting data presented here has been supplied by United Sporting Arms:

.41 MAGNUM
NOTE: While the .41 magnum never has caught on as a successful silhouette cartridge, both the T/C Contender and various revolvers chambered for the .41 magnum cartridge have been used enough for silhouette data to be worked up.

.44 Magnum

CARTRIDGE: .44 magnum
GUN: Dan Wesson 44VH8 and Ruger .44 Super Blackhawk
BARREL AND LENGTH: DW — 8-inch; Ruger — 10½-inch
PRIMER: Federal 155
CASE: Federal
BULLET: see below

These tests are based on ten-shot groups fired at fifty meters from sandbag rest position.

BULLET	POWDER	WEIGHT IN GRAINS	AVERAGE MUZZLE VELOCITY FPS 8" DW	AVERAGE MUZZLE VELOCITY FPS 10½" RUGER
220 Sierra FPJ	H-4227	23.5	1313	1352
220 Sierra FPJ	H-4227	24.5	1370	1403
220 Sierra FPJ	2400	21.0	1277	1336
220 Sierra FPJ	H-110	25.5	1396	1449
240 Hornady JTC-SIL	AA-9	23.0	1436	1475
240 Hornady JTC-SIL	H-110	25.0	1409	1451
240 Hornady JTC-SIL	2400	21.5	1374	1419
240 Hornady JTC-SIL	H-4227	23.0	1307	1336
240 Hornady JTC-SIL	IMR-4227	23.0	1302	1305
240 Speer FMJ	H-110	25.0	1386	1439
240 Speer FMJ	AA-9	23.5	1438	1490
240 Speer FMJ	H-4227	23.0	1285	1288
240 Speer FMJ	IMR-4227	23.0	1270	1292
240 Speer FMJ	IMR-4227	24.5	1346	1351
250 Sierra FPJ	AA-9	21.0	1352	1378
250 Sierra FPJ	2400	20.0	1272	1294
250 Sierra FPJ	H-4227	21.0	1199	1234
250 Sierra FPJ	IMR-4227	23.0	1317	1223
250 Sierra FPJ	H-110	23.0	1356	1396
250 Sierra FPJ	H-110	24.0	1402	1467
250 Sierra FPJ	H-110	24.5	1432	1494

Note: All data and information in this book is the result of safe and careful testing by the author and other contributors submitting the material contained herein. Since neither the author, DBI Books, Inc., nor any of the contributors has any control over the components, equipment and techniques used with this published information, no liability or responsibility for any injury or damage that occurs is either implied or assumed.

This load data may be used in other comparable revolvers chambered for the .41 magnum cartridge, although results may vary widely due to barrel length, cylinder gap, cylinder exit holes, forcing cone shape and other variables.

CAUTION: When using Smith & Wesson revolvers, start with a fifteen percent *lighter* powder charge for all loads listed here.

.44 MAGNUM

The .44 magnum silhouette load data presented here is for two of the most popular revolvers used in the sport, the Dan Wesson .44 VH8 with eight-inch barrel and the .44 Ruger S411N Super Blackhawk.

INTERARMS .357 AND .44 MAGNUM

Nestled in gently rolling hills forty miles southwest of our Nation's Capitol, there is a little town by the name of Midland, Virginia. This is the home of twenty of the Interarms

This five-shot group was fired by David Bradshaw with a Dan Wesson 44VH8 at 100 meters. Aimpoint sight is not allowed in competition, but it has been found valuable in tests and in checking out load data for any handgun.

.45 Long Colt

CARTRIDGE: .45 Long Colt
GUN: Ruger Blackhawk BN 45
BARREL AND LENGTH: 7½-inch
TWIST: 1:16
PRIMER: CCI 350 Mag Pistol
CASE: Winchester
BULLET: see below

These tests are based on ten-shot groups fired at fifty meters from sandbag rest position.

BULLET	POWDER	WEIGHT IN GRAINS	AVERAGE MUZZLE VELOCITY FPS	REMARKS
200-gr. Speer HP	2400	20.4	1302	
200-gr. Speer HP	HS-6	14.5	1298	
200-gr. Speer HP	Unique	12.0	1328	maximum
200-gr. Speer HP	SR-4759	25.6	1339	
200-gr. Speer HP	231	11.2	1271	
200-gr. Speer HP	Win. 473AA	11.6	1183	
225-gr. Hornady HP	2400	19.5	1228	
225-gr. Hornady HP	HS-6	14.1	1198	
225-gr. Hornady HP	Unique	11.0	1187	
225-gr. Hornady HP	SR-4756	10.9	1163	
225-gr. Hornady HP	231	10.5	1169	
225-gr. Hornady HP	Win. 473AA	11.4	1115	
250-gr. Speer HP	Win-296	20.6	1265	
250-gr. Speer HP	HS-6	13.2	1175	
250-gr. Speer HP	H-110	20.1	1253	
250-gr. Speer HP	AA-5	13.5	1142	
250-gr. Speer HP	Unique	10.5	1130	
260-gr. Speer HP	Win-296	20.6	1202	
260-gr. Speer HP	AA-5	10.2	1014	
260-gr. Speer HP	HS-6	13.2	1126	
260-gr. Speer HP	HS-7	15.0	1163	
260-gr. Speer HP	H-110	20.2	1179	

Note: All data and information in this book is the result of safe and careful testing by the author and other contributors submitting the material contained herein. Since neither the author, DBI Books, Inc., nor any of the contributors has any control over the components, equipment and techniques used with this published information, no liability or responsibility for any injury or damage that occurs is either implied or assumed.

David Bradshaw holds Ruger .44 mag silhouette model with a 10½-inch barrel. The handgun has recoiled upward after shot has been made.

Virginian series of single-action revolvers. The cream of these revolvers is the Silhouette Dragoon Model, available in both .357 and .44 magnum calibers. Production of the Virginia Dragoon was discontinued in 1984, but there are a lot of them being used in silhouette and it is a highly sought revolver.

All Virginian model revolvers utilize basic Colt Peacemaker lockwork. While there are six chambers, one never loads more than five. The hammer is lowered on an empty chamber. (This, of course, is SOP for all revolvers fired in IHMSA competition.)

Construction of the Silhouette Dragoon is stainless steel throughout. Trigger and bolt (stop) springs are leaf. The trigger spring may be bent to lighten letoff without fear of breaking the spring. An adjustable trigger stop is provided. Patient, sensitive, knowing individuals will have no trouble getting the trigger down to a clean, light break. Beginning shooters should leave it just as it comes from the factory.

Diameter of the 10½-inch barrel is .780 inch, its full length exactly that of Ruger SRM and KS411N revolvers. Barrels of both .357 and .44 Silhouette Dragoons are button rifled one turn in eighteen inches right hand (1:18 RH). The carbide button skids somewhat during its squeeze through the bore, resulting in an actual twist closer to 1:19 inches.

In accordance with the findings of successful competitors in high-power rifle, benchrest and IHMSA, groove diameter of the barrel shall not exceed that of the bullet. Groove diameter of the .357 magnum Silhouette Dragoon is .355 inch (bullet .357). Groove diameter of the .44 Silhouette Dragoon is .428 inch (bullet .429 to .430).

Chambers and exit holes are held to SAAMI minimum dimensions and are roller burnished in separate operations. Roller-burnished chambers facilitate extraction of fired cases. Roller-burnished chamber exit holes probably reduce in-cylinder bullet abrasion, for spitting and copper wash around the frame windows and along the cylinder is reduced.

Chambers are counter-bored. Cylinder lockup is tighter than that of any revolver, possibly excepting the Colt Python, which advances the hand against the cylinder ratchet at the moment of hammer fall. No other single- or double-action revolver I have tested approaches the Silhouette Dragoon for tight lock-up

The front sight is a patridge type drafted across its top and back to reduce glare. It is .100 inch wide.

The rear sight features a back-drafted slide, the notch of which is .090-.095 inch wide by .070 inch deep. There are sixteen clicks per revolution for elevation and sixteen clicks per revolution windage. Directional indicators ("U"-up, "R"-right), are stamped on the sight body to help guide the shooter through those moments of panic provided by changes in wind and light.

A Pachmayr presentation grip is supplied with each Silhouette Dragoon to supplement the walnut stocks which are hand finished to the grip frame at the factory.

Lock time on the Silhouette Dragoon is long, hammer fall hefty. Some shooters cannot handle so long a hammer fall.

Twice I have recorded 39x40 with the .44 Silhouette Dragoon: bought it on a turkey the first time; slipped a slug over my ninth ram the second. Federal 220-grain silhouette ammo was used on both outings. On several occasions, when all the vital ingredients of accuracy were on the menu, five-shot groups of three inches and under have decorated the one hundred-meter target. As is to be expected, recoil of the .44 SD is heavy.

Recoil of the .357 SD is light. Hornady .358 rifle bullets may be fired in the .357 Silhouette Dragoon in cases trimmed to 1.020 inch. I use Federal .38 Special nickel brass; head thickness is the same as for .357 brass, less trimming is required, and case life — with reasonable loads — is good.

However, thus far, I have not achieved an accurate load with the Hornady 200-grain .358 spire-point. Ron Reiber of Hornady thinks the twist is too slow and the velocity too slow to stabilize this rifle bullet. Perhaps he is right. (While some silhouette acquaintances tell me the Hornady 200 SP shoots like fury in the Dan Wesson 40 Super Mag, my shooting does not bear this out.)

The Hornady 200 round-nose, with a ballistic coefficient of .201, does not have the down-range velocity retention of the spire-point. However, without accuracy from the spire-point, the point is moot.

A competitor at a match held on an Alaskan range used his S&W Model 25 chambered for .45 Long Colt.

This load works well in the test .357 SD: Hornady 200 RN .358, 11.7 grains 2400 powder, Federal .38 Special case trimmed to 1.021 inches, Federal 205M small rifle primer. Velocity averages 955 fps for six shots, with an extreme spread of 31 fps. Standard deviation is 11 fps.

This is still 400 fps below an accurate load with the same bullet fired from the Dan Wesson M40 Super Mag, which reveals a great lie that is presently being perpetrated by PFTs (Phony Fountainheads of Truth) — make that two lies: that the .357 Super Mag/Maximum is too much too soon and that no safe handloads have been developed for it. Fact is, the .357 Super Mag/Maximum has blown conventional .357 magnums off the firing line. Contrary to PFTers, who demagogically denounce the accomplishments, the .357 Super Mag has all but shut the door on the old .357 magnum and is closing in on the .44 mag, too.

All of this indicates that the Interarms .357 Mag Silhouette Dragoon is a beautiful revolver whose cartridge is shy on the stomping end. Chief weakness of the Virginian .357 SD is that it is not elongated to Super Mag dimensions.

The .44 Silhouette Dragoon is the accuracy rival of a Dan Wesson or Ruger of the same chambering. Its rear sight roughly equals that of the DWA M44. A look at the average velocities as recorded from the .44 Silhouette Dragoon reveals:

Federal 44A 240 JHP 1343fps
Federal 44C 220SIL 1390fps
Hornady #4425 240 JTC-SIL, 23/296, Fed
   155 primer, Fed case . . . . 1273 fps
Hornady #4425 240 JTC-SIL, 24/296,
   Fed 155 primer, Fed case . . . . 1421 fps

These velocities are lower than the same ammunition fired in a Smith & Wesson M-29 with 10⅝-inch silhouette barrel, a Dan Wesson M44 eight-inch, or the Ruger KS411N 10½-inch. A shallow eleven-degree forcing cone, in conjunction with one-half inch of freebore, is incorporated into the barrel. According to Interarms' Rod Sward, this freebore does much to insure bullet/bore concentricity. That the .44 Silhouette Dragoon shoots is beyond question. But the Dan Wesson and Ruger also shoot, and they are freebored. Since chamber exit holes measure a heel-stabilizing .430 inch, it is likely that the freebore is not necessary.

Sight settings for Federal 220 Silhouette read: C-13, P-18, T-23, R-29. As with all sights used in silhouette competition, it is wise to lubricate elevation and windage screws with BreakFree. Sights take a constant beating from adjustment, paint, sight black and the heat of carbide lamps.

The Interarms Silhouette Dragoons are finely made, hand-finished revolvers that contrast sharply with some better known products. All Silhouette Dragoons are test fired for accuracy. If they do not satisfy Rod Sward, they are not shipped. That's as close as a manufacturer can get to guaranteeing accuracy.

.45 LONG COLT

While seldom used in silhouette competition now, this 115-year-old cartridge still is alive and kicking. Thompson/Center chambered for it for a few years and Ruger is still offering it as their BN45 Blackhawk with a 7½-inch barrel. Smith & Wesson still catalogs it as their Model 25. Dan Wesson will be offering the .45 Colt in 1988 on the same frame as their .44 magnum.

Fortunately, three of these handguns, the Contender single-shot, the Ruger and the Dan Wesson revolvers are capable of withstanding higher pressures than earlier .45 Colt revolvers.

The data presented here is for those who are interested in shooting silhouettes or handgun hunting.

CAUTION: When using Smith & Wesson revolvers, start with a fifteen percent *lighter* powder charge for all listed loads.

The author's cigar is not quite as long as the rear-grip Remington XP-100 chambered for 7mm IHMSA International. Gates, an inveterate experimenter and wildcatter, has developed several of the popular silhouette cartridges.

They're Still Seeking The Ultimate For Long-Range Handgunning

THE UNLIMITED SILHOUETTE HANDGUN

CHAPTER 12

Robert Gates (left) and Elgin Gates display their early unlimited silhouette handguns. Pistol in latter's right hand is the first unlimited silhouette gun ever created. From this 7mm/.223, additional wildcats were developed.

WHAT IS an unlimited silhouette handgun? The answer was clear in my mind the night we founded IHMSA on October 2, 1976. I had designed and built the first unlimited class prototype silhouette pistol ever created and fired it on October 7, 1975, just five days short of a year earlier.

It had been obvious at the first handgun silhouette match ever held in September, 1975, in Tucson, Arizona, that none of the handguns then in existence were equal to the task of consistently knocking down the heavy steel silhouettes at ranges previously unheard of for handguns.

It was equally clear that we needed a new breed of handguns, as powerful and as accurate as rifles, but which would be legally accepted as handguns under the law.

My motion to create an unlimited category had been discussed at length, then accepted by unanimous vote. The stage was set for some marvelous things to come in the handgun world.

At that time, there was only one pistol on the market that could truly qualify as a long-range handgun. It was the Remington XP-100. In .221 Fireball caliber, it had been introduced in 1963. It was touted then as a varmint pistol and provoked a good deal of interest in its early days, but still was a popgun insofar as being effective for the newly created silhouette game. The XP-100 was simply a Remington Model 600 rifle action with a 10¾-inch barrel installed and a moulded nylon handgrip stock added. The factory open sights that came on it were less than adequate, but with a correctly installed scope, accuracy with this rigid bolt-action system was excellent.

By some quirk of fate, even though readily available, there had not been a single XP-100 at that first handgun silhouette competition in 1975. Why? Even then the competitors probably realized that, in its varmint caliber of .221, it wouldn't be effective against the heavy steel silhouettes. They were right. Secondly, the words, "unlimited gun," as related to silhouette shooting, hadn't been created until I coined the term in proposing the unlimited category of competition at the founding meeting of IHMSA a year later.

My first experiments began immediately after returning home from the 1975 match, using the easily worked-on Thompson-Center Contender. Sixteen days later, I had cobbled together the first unlimited silhouette handgun ever created. It was chambered in 7mm/.223. The cartridge would be adopted five years later by Thompson-Center as the 7mm T/C and would become the most successful production cartridge in the history of silhouette shooting.

Back to the Remington XP-100 in .221 Fire Ball: Once the newness wore off by the mid-1970s, Remington came within a whisker of discontinuing it. That's when the silhouette game came to town and created so great a demand for the XP-100 that the factory was hard put to keep up

This silhouette shooter demonstrates his Creedmoor position, utilizing a rebarreled and rechambered Remington XP-100 bolt-action .358 Winchester.

For his XP-100 rebarreled to full-length .308 Winchester, this shooter prefers a hooded front sight and Micro rear sight. The stock is of walnut, not the original plastic.

Registrar at a sanctioned IHMSA match weighs an unlimited gun that is chambered for .30/.223. Stock is of light fiberglass filled with foam to keep gun under 4½-pound limit.

with the orders. For reasons of their own, probably related to product liability and insurance, Remington would not sell the actions separately. With the number of them being rebarreled to silhouette calibers, there must be thousands of .221 Fire Ball barrels gathering dust and rust on gunsmiths' shelves around the country.

As soon as the realization developed among competitors that the XP-100 action was superior for creating accurate long-range handguns, the great unlimited race began. As the weeks and months slipped by, XP-100 actions were rebarreled in every caliber imaginable, from .25 up to the full-length .458 Winchester magnum.

At first, the demand was for big boomers and every gunsmith interested in the silhouette game tried to build something bigger and more powerful than the next guy. First, they were using cut-down or shortened versions of

Author test fires an unlimited pistol from a sitting position. Gun, chambered for 7mm/.223, was extremely accurate, but the author felt the cartridge was under-powered for limited competition on silhouettes.

Gates tests out Contender that was an early unlimited model. It was chambered for .308x1½. Cartridge did not catch on.

some of the well known existing rifle cartridges such as the .30/06, .308, .300, .338, .358, .375, .45-70 and the .458, to name a few. Some of these conversions proved to be quite successful and became top winners.

Of the dozen or so of my own unlimited creations, created in those early days, one of them — a 7.62mm case shortened from 2.01 to 1.875 and necked to 7mm after long and careful testing — was given a thirty-eight-degree shoulder borrowed from benchrest technology. I called it the 7mm IHMSA International — soon shortened simply to 7mm Int. It would prove to be the most successful unlimited cartridge available to this day. Federal Cartridge Corporation tooled up and ran off half a million match grade cases to supply the silhouette demand. Incidentally, a number of gunsmiths chambered rifles for the 7mm Int and it has become a potent hunting cartridge.

Author's wife, Dollie Gates, tries her hand with unlimited 6.5mm/.223 Contender, while author acts as her coach. An increasing number of competitors today are housewives.

IHMSA international title shoot has drawn more than 1000 shooters in each of the past seven years.

Realizing that the XP-100 action could handle anything you could close the bolt on, gunsmiths soon were rebarreling them for full-length rifle cartridges instead of the shortened-case versions.

By 1981, common sense began to prevail and most of the big-caliber handguns were retired as heirlooms or conversation pieces to hang over the fireplace. The common sense came with realization that accuracy was the key ingredient in taking down silhouette targets at up to two hundred meters. You had to hit 'em. The big boomers weren't as accurate as the smaller calibers; it was as simple as that.

Right from the beginning, I had concentrated on 7mm and .30 as the most likely calibers. Ballistic science had long known of the superior ballistic coefficient and sectional density advantages of the 7mm projectile and, by late 1976, I was fully committed to 7mm as being the ultimate silhouette caliber for unlimited handguns.

This whole preoccupation of filling that empty area between the existing pistol cartridges of the mid-1970s and the full-length rifle cartridges with something to successfully shoot silhouettes became a mania with gunsmiths and shooters alike.

Most of us started with the smaller calibers for unlimited

These unlimited guns are circa '77. At top, gun uses original factory stock of Zytel, but is rebarreled to 6.5mm International. It has Micro rear sight, Lyman front. Lower gun with fancy walnut stock has been chambered in .35 IHMSA International.

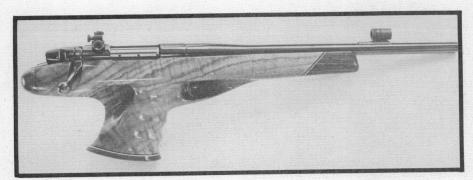

Only 225 Weatherby unlimited guns for silhouette competition were made, most in .308 WCF full length. A few were chambered in .22-250. All are on Weatherby Mark V action.

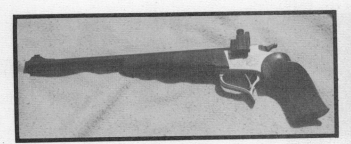

This state-of-the-art gun is a Contender with Armorloy-finished receiver, Herrett stocks, custom Hart match grade barrel; chambered in 7mm International Rimmed.

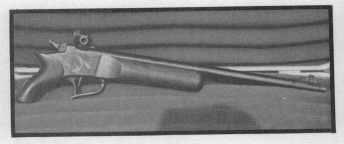

This unlimited T/C in 6mm/.222 has a 15-inch barrel and an extra-small grip for a woman's hand. Distaffers have taken to the silhouette game with unbridled enthusiasm.

guns, then the pendulum swung over to the boomers. The bigger and more powerful, the better. Finally, it swung back to the mid-range calibers with the XP-100 or similar bolt-actions preferred.

Remington finally acknowledged the fact that the silhouette game had come to stay and, in 1980, the company introduced the fourteen-inch-barrel silhouette model as their XP-100 7mm BR, using a 1½-inch version of their small primer-pocketed .308 Bench Rest case.

As mentioned, one of the earliest pistols to be experimented with for unlimited cartridges was the T/C Contender. It was easy to work with because of its detachable barrel feature and, even when the bolt-actions took over, the Contender never completely faded away as an unlimited competition gun.

Defying all the logic that benchrest shooters have developed for their sport — that it takes a rigid bolt-action gun to shoot accurately — the Contender is still present and, in some cases, highly competitive. My personal belief is that it takes more skill to upgrade a Contender that will shoot with extreme accuracy, but it is being done by one or two skilled gunsmiths. Even a few factory fourteen-inch Contenders do quite well. Rechambered T/C fourteen-inch barrels in 7mm Int-R, the rimmed version of my 7mm

Early experimental XP-100 by the author has fluted Douglas air gauged barrel; caliber is .30/.223. (Right) Rear grip XP-100 prototype uses the first silhouette electronic trigger.

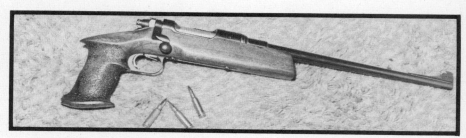

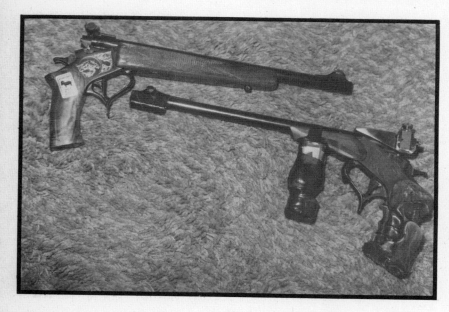

Using basic Contenders, author built these experimental prototypes. Top gun is 7mm/.222; bottom has weight taped to the end of barrel to reduce the recoil jump. Chambering for this one is 7mm/.223, the wildcat Thompson-Center would adopt in 1980 for standard production chambering.

IHMSA International, are consistent unlimited trophy winners to this day.

A great deal has been learned over the past ten years about how to select the unlimited gun features of your choice.

Bolt-action guns outnumber the break-open unlimited guns by a wide margin. The reasons are many and understandable.

1. A few years ago, used XP-100s were numerous and rather inexpensive to purchase.

The original factory XP-100 in .221 Fire Ball chambering was the only long-range handgun available when the game started in 1975. Gun had been introduced by Remington in 1963. The .221 bullet was too light, but the action was considered superb. Thousands were bought, rechambered.

Finally, in 1980, Remington introduced the XP-100 model specifically designed for silhouette competition. This one is chambered for the 7mm BR, a short case version.

During a Hawaii match, competitor fires his Remington 7mm BR model in unlimited match. Since Remington made BR brass available in 1986, the caliber has become popular.

2. Today, between the .221 Fire Ball and 7mm BR, the XP-100 offers bolt-face size for any practical silhouette application.

3. The 7mm BR can be rechambered to 7 IHMSA or to 7mm/.308 for little money.

4. The 7mm BR itself is highly competitive out of the box. Only sights need to be added.

5. Any competent gunsmith can make a bolt-action handgun that shoots well.

6. Custom stockmakers give the shooter the choice of center grip or rear grip.

7. The bolt-action is strong, safe and good looking.

METALLIC SILHOUETTE SHOOTING

This is a vertical silhouette range. Almost any type of terrain can be used. Indian Creek, Indiana, is the functional installation's site.

During match in Goliad, Texas, Dave Bradshaw fires Weatherby that has been chambered for full-length .308. He uses what is called a Creedmoor (freestyle) position for the match.

The late Seventies and early Eighties offered certain challenges in silhouette shooting that aren't seen often now. We still hear about hard-set silhouettes occasionally, but they used to be the rule, not the exception. You'd find them with all sizes of feet, nothing uniform, set in the middle of the rail, cement blocks or railroad ties, even in the dirt; whatever was handy and inexpensive. (I remember a February match when railrod ties, soaking wet, were used. The metal critters would freeze to the ties so hard you couldn't even kick them off with your feet.)

The trend then was to build bigger guns with more and more power. Anyone shooting less than a .308 with 200-grain bullets usually was considered a sissy. We got caught up in trying to impress and outdo ourselves with how ridiculous we could make them. Mild steel targets were used then and many a harsh word was exchanged between the match director and the big gun shooter. I don't remember who it was that used a .45/70 Contender, 350-grain

Action on the line at this match in Idaho is fairly informal, although constant check on safety measures is maintained by the range officer.

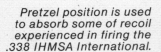

Pretzel position is used to absorb some of recoil experienced in firing the .338 IHMSA International.

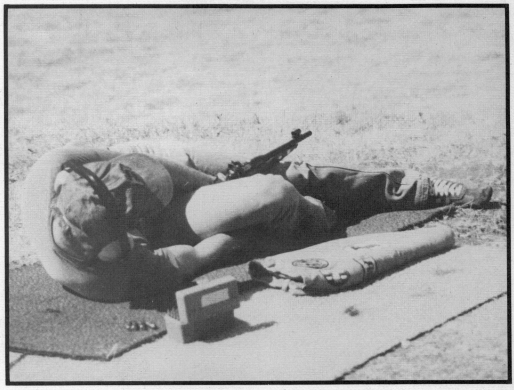

cast bullets with the nose drilled out and filled with 10.0 grains or so of Bullseye powder and a primer glued into the end. It sure upset the match directors, though!

The guns and the sport have settled down a lot in the past few years for the benefit of everyone, but it was really exciting for a while. Better target materials, better stands, narrower feet on the animals and the new "ram topple" rule all have tended to reduce our gun needs to a much more reasonable level. The latest trend is to build and shoot a caliber that will do the job reliably and punish the shooter as little as possible.

The targets are hit a lot more often now and the chances of their falling are much greater, but we lost something when we no longer had to shoot through the target and no longer set the sagebrush and grass on fire in front of the shooter with muzzle flash. Oh well, good sense usually prevails.

Today's shooters are capable of extremely accurate

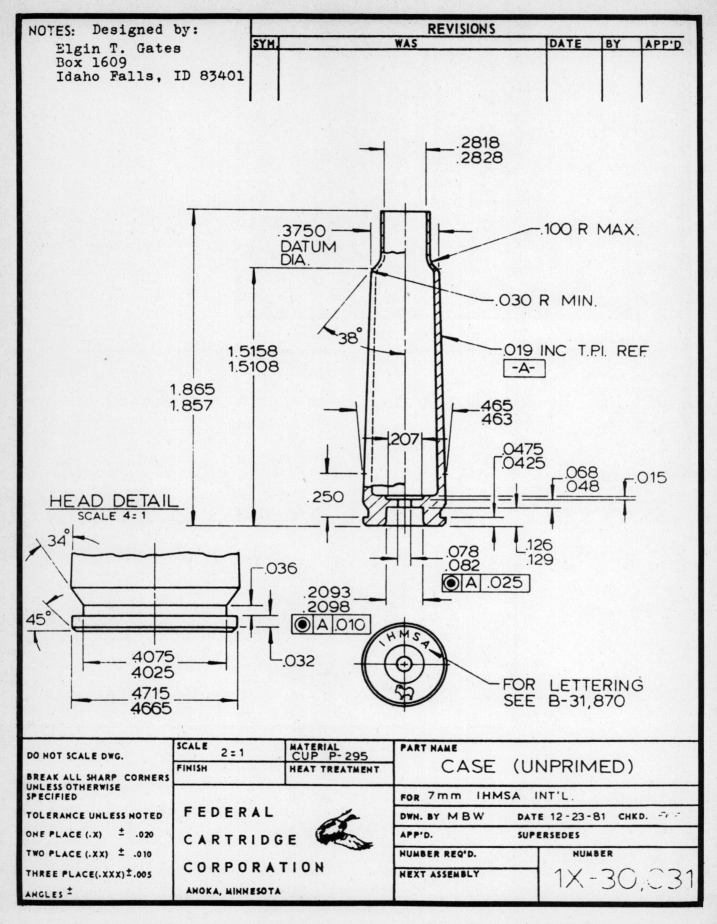

Left: Federal's specs for the 7mm International cartridge designed by author. The company produced half a million cases to meet silhouette demand. (Above) These Douglas premium barrels are 15 inches in length and chambered, threaded to fit XP-100 actions. They were made available to members through silhouette association headquarters.

shooting and our own research and development have made us all much more knowledgeable of our needs for the silhouette game. We have developed track records for many successful cartridges, but still the biggest question facing someone building his first unlimited is, "What caliber should I use?" That person will ask other shooters and the answers given are as numerous and varied as there are shooters and calibers.

The problem is that most of us usually recommend what we personally use. That may be fine for us, but not necessarily correct or ideal for the other person.

I'm going to attempt some advice to the new unlimited-gun builder; not that I'm any smarter than anyone else, it's just that I have tried lots of guns and calibers and have probably made more mistakes than most people. This is not a complete list, but I have owned or still have the following calibers in bolt-action guns: .17/.223, 6x47, 7mm T/C, 7mm BR, 7/.308, .308, 7x57, .45/70, 6.5 IHMSA, 7mm IHMSA, 7mm R, 6.5 Rem mag, .350 Rem mag and .458 Win. mag. What I recommend is that one take the following information into consideration before making a choice:

Accuracy:
1. Any cartridge frequently used to win in silhouette competition is capable of excellent accuracy.
2. Most shooters can maintain their own level of shooting better with mild recoil.

Bullet Selection:
1. The 7mm probably offers the best selection.
2. The .30 caliber probably offers the second best selection.
3. Bullet cost is important as you will shoot a great deal.

Knockdown Reliability:
1. Forget about bullet energy. It's a poor way to analyze the target knockdown factor. Momentum is a much more efficient method.
2. I recommend a momentum factor of at least .6 for an unlimited gun, for reliable knockdown.
3. "Reliable knockdown" does not mean that every silhouette hit will always fall without exception. It means that it will take down about 99½ percent of the targets. No

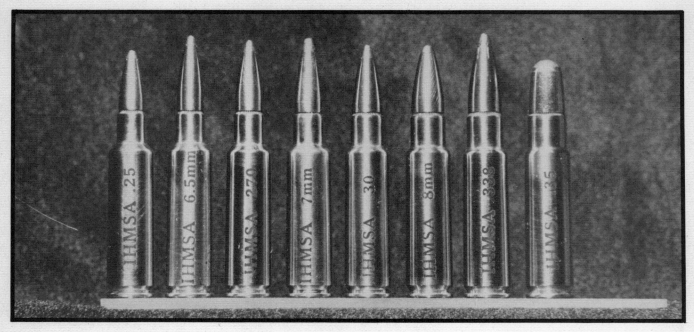

This eight-caliber series of International silhouette cartridges was designed in 1976 soon after the birth of the silhouette sport. All have case lengths of 1.875 inches, as compared to 2.01 length of parent 7.62mm case. From left, the calibers are: .25, 6.5mm, .270, 7mm, .30, 8mm, .338 and .35. Mid-range calibers are more popular.

For comparison (from left) are .30x1½, 7mm/.308x1¾, 7mm IHMSA International, 308 full length, 7x57 full length and the standard .30/06 cartridge, so familiar.

The 7mm International headstamp reads "IHMSA," features the silhouette ram imprinted into the brass on bottom.

cartridge can absolutely guarantee one hundred percent knockdown. There are always unexplained exceptions.

4. Unlimited guns shooting 140-grain bullets, with velocity of about 1900 fps and a reasonable coefficient, give about minimum reliable knockdown momentum.

5. The type of bullet construction has little meaning. They all seem to work quite well.

Cartridge Efficiency:

1. "Overkill" cartridges usually are not too efficient and cost more to shoot than an efficient one.

2. Efficiency simply means doing the needed job as economically as possible.

3. The 7mm IHMSA cartridge is optimum in case capacity needed for usable efficiency.

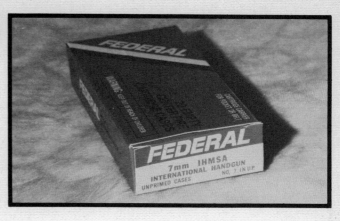

The 7mm IHMSA International cases were manufactured and packed by Federal in two lots of 250,000 rounds each. They were made to Gates' specs for the silhouette game.

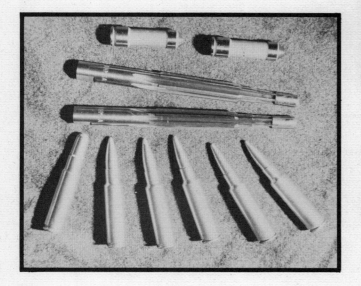

The go-no-go gauges, chambering reamers were built to chamber Douglas and Shilen barrels for installation on Remington XP-100 actions for unlimited silhouette guns.

Remington's .221 Fire Ball XP-100 barreled action had a 10-inch barrel. During the first four years of the new silhouette sport, this was the preferred action, but it invariably was rebarreled for high performance rounds.

4. A 7 T/C will meet momentum standards with a 139-grain Hornady bullet and 27.0 grains of Winchester 748 powder.

5. My .458 Win. mag takes 500-plus-grain bullets and it takes over one pound of powder to load one hundred rounds. Overkill? Yep! Efficient? Nope!

Felt Recoil:
1. There are no trophies in the silhouette game for:

   a. The shooter who can stand the most punishment.
   b. The gun that produces the most muzzle flash and concussion.
   c. The shooter with the worst flinch.

2. Other factors being equal, the bigger the bore and the heavier the bullet, the more felt recoil.

3. Shoot as many guns as possible and pick one that you feel totally comfortable with. Most silhouette shooters are quite free in letting others try their guns.

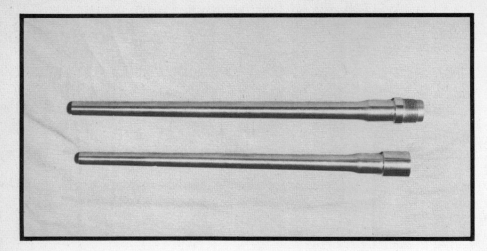

These Douglas premium barrels have been turned, tapered and prepared for fitting on the XP-100 actions.

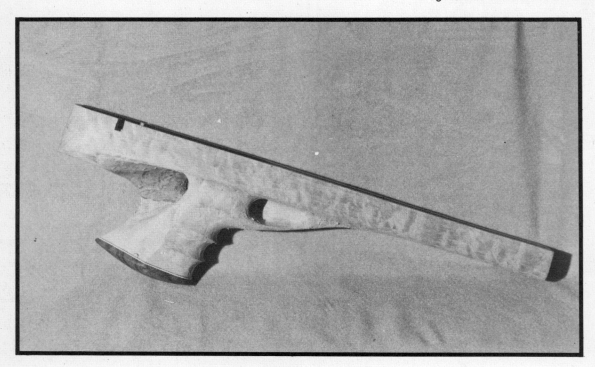

Below: Unfinished thumbhole stock is of maple, designed for XP-100. George Peterson supplies them to gunsmiths and silhouette shooters

4. Ask yourself this question, "Would I look forward to shooting that cartridge in an eighty-round match?" If you pull the trigger and hope that it doesn't go off, your accuracy is bound to suffer.

5. Consider a muzzle brake even on a cartridge that doesn't bother you. Besides recoil, they limit muzzle jump.

Open Sights:

This recommendation for sights is for the shooter looking for high quality at a reasonable price. There are many good sights available, some of them designed for special purposes, and the price range is tremendous. I recommend hoods, both front and rear, if you do not shoot under a covered range. They help reduce light condition changes. The sights that I recommend take ease of hood mounting into consideration.

1. Front Sight:

a. Use two screws to mount the front sight. If needed, drill and tap the second hole.

b. A choice of post widths should be available from the manufacturer. Apertures should be another option.

c. Lyman and Redfield are both good choices. Opening size and cost are the biggest differences between them.

d. The Redfield Olympic offers a quick-change light reducer and two mounting distances.

2. Rear Sight:

a. There is no need to use a rear sight that is any more mechanically refined than the Williams or the Bo-Mar. Two-thousandths-of-an-inch click adjustment is adequate for an unlimited gun for any type of shoot-off you may encounter.

b. The Bo-Mar sight is made out of steel, has two

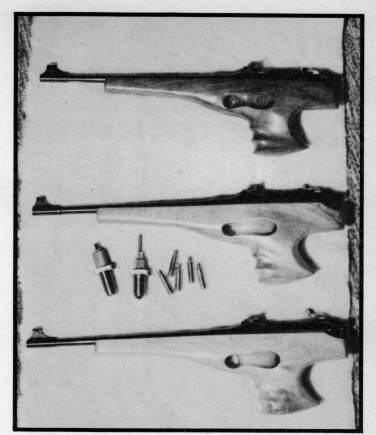

These finished unlimited silhouette pistols are ready for action. All are chambered for 7mm International IHMSA cartridge. Dies are manufactured by RCBS.

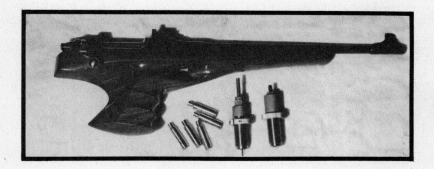

Custom-built walnut stock has been installed on XP-100. Finger grooves have been cut to fit the hand of the silhouette shooting owner.

thousandths click movement, is consistent, positive and durable.

    c. The Williams is made of aluminum and is lightweight, has sight movement of one-thousandth per click and is consistent and positive. It's not as durable as the Bo-Mar. Because of the better click adjustment movement, this sight is ideal for .22 LR silhouette.

    d. The Bo-Mar is top-mounted and requires no stock cutting, but must be mounted on the front of the receiver.

    e. The Williams is a side mount and may be used either on the receiver front or rear, but usually requires stock modifications.

Stocks:

1. The choice between rear grip or center grip is strictly a personal preference, both offering certain advantages. Try both types before you decide which one is best for you.

2. Thumbholer or open rear grip? The open grip is probably the more comfortable for the majority of shooters, as well as being slightly lighter. Weight is often of concern for the unlimited gun builder.

3. Wood or glass? There are many options available and several things might be taken into consideration in making your decision:

    a. Kevlar is the strongest material for stocks, glass probably the second and wood the least strong. However, stock strength is not critical. Any of them will do very well.

    b. Wood stocks are hard to beat in beauty.

    c. Foam-filled glass and Kevlar are usually the lightest in weight.

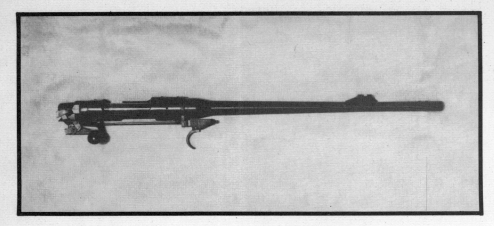

In 1980, Remington introduced a 7mm BR silhouette pistol, making barreled actions available to a growing silhouette fraternity.

Oklahoma City gunsmith Jack Dever built this rear-grip limited edition unlimited pistol. He utilized XP-100 actions and Shilen stainless steel barrels. The gun was sold in a specially-fitted custom case.

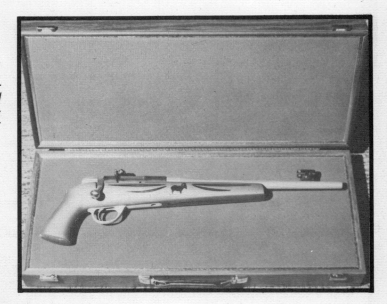

Jack Dever made only twenty-five of the custom guns. This one — No. 1 of the series — is chambered for the .30 International cartridge. All of the guns in this series are considered to be valuable collector items.

d. Glass stocks may seem easier than wood to finish, but it really depends on which you would rather do. Glass usually needs the pinholes filled and then to be spray-painted.

e. The factory Remington stock can be customized with "glass" Bondo and painted. The poor man's way, but adequate.

Barrel Selection:

This area is highly controversial, as everyone has an opinion and all have merit, but these are my recommendations:

1. Custom-made barrels may be necessary for special reasons such as: custom twists, custom chambering, special outside dimensions, metallurgy and so on.

2. For accuracy, custom barrels have little to offer the silhouette shooter. We can't use benchrest accuracy potential. When is the last time you saw a benchrest gun with open sights?

3. Because we often are forced to shoot our guns when they are sizzling hot, we often see custom barrels that "wash out" sooner than factory barrels.

4. There are probably more matches won with factory barrels than all the custom-made ones combined.

5. Remington barrels are hammer-forged, I believe, the only ones that are readily available.

6. I would recommend staying with a Remington barrel unless you have a special reason that demands a custom-made one.

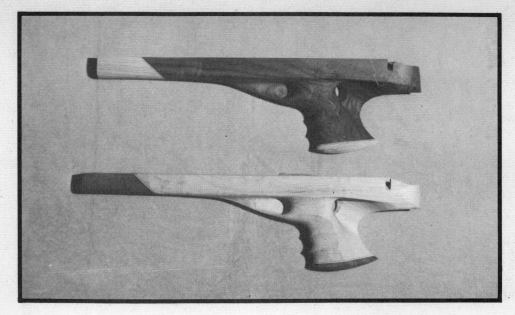

Unlimited gun kits, featuring unfinished wood stocks, were available from headquarters of IHMSA for several years.

From left: 7mm BR silhouette cartridge; 7mm IHMSA International version; and the .308 full-length round. These are favorites among the modern breed of silhouette competitors.

Stock-Action Mounting System:
1. In any stock use only the front screw.
2. If it's a factory stock, cut off the forend tip. They're usually crooked.
3. Aluminum V-bar bedding is adequate, but not my first choice.
4. I recommend glass bedding as the best system. It's solid and custom fits that particular action perfectly.
5. Glass bed from the tang to well in front of the recoil lug.
6. A free-floated barrel does not always shoot better than one with pressure. I recommend that you experiment to find out which your gun prefers. Go with your gun's preference, not yours!

As you probably can tell by now, I recommend building unlimited guns following the current trends. It makes all kinds of sense to build it to do the job effectively, but not to beat the shooter to death. But, I'll always remember the old days with fond memories. Those were days of shooting clear through the rams without knocking them down, raising the other guy off his rug with concussion from your gun, taking your new ram-slammer to the range mounted on its training wheels, seeing who could get the biggest ball of fire out the muzzle, hitting the rail and knocking all the animals down, listening to the alibis.

Why did you guys have to come along, bringing common sense with you? We were having fun!

THE BRUTUS STORY

CHAPTER 13

...With Pertinent Observations On Loading The Really Big-Bore Silhouette Guns!

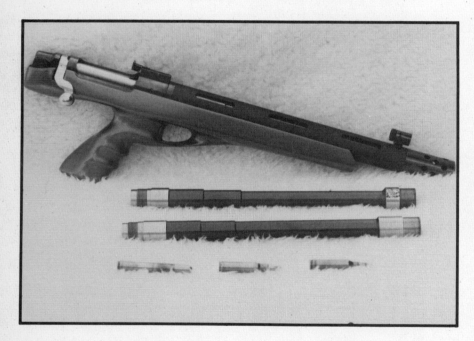

Brutus was meant to be the ultimate silhouette handgun, but when it was completed, the weight exceeded that allowed in the rules; so it became the ultimate handgun for hunting!

THE PIECE DE RESISTANCE of the IHMSA handgun silhouette game is the unlimited pistol. Anything goes in the way of modifications so long as the gun meets the weight limit of 4½ pounds and the barrel length and sight radius limit of fifteen inches.

The unlimited gun rule is in stark contrast to the production gun rule that allows only the manufacturer to improve his product. For unlimited competition, the sky is the limit. If you can afford a $5000 unlimited gun with all the engraving, frills and gold inlay that goes with it, more power to you.

On the other hand, price alone does not guarantee you will win in competition. The standard factory-built Remington XP-100 7mm BR pistol is capable of shooting better scores than the ability of any shooter allows.

In the year following the first handgun metallic silhouette competition, a few of us experimented with ways to come up with high performance handguns. The results were spectacular when compared with the handguns that had been manufactured for the past hundred years. The new long-range pistols won all of the marbles at the 1976 championships in El Paso, Texas. It was obvious that the standard manufactured handguns of the day were badly outclassed.

At the founding meeting of IHMSA, I offered a motion to create a category of unlimited pistols. The motion passed unanimously. That was in October, 1976. Six months

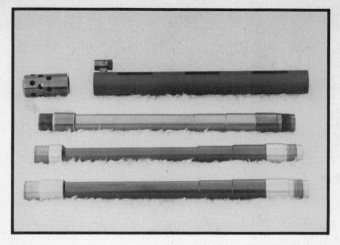
From top are Brutus muzzle brake and barrel shroud; the .458 Win. mag barrel; 6.5 Rem. mag barrel; and barrel for the .350 Remington magnum. Barrels were color-coded.

The lineup of cartridges for which the various Brutus barrels were chambered are (from left) Winchester .458 magnum; .350 Remington magnum; 6.5mm Rem. mag.

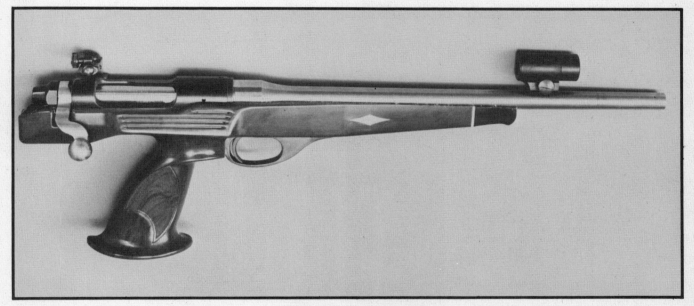
This unlimited test gun, chambered in .30 International, uses a Douglas premium air gauge stainless steel barrel. The barrel length has been held to 15 inches to meet the competition requirements. Action is Remington's XP-100.

later, as word spread around the country, the great unlimited handgun race was going all out.

Unlimited guns, mostly rebarreled XP-100 actions, were chambered for every cartridge imaginable, from shortened versions of various rifle cartridges on up to the full length .458 Winchester magnum.

The purpose of this chapter is to describe the creation of what may be the ultimate unlimited pistol, and to provide load data for some of the most popular unlimited calibers that have been used in IHMSA silhouette over the past ten years.

Bill Bartram of Orem, Utah, chairman of IHMSA's technical committee, came up with the idea of an interchangeable-barrel unlimited gun on an XP-100 action capable of flattening the most stubborn steel ram. At the same time, the idea was to create a long-range hunting pistol that would handle any big-game trophy on the face of the earth. The name Bartram selected for this gun was Brutus. Ultimately, Brutus failed to meet the IHMSA weight rule, but the end product was a fantastic hunting pistol.

As a result of Brutus, one manufacturer, claiming the perennial title of "the world's most powerful handgun," had to tone down his claim to "the most powerful production revolver."

Bartram got together with his gunsmith friend, Gil Biggerstaff of Salt Lake City, to set the criteria for the gun. They had been working on muzzle brake designs for an XP-100 chambered in full length .308. Now was the time to build

Left: Author chambers an unlimited barrel in his shop. (Below) Barrel is threaded to fit the Remington XP-100 in creating unlimited gun.

Three popular unlimited silhouette cartridges are (from left): 7mm BR, 7mm International and the 7mm/08. Test gun is chambered for the last.

Brutus and refine their muzzle brake ideas at the same time.

At the beginning of the project, Bartram and Biggerstaff laid out some preliminary ideas they wanted to accomplish in the design and features for the gun.

1. The .221 Fireball bolt would be easier to open up and install an extractor in, than the Remington .308-based bolt that also is used in some XP-100 models.

2. The Mauser 91 extractor would best serve the purpose, as it would work on the magnum-based cartridges and also on rimmed calibers based on the .30-30 case.

3. The gun would be useable with factory-loaded ammunition. Bartram had a pet peeve about guns chambered for example, for a .375 H&H magnum, but which must be loaded down to performance levels of a .375 Winchester to be comfortable to shoot.

4. Barrels and chamberings:

a. 7R — A silhouette handgun cartridge based on a reduced-capacity .30-30 case and necked down to 7mm. Excellent for silhouette and small animals up to whitetail deer size.

b. 6.5 Remington mag — Excellent for long distance shooting, fast and flat shooting for game size up to mule deer.

c. .350 Remington mag — Ideal for game animals up to elk, bear and moose, with proper bullet selection.

d. .458 Winchester mag — Not the most powerful cartridge in the world, but adequate for most anything that breathes.

Bert Stringfellow, ardent designer of silhouette production handguns, checks 6.5mm unlimited gun he built.

State-of-the-art unlimited models were built by Frank Scotto, who is chairman of the IHMSA evaluation committee. Gun at top is rear-grip model; at bottom is one with center-grip configuration. Both handguns are chambered in 7mm International.

5. Interchangeable barrels — Gil was challenged to make this gun so that it could be broken down and the barrels changed with tools no more sophisticated than a rock and a stick.

6. The gun must utilize the same set of sights and scope mount for all barrels.

Bartram's demands kept Gil Biggerstaff quiet for several weeks, but one night about midnight, the phone rang and Gil quietly said, "I've got it figured out." The reality of our dream gun had begun.

Besides the challenges, there were a lot of unknowns that had to be worked out. How heavy should the gun be? Despite the muzzle brake, could a man actually handle the recoil of a .458 Winchester magnum? Would a handgun stock be strong enough to handle a cartridge that can generate over 5000 pounds of energy? Was the muzzle brake design actually good enough? Could .458 Winchester magnum factory-loaded ammo be extracted in that short action that was designed for a .221 Fire Ball?

Bartram had heard of three other handguns that had been built up on bolt actions, but none of them were successful to his way of thinking — shortened cartridge cases, way underloaded, etc. In other words, not truly .458 Winchester mags. Gil and Bartram agreed this one was going to be a full house .458 Winchester magnum and it would handle all factory loadings.

Biggerstaff is not a full-time gunsmith, nor does he have access to a fully equipped machine shop. He is a part-time gunsmith who works out of his house in the evenings. He

Competitor's big-bore unlimited gun recoils after being fired from the Creedmoor position. The gun which he is using is rear-grip XP-100 model.

owns a small lathe and a drill press, which he taught himself to use. Any other machining he does on borrowed equipment. What he really has to offer is a mechanical mind, vivid imagination and magic fingers. Many gunsmiths do not have these talents to offer.

The dust was wiped off the .221 Fireball XP-100 and it was delivered to Gil the following Saturday. He started ordering barrels and parts and, while waiting for the stuff, started in on the machine work. The bolt face needed to be opened up to accommodate the magnum cases. The extractor needed to be installed, the bolt release maxed out, ad infinitum. To be able to extract a live factory round, Gil had to cut a groove into the right-hand side of the action to allow the nose of the bullet to clear. The recoil lug is pretty small on the XP-100, so he hand-made a huge dog leg-type lug that offered a much larger exterior surface to which to bed the stock.

Seamless aluminum tubing was used as a barrel shroud, 1¾-inch inside dimension and 2⅛-inch outside dimension. The shroud mounted the front sight and was made to index on two pins mounted on the recoil lug. The shroud was slotted and a black anodized finish completed the job. The trigger was straightened and fine-tuned in adjustment.

Bartram phoned George Peterson of Western Gunstock, and asked if he might be able to make a wood stock for an XP-100 with a wide forend.

"I need one for 2⅛ inches," Bartram said.

"Well, Bill, my standard stocks have a forend that's 2¼-inches."

"You don't understand, Geroge, I need a 2⅛-inch barrel *channel,* not total width."

"Is this another one of your weird ideas, Bill?"

"Nope, just a full house .458 Winchester magum."

A long pause, then, "I'll make it, but on two conditions: First, you acknowledge I've told you it won't work. Second, when you blow the stock in half, you don't tell anyone where you got it!"

"It's a deal, but what if it does work?"

"If it turns out okay, you can tell people what a fine stock I make."

"No fancy wood, George. I plan on glassing it for additional strength."

Two weeks later, Bartram received the stock and put on

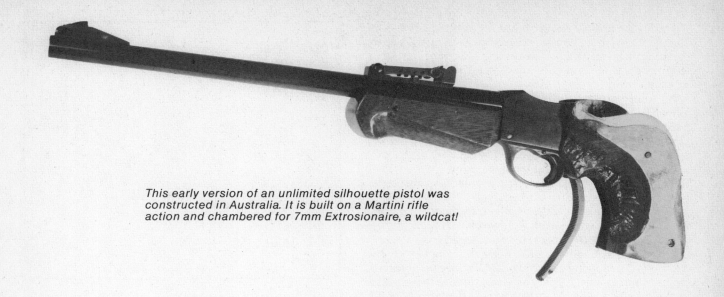

This early version of an unlimited silhouette pistol was constructed in Australia. It is built on a Martini rifle action and chambered for 7mm Extrosionaire, a wildcat!

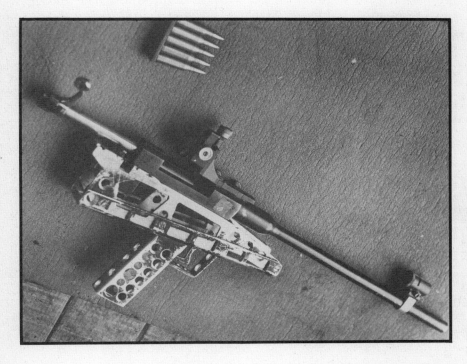

This unlimited gun, built in Finland by the Rautiainen brothers, has Sako barrel, Tikka action and Anschutz sights. It is chambered for .243 and has been found extremely accurate.

three layers of fiberglass cloth and painted it gold.

The barrel blanks came in and Gil left them as 1¾-inch bull barrels for weight. Both ends were threaded, one end for the receiver and the other end for the muzzle brake. A Bo-Mar rear sight was installed on the reciever and a Lyman 17A front sight mounted on the shroud. The muzzle brake chamber was machined and the exit holes drilled, with outside dimensions the same as the shroud. Then the gun was assembled and it was ready for testing.

During the time the gun was being built, word leaked out about it and some well-meaning people thought it wise to do one or more of the following:

a. Question the builders' sanity.
b. Insult their intelligence.
c. Repeat secondhand horror stories.
d. Remind them of the frailty of human bone structure.
e. Wanted to be present when the gun was tested.

The decision was made to test the gun in the .458 Winchester magnum chambering. If it worked okay, then the 7R, 6.5 magnm and the .350 Remington magnums would be a snap. They started out with some cast-bullet handloads that Bartram made up. Bartram admitted he was a bit over-cautious and that the first few loads were a little on the mild side. But it wasn't long before they were shooting maximum cast bullet loads. No problems were encountered, so they tried 400-grain jacketed-bullet handloads and loaded up through the hottest loads found in the manuals. Still with no problems.

During the testing, about twenty-five other shooters had assembled. At the silhouette range you can drive right up to the firing line, and people were driving up in ones and twos, ten to twelve vehicles, only a few feet from where testing was under way.

Bartram pulled out the last reamining few rounds of .458 Winchester magnum ammo that still needed to be tested: 515-grain copper-clad steel bullets, Winchester's Safari loads, made for African big-game. Hot stuff. They looked at each other and Bartram asked, "What do you think?"

Gil replied, "That's what we're here for."

They flipped a coin. Gil won the dubious pleasure of being the one to test the ultimate load.

They had been testing the .458 in Creedmoor position, which is a bit punishing even with normal guns, and really didn't know what to expect from the Safari load, except that it kicked like hell in a rifle. Bartram taped two elbow pads to Gil's shooting arm and put about twenty layers of tape around his wrist. Gil lay down and loaded the gun. He looked around to see what their friends thought about all this. They seemed pretty unconcerned, and even nonchalant, hunkering down behind those pickups. Brave, but

At this silhouette shoot on a range in Idaho, one can find any number of unlimited category handguns that are limited in design only by imagination of the creator.

6.5mm International

CARTRIDGE: 6.5mm International
GUN: XP-100
BARREL AND LENGTH: Douglas premium, 15 inches
TWIST: 1:8
PRIMER: Federal 210 M
CASE: IHMSA Federal
BULLET: See below

These tests are based on ten-shot groups fired at fifty meters from sandbag rest position.

BULLET	POWDER	WEIGHT IN GRAINS	AVERAGE MUZZLE VELOCITY FPS	REMARKS
100-gr. Sierra SPFB	AA-2230	34.0	2594	
100-gr. Sierra SPFB	AA-2520	35.0	2608	
100-gr. Sierra SPFB	H-322	33.1	2574	most accurate
100-gr. Sierra SPFB	AA-1680	35.0	2604	
120-gr. Sierra SPFB	H-335	34.0	2427	
120-gr. Sierra SPFB	AA-2520	35.5	2406	
120-gr. Sierra SPFB	H-322	30.6	2344	accurate
120-gr. Sierra SPFB	H-4198	28.2	2307	
140-gr. Hornady SPFB	H-4831	39.5	2302	
140-gr. Hornady SPFB	H-335	31.0	2217	
140-gr. Hornady SPFB	AA-2520	30.8	2264	accurate
140-gr. Hornady SPFB	H-4198	25.1	2063	
160-gr. Hornady RN	H-4831	37.5	2017	
160-gr. Hornady RN	H-335	28.2	1984	
160-gr. Hornady RN	H-4198	23.1	1788	
160-gr. Hornady RN	AA-2520	29.1	2003	accurate

Note: All data and information in this book is the result of safe and careful testing by the author and other contributors submitting the material contained herein. Since neither the author, DBI Books, Inc., nor any of the contributors has any control over the components, equipment and techniques used with this published information, no liability or responsibility for any injury or damage that occurs is either implied or assumed.

not stupid, as one of them said later.

"We *knew* the gun would work, that our calculations were correct and the muzzle brake was effective, but there was still a tiny bit of doubt left in the subconscious mind. *Wham!* The gun went off! Gil was still in one piece and unharmed. We had a successful hunting handgun." Bartram related.

The only change made to the gun was to reduce the outside dimension of each barrel, as the gun was too muzzle-heavy. Total weight of the gun was reduced to 6½ pounds. The barrels were color coded for easy identification. Everything they had hoped to accomplish with this gun was done. Barrels are changed, indexed and headspaced with no tools and the stock remains intact during the changing of barrels.

"The cartridge and the gun itself intimidates the vast majority of potential shooters," Bartram told me. However, Gil and I have named it the .458 Brutus to enchance

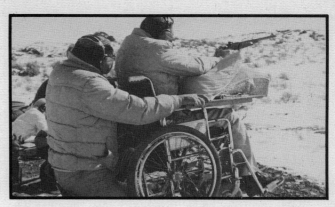

Firing from his wheelchair, this competitor favored the Super 14 Contender in 7mm International Rimmed caliber.

7mm International

CARTRIDGE: 7mm International
GUN: XP-100
BARREL AND LENGTH: Shilen Stainless 15 inch
TWIST: 1:8
PRIMER: Federal 210 M
CASE: IHMSA Federal
BULLET: See below

These tests are based on ten-shot groups fired at fifty meters from sandbag rest position.

BULLET	POWDER	WEIGHT IN GRAINS	AVERAGE MUZZLE VELOCITY FPS	REMARKS
139-gr. Hornady SPFB	AA-2230	32.0	2184	
139-Gr. Hornady SPFB	AA-2460	32.0	2214	accurate
139-gr. Hornady SPFB	H-322	33.2	2249	
139-gr. Hornady SPFB	H-4198	30.2	2207	accurate
154-gr. Hornady SPFB	AA-2230	33.0	2148	
154-gr. Hornady SPFB	AA-2520	34.0	2173	accurate
154-gr. Hornady SPFB	H-322	32.1	2147	
154-gr. Hornady SPFB	H-4198	29.5	2160	
160-gr. Speer SPFB	AA-2460	32.0	2037	
160-gr. Speer SPFB	AA-2520	32.6	2104	accurate
160-gr. Speer SPFB	H-322	32.0	2174	
160-gr. Speer SPFB	H-4198	28.6	2088	
168-gr. Sierra HPBT	AA-2230	31.0	2006	
168-gr. Sierra HPBT	H-335	23.0	2045	accurate
168-gr. Sierra HPBT	IMR-4895	33.2	2086	
168-gr. Sierra HPBT	H-322	31.2	2063	
168-gr. Sierra HPBT	IMR-4198	28.2	2057	
175-gr. Sierra SPBT	IMR-4895	32.0	2011	
175-gr. Sierra SPBT	H-322	30.1	1916	
175-gr. Sierra SPBT	IMR-4198	27.2	1894	accurate
175-gr. Sierra SPBT	H-335	32.1	1923	

Note: All data and information in this book is the result of safe and careful testing by the author and other contributors submitting the material contained herein. Since neither the author, DBI Books, Inc., nor any of the contributors has any control over the components, equipment and techniques used with this published information, no liability or responsibility for any injury or damage that occurs is either implied or assumed.

METALLIC SILHOUETTE SHOOTING

its reputation. What is Brutus really like to shoot? Actually, nothing like you might think. The 7R recoils like a pellet gun; the 6.5 Remington magnum feels much like a warm .38 Special revolver; and the .350 Remington magnum like a .357 magnum.

"The .458 Winchester magnum with standard factory loadings recoils much like a 12-gauge shotgun or a black powder rifle. It pushes at you, but doesn't kick sharply. The Winchester Safari loads clean out your sinuses, but are not really punishing. At a retail price of over $55 per box of twenty, you don't do much target practicing with them anyway."

Bartram took Brutus to a silhouette match once and entered it as an unofficial "score-only gun," promising to disqualify himself if any target damage became apparent. Using 350-grain cast bullets at velocities of 2240 feet per second, he shot thirty-seven out of a possible forty animals.

"Missed two turkeys at 150 meters and one ram at two hundred meters," Bartram said. "I felt pretty good about the capability of the .458 Winchester magnum. However, the target setters complained about having to walk a hundred yards or so to retrieve the chickens. They threatened to gang up on me, if I ever shot Brutus at another silhouette match."

South Dakota shooter Jim Larson fires a match, using an unlimited 6.5mm International rear-grip model, while hits are spotted for him by another shooter, Dave Logosz.

Many people have put a combined total of about 1500 rounds through Brutus now in .458 Winchester magnum and the following scenario always happens:

1. I sincerely try to explain what the recoil feels like, (there is no torque or twisting of the gun) and just what to expect when the trigger is pulled.

.30 International

CARTRIDGE: .30 International
GUN: XP-100
BARREL AND TWIST: Douglas premium air gauge stainless 15-inch
TWIST: 1:9
PRIMER: CCI-200
CASE: IHMSA Federal
BULLET: see below

These tests are based on ten-shot groups fired at fifty meters from sandbag rest position.

BULLET	POWDER	WEIGHT IN GRAINS	AVERAGE MUZZLE VELOCITY FPS	REMARKS
150-gr. Sierra SPBT	RE-7	30.5	2246	
150-gr. Sierra SPBT	H-322	34.1	2164	accurate
150-gr. Sierra SPBT	IMR-4895	36.0	2304	
165-gr. Hornady SPBT	H-322	34.0	2164	
165-gr. Hornady SPBT	AA-2230	34.0	2174	accurate
165-gr. Hornady SPBT	AA-2520	34.2	2109	
180-gr. Speer SPBT	H-322	33.0	2104	
180-gr. Speer SPBT	AA-2230	34.0	2071	
180-gr. Speer SPBT	AA-2520	34.0	2106	accurate
190-gr. Speer Match BT	H-322	32.1	2015	
190-gr. Speer Match BT	AA-2520	32.4	2023	accurate
190-gr. Speer Match BT	AA-2230	34.0	2016	
200-gr. Sierra MKHP	H-322	31.0	1890	
200-gr. Sierra MKHP	AA-2520	30.8	1774	accurate
200-gr. Sierra MKHP	AA-2230	30.1	1706	

Note: All data and information in this book is the result of safe and careful testing by the author and other contributors submitting the material contained herein. Since neither the author, DBI Books, Inc., nor any of the contributors has any control over the components, equipment and techniques used with this published information, no liability or responsibility for any injury or damage that occurs is either implied or assumed.

Handgun hunting cartridges developed by J.D. Jones on .444 Marlin case are (from left): .308, 8mm, .338 (on .303 British case); .358, .375, .411, .416 and .430. Last cartridge is the standard .444 Marlin parent case. The .375 JDJ is a standard with big-game handgunners.

2. No one ever believes me.
3. After the first shot, they look up in surprise and say, "Hey, that wasn't bad."
4. They always ask if they can shoot it some more.

Brutus Nomenclature
Weight — 6½ pounds
Calibers — 7R, 6.5 Remington magnum, 350 Remington magnum and .458 Winchester magnum
Barrel length — 15 inches with muzzle brake. 13 inches without muzzle brake.
Value — $3500
Stock — Western Gunstock
Sights — Rear, Bo-Mar. Front, Lyman 17A.

Handgun metallic silhouette and handgun hunting have a lot in common. One complements the other. There have been self-made handgun hunters since the handgun was

7mm/.308 (7mm x 08)

CARTRIDGE: 7mm/.308 (7mmx08)
GUN: XP-100
BARREL AND LENGTH: Douglas Premium 15-inch
TWIST: N/A
PRIMER: 210 M Federal
CASE: WW
BULLET: See below

These tests are based on ten-shot groups fired at fifty meters from sandbag rest position.

BULLET	POWDER	WEIGHT IN GRAINS	AVERAGE MUZZLE VELOCITY FPS	REMARKS
139-gr. Hornady SPFB	AA-2520	36.0	2360	
139-gr. Hornady SPFB	H-322	35.0	2329	
145-gr. Speer SPFB	AA-2520	35.1	2274	
145-gr. Speer SPFB	H-322	34.1	2289	accurate
154-gr. Hornady SPFB	AA-2520	34.5	2263	
154-gr. Hornady SPFB	H-322	34.1	2293	
160-gr. Speer SPBT	AA-2520	33.2	2097	
160-gr. Speer SPBT	H-322	32.4	2103	
168-gr. Sierra HPBT	AA-2520	33.0	2140	
168-gr. Sierra HPBT	H-322	32.0	2159	accurate
175-gr. Sierra SPBT	AA-2520	32.2	1974	accurate
175-gr. Sierra SPBT	H-322	31.4	1997	

Note: All data and information in this book is the result of safe and careful testing by the author and other contributors submitting the material contained herein. Since neither the author, DBI Books, Inc., nor any of the contributors has any control over the components, equipment and techniques used with this published information, no liability or responsibility for any injury or damage that occurs is either implied or assumed.

invented, but on the other hand, literally thousands of shooters who have been turned on by the silhouette sport have joined the ranks of handgun hunters.

Undoubtedly, the foremost authority in the world on the technical aspects of handgun hunting is J.D. Jones, founder of Handgun Hunters International, an organization of several thousand handgun hunters. Jones is an experienced silhouette shooter and is a former IHMSA state director for Ohio.

Other noted handgun hunters such as Larry Kelly, Lee Jurras and Hal Swiggett, to name just three, are members of HHI as well as being recipients of the Outstanding American Handgunner Award, the "Oscar" of the handgun world. J.D. Jones won the award in 1983.

Other contributors to the lore and the legend of handgun hunting — and winners of the OAHA award — are Colonel Charles Askins and Bill Jordan, along with departed legends Elmer Keith, Skeeter Skelton and Steve Herrett. I have been privileged to know all of them.

J.D. Jones has developed cartridges on the .225 Winchester case, which is on left. Others shown are the .226, 6mm, .257, 6.5mm, .270 and 7mm JDJ. The last cartridge is the 7mm JDJ #2. It uses the .307 Winchester case with a forty-degree shoulder angle.

7mm BR Remington

CARTRIDGE: 7mm BR Remington
GUN: XP-100
BARREL AND LENGTH: Factory 14 inch
TWIST: N/A
PRIMER: CCI BR-2
CASE: Remington 7 BR
BULLET: see below

These tests are based on ten-shot groups fired at fifty meters from sandbag rest position.

BULLET	POWDER	WEIGHT IN GRAINS	AVERAGE MUZZLE VELOCITY FPS	REMARKS
130-gr. Sierra SPFB	AA-2520	30.1	2149	
130-gr. Sierra SPFB	AA-2230	30.1	2138	accurate
130-gr. Sierra SPFB	H-322	28.0	2201	
140-gr. Sierra SPBT	AA-2520	28.5	2115	
140-gr. Sierra SPBT	AA-2230	29.0	2104	
140-gr. Sierra SPBT	H-322	26.5	2080	
154-gr. Hornady SPFB	AA-2520	28.0	1984	
154-gr. Hornady SPFB	AA-2230	28.0	1967	
154-gr. Hornady SPFB	H-322	26.0	1974	accurate
160-gr. Speer SPBT	AA-2520	27.1	1976	
160-gr. Speer SPBT	AA-2230	27.1	1897	
160-gr. Sierra HPBT	H-322	25.0	1878	
168-gr. Sierra HPBT	AA-2520	25.4	1903	most accurate
168-gr. Sierra HPBT	AA-2230	26.5	1863	
168-gr. Sierra HPBT	H-322	24.1	1845	

Note: All data and information in this book is the result of safe and careful testing by the author and other contributors submitting the material contained herein. Since neither the author, DBI Books, Inc., nor any of the contributors has any control over the components, equipment and techniques used with this published information, no liability or responsibility for any injury or damage that occurs is either implied or assumed.

J.D. Jones, as an integral part of his handgun hunting organization, has created and developed a highly successful series of cartridges designed specifically for handgun hunting. By extension, virtually all of them are suited to the unlimited category of the silhouette game and are constantly used therein.

(For membership information on Handgun Hunters International, write to HHI, P.O. Box 357 Mag, Bloomingdale, OH 43910.)

Frank Barnes is another cartridge innovator who started early, developing his .308x1½ Barnes in 1961. The cartridge is still in use today in the IHMSA unlimited category and shows up regularly as a winner.

Barnes undoubtedly was the first to create the .458x1½-inch and the .458x2-inch cartridges in 1962, both of which have been used in the silhouette game in rebarreled XP-100s.

Barnes also created the .45 Silhouette in 1984, another 1½-inch cartridge made by cutting down the .45-70 case.

Load data for the more popular unlimited silhouette cartridges is presented here, starting with the three most used of the IHMSA International series developed by the author in 1975-75. For simple identification, the cartridges are designed as 6.5mm, 7mm and .30 Internationals.

Unlimited load data for the 6.5mm/.223, 7mm/.223, the 7mm/.222 magnum and additional data on the 7mm International can be found in Chapter 10.

Special JDJ cartridges are (from left): 6.5mm/.308; .411 Whammy, .350 Rem. mag necked to .41 caliber; 12.9x50.8 JDJ, a 2.0-inch .460 Weatherby case with a 550-grain cast bullet. The last cartridge is the same, but is loaded with a 600-grain Barnes bullet.

.308 Winchester Full Length

CARTRIDGE: .308 Winchester full length
GUN: XP-100
BARREL AND LENGTH: Shilen 15-inch
TWIST: N/A
PRIMER: Federal 210 M
CASE: Winchester
BULLET: See below

These tests are based on ten-shot groups fired at fifty meters from sandbag rest position.

BULLET	POWDER	WEIGHT IN GRAINS	AVERAGE MUZZLE VELOCITY FPS	REMARKS
150-gr. Sierra SPBT	AA-2520	39.8	2317	
150-gr. Sierra SPBT	AA-2230	38.6	2287	
150-gr. Sierra SPBT	H-322	39.5	2307	
165-gr. Hornady SPBT	AA-2520	38.0	2170	
165-gr. Hornady SPBT	AA-2230	39.0	2116	
165-gr. Hornady SPBT	H-322	36.0	2184	
180-gr. Speer SPBT	AA-2520	38.0	2187	
180-gr. Speer SPBT	AA-2230	39.0	2168	
180-gr. Speer SPBT	H-322	37.0	2177	
190-gr. Speer Match AT	AA-2520	36.0	2024	
190-gr. Speer Match AT	AA-2230	37.0	2016	
190-gr. Speer Match AT	H-322	34.0	1997	
200-gr. Sierra MICHP	AA-2520	35.0	1952	
200-gr. Sierra MICHP	AA-2230	35.0	1968	
200-gr. Sierra MICHP	H-322	33.0	1944	

Note: All data and information in this book is the result of safe and careful testing by the author and other contributors submitting the material contained herein. Since neither the author, DBI Books, Inc., nor any of the contributors has any control over the components, equipment and techniques used with this published information, no responsibility for any injury or damage that occurs is either implied or assumed.

CAST BULLETS FOR SILHOUETTE SHOOTING

CHAPTER 14

Cast bullet shooting in the silhouette game can effect a considerable monetary saving. Cast bullets are about one-third the cost of factory-produced jacketed bullets. More and more of them are being used in silhouette guns.

SILHOUETTE SHOOTING is a reloader's game and well over four million rounds are fired downrange every year. That adds up to a lot of consumable components being used, such as powder, primers and bullets.

The biggest expense, of course, is jacketed bullets. During the ten years the silhouette game has been in existence, bullet prices have gone up and up; in many instances, as high as five hundred percent.

Devotees of cast bullets, found in every shooting sport, are increasing rapidly in numbers in the silhouette sport, as the price of manufactured bullets continues to move upward.

Price is one reason why silhouetters have turned to cast bullets; shooter satisfaction is another. A lot of the enjoyment in shooting silhouettes comes from knocking the targets down with your own brew of brass, powder, primers and bullets. It's even more fun when you make your own bullets.

Some of the most gratifying moments I've had in the silhouette game were in shooting good scores with bullets that I made on my own.

Casting bullets also gives tremendous versatility to both the weight of the bullet and its diameter. Bullets can be sized to fit a particular barrel and cylinder combination for revolvers, and barrel and chamber dimensions in single-

Other Than Personal Satisfaction, This Type Of Bullet Expands Availability

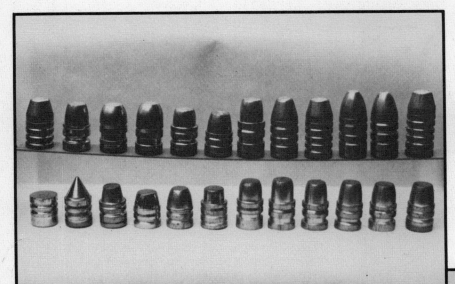

With twenty-four different moulds available for the .44 caliber, a lot of experimenting is possible in the weight range of 180 to 350 grains.

For the .45 Colt are: the 300-grain Lyman #457191; NEI #310451 loaded in .45 Long Colt case trimmed to .44 Special length; Lyman #454424 250-grain and Saeco 220-grain bullet.

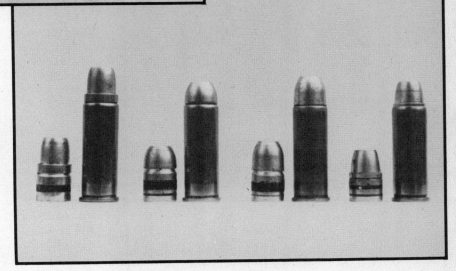

shots. This is a luxury not allowed with jacketed bullets. Even more important is the use of varying weights of bullets.

Both my ten-inch Dan Wesson and my 10½-inch Abilene will shoot over chickens with the sight bottomed out and using 240-250-grain bullets. This leaves me with the choice of either going to a match knowing I will have to hold six inches under the chickens, or finding a bullet that will shoot chickens with a six o'clock hold at fifty meters. Having twenty-four different bullet moulds for .44 caliber in my loading room, it is no great problem to find a 200-grain bullet that shoots to the proper point at fifty meters.

More importantly, at the other end, I have a 10½-inch Ruger Super Blackhawk that runs out of rear sight before I even get to the rams. It is no great problem to hold under chickens at fifty meters, but trying to hold over rams at two hundred meters gets pretty iffy. The answer has been the use of a 310-grain cast bullet in this particular .44 for rams.

In .44 caliber alone, I have acquired enough moulds that I could experiment the rest of my life and still only scratch the surface. Of my .44s, I have six moulds that throw bullets in the 300-grain range; three in the 215-grain range; nine in the 250-grain; three in the 300-grain; and three in the 350-grain range. There is no situation for which I could not find the proper bullet.

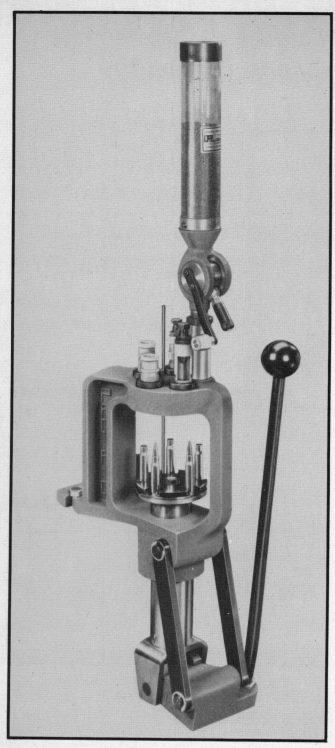

After the cast bullets have been sized properly, they can be loaded with any press, like this Hornady model.

This five-shot group on a javelina target was made with a ten-inch Dan Wesson .44 mag. Cast bullets were from a NEI #429 mould, with 21.5 grains of Winchester 296.

There are numerous designs available in .44 caliber, with one of the old standbys and most popular bullets being the semi-wadcutter design that can be traced back to the late Elmer Keith. I have these type of designs from Lyman, NEI, RCBS, H&G and Saeco. Under the management of Richard Beebe of Redding, who took over Saeco and infused his own ideas of quality control, this design no doubt will be the best of the lot. My Saeco moulds are of the original, less-than-top-quality types and I have not been able to find any notable difference in the shooting qualities of the five brands listed above.

In addition to their old designs, Saeco, under the expertise of Beebe, has two excellent .44 moulds designed especially for the silhouette shooter, casting 250- and 265-grain silhouette bullets. Both of these have flat points that transmit a lot of impact energy to the targets. It is no secret that silhouette shooters are partial to heavy bullets in .44 caliber, be it the .44 Special or the .44 magnum. These are excellent for dropping stubborn rams and for hunting live game.

Especially in .357 caliber have I found the usefulness of casting bullets. The answer for the question of what bullet to use in the .357 for silhouettes is the 200-grain cast bullet. I have had excellent results with two of these heavyweight bullets: the fairly new Lyman 210-grain gas check and the RCBS 35-200FN. The latter originally was designed for the .35 Remington rifle, but has turned out to be a good cast bullet for long range shooting in the .357 magnum.

For the .357 Super Mag, the best two are the #356 Saeco, which turns out 200-grain flat-point gas check bullets, and the #292 Saeco that casts 200-grain truncated-cone bullets. These bullets are also excellent in the Thompson/Center Contender.

For the .45 Colt, I have had good results with three bullets in the Ruger Blackhawk. These three are the Lyman 457191, a 300-grain bullet originally designed for the .45-70; the Lyman 454424 that turns out a 250-grain SWC;

Cast bullets have become popular in revolver shooting circles. The group of six-guns includes Dan Wessons in .357 magnum, .357 Super Mag and .375 Super Mag; Rugers in .357 magnum, .44 magnum and .44 Super Mag; plus a S&W .357 magnum. All digest the cast bullets with ease and with accuracy.

and the Saeco #15, a 300-grain FP. Also, the 310451, a 290-grain SWC from NEI, is good. Using this bullet, I have to trim my cases slightly, as the shoulder of the bullet catches the step in the Ruger cylinder. As with the .357 and .44 magnums, the need of the .45 Long Colt is a heavy bullet at moderate velocities.

My choice for the .375 Super Mag is the new Saeco #375 mould that casts a 240-grain truncated-cone bullet. As yet, there isn't a wide variety of bullet moulds available in .375 caliber, but as silhouette downing continues to gain popularity, I'm sure other useful moulds will be offered.

Are cast bullets as accurate as jacketed bullets? Some six-guns will shoot cast bullets even better than jacketed bullets. If care is used in producing cast bullets, making sure bases are completely filled out with no pin holes, there is no reason why they shouldn't be just as accurate as jacketed bullets. Bases must be perfect in gas checked bullets also. A gas check over a badly formed base will not shoot well at all. Some cast bullet aficionados go to the extra step of weighing their bullets and separating them into weight ranges. If a bullet weighs considerably less than others, it is because it has air bubbles inside. Weighing each bullet will catch these and avoid fliers.

The key to using cast bullets is care plus experimenting to find the right combination. I will continue to shoot both cast bullets and jacketed bullets; when time is no problem,

The array of silhouette targets downrange is being reset and painted by target setters. In this match, an assortment of cast bullets fired in revolvers achieved most of the hits being covered for the upcoming rally.

Check any group of shooters on the line and you'll find any number of them shooting bullets they've cast.

As more shooters cast their own, more efficient casting equipment like this RCBS Pro-Melt furnace has appeared.

I go with the cast; when time is short, I'll take the easier way out and opt for the jacketed variety.

One extra bonus is given with cast bullets. They will shoot to the same velocity as jacketed with less pressure and less powder, plus be much easier on the barrel. There are many excellent jacketed bullet designs available on the market, but there are no heavyweight bullets available for either the .44 magnum or .45 Colt. Only cast bullets can fill this gap.

There has been quite a bit of dialogue lately concerning what diameter to size cast bullets. For years, six-gunners have been driving pure lead slugs through their revolver barrels, miking the resulting slug to see what would be the proper size bullet diameter to use. However, as most knowledgeable cast bullet shooters have known for years, this is not enough. There is another factor quoted from *Six-gun Cartridges And Loads* by Elmer Keith, published in 1936. "However, it must be loaded with bullets sized just right for the individual gun, and not more than .001 inch or .002 inch over groove diameter, and the cylinder throats must be large enough to allow the bullets to pass through easily by hand."

So we have two important factors at hand: groove diameter and throat diameter of the cylinder. These also can be factors in choosing jacketed bullets, especially if the groove diameter happens to be on the large size. Since I had two diameters of sizing dies for .38 Special-.357 magnum-.357 Super Mag and four sizes for the .44 Special-.44 magnum, I decided to do some experimenting to see just what sizes worked best. This was not an experiment to find the most accurate loads, but rather to see what difference just the size of the bullet made with all other factors being kept equal, at least as much as humanly possible.

I decided to try three different categories of six-guns, namely, .357 magnum, .357 Super Mag and .44 magnum. All bullets were sized in my Star Lubrisizer using Mi-

Bullets for .375 Super Mag are (from left): 220-grain Hornady jacketed type; NEI 210375 GC; Lyman #375449 GC; and Lyman #358627. Last is just being made for the .375.

This recently introduced Redding #25 turret press has been set up for loading cast bullets in cases for the .375 Super Mag. Silhouette has brought new developments.

crolube. If you are not acqainted with the Star, you are missing a quality piece of equipment for the bullet caster. It is possible to size bullets at least three times as fast in the Star as with conventional sizers, as the bullet is handled only once, with the finished lubed and sized bullet dropping out the bottom into a waiting container.

For the .357 magnum, I selected a long-time favorite bullet, Lyman's #358429, a plain-based bullet that weighs 168 grains with my hard alloy. This bullet was designed by Elmer Keith before the birth of the .357 magnum, consequently the nose is too long to allow crimping in the groove when using .357 cases and still allow overall length to stay within the bounds of most .357 cylinder lengths. Therefore, I load this bullet in .38 Special cases. The load chosen was another oldie: 13.5 grains of 2400, cases were Remington, with CCI 550 magnum primers being used. Three revolvers were chosed for this part of the test: a Dan Wesson .357 ten-inch HB, a Smith & Wesson .357 Model 27 8⅜-inch and a Colt Python .357 six-inch. Since I would be using bullets sized to .356 and .358 inch, I first checked

.357 MAG	SIZE	AVG. MV	AVG. VS*	AVG. HS*	AVG. GRP	BEST GRP
S&W .357 8⅜"	.356	1422	1½"	1⅝"	2"	1½"
	.358	1436	1¼"	1⅛"	1⅝"	1½"
Colt Python 6"	.356	1285	2⅜"	2½"	2¾"	2½"
	.358	1298	¾"	1¼"	1¼"	1⅜"
DW .357 10"	.356	1386	2½"	1¾"	2⅝"	2"
	.358	1395	⅞"	1"	1⅛"	⅝"

VS-Vertical Spread — HS-Horizontal Spread

As can be seen, little difference is noted in using both sizes in the S&W, while the difference in the use of .358 bullets over .356 bullets is widespread in both the Colt and DW. Groups in the Colt and DW averaged less than one half, .358" compared to .356".

Turning to the .357 Super Mag, I chose Lyman's #358647, a SWC, gas-checked bullet of 210 grs., designed specifically for silhouetting. Revolvers used were Ruger's 10½" Maximum, and DW's 8" Super Mag. Federal IHMSA cases were used with CCI Small Rifle primers, and a charge of 19.0 grs. of WW296. The Ruger had a groove diameter of .356 and would not accept .358 bullets in the cylinder throat; the DW had a groove diameter of .357 and would accept .358 bullets when pushed through the cylinder throats by hand.

.357 SUPER MAG	SIZE	AVG. MV	AVG. VS	AVG. HS	AVG. GRP	BEST GRP
Ruger 10½" Maximum	.356	1443	1½"	1⅞"	1⅞"	1⅜"
	.358	1478	⅞"	1⅛"	1⅛"	⅞"
DW 8" Super Mag	.356	1378	1½"	1⅝"	2⅛"	1⅞"
	.358	1396	⅞"	1"	1⅛"	¾"

Note that MV is not only higher with the .358 size, also group sizes are almost one-half of those fired with .356 bullets.

Switching to the .44 magnum, I chose Lyman's #43244, a gas-checked SWC of 245 grs. I had also planned to use Lyman's #429215, but it cast too small for all the sizes I wanted to try, namely .428, .430 and .432". Three silhouette six-guns were chosen for testing, Ruger's 10½ Stainless, DW's 10" .44, and S&W's 10⅝" Silhouette Model. Cases were Winchester-Western, 20.0 grs. 2400 and CCI 350 magnum primers.

to see which size would pass through the chamber throats. The S&W would not accept the .358 sized bullet, while both the Colt and DW allowed the bullets to be pushed through the cylinder easily by hand. In measuring groove diameters, the DW and the S&W both measured .357 inch while the Colt measured a very tight .354; call it .3535 inch.

All loads were fired from sandbags at twenty-five yards, temperature, eighty-five degrees, with winds of twenty-five to thirty miles per hour, strong enough that I had difficulty staying steady. The accompanying chart tells the story.

Some of my favorite cast bullet loads for revolvers are shown in the accompanying table.

One interesting facet of cast bullet shooting is the willingness of silhouetters to share their techniques, favorite bullet moulds, load data and so on.

.44 MAG	SIZE	AVG. MV	AVG. VS	AVG. HS	AVG. GRP	BEST GRP
Ruger 10½" Stainless	.428	1328	1⅜"	1⅛"	1½"	1⅜"
	.430	1355	1"	1"	1⅜"	1⅛"
	.432	1349	1"	⅞"	1¼"	1⅛"
S&W 10⅝" .44	.428	1290	2"	1¼"	2"	2"
	.430	1327	1¼"	1⅜"	1⅞"	1¾"
	.432	1326	1⅝"	1¼"	1⅝"	1½"
DW 10" .44	.428	1291	2"	1"	2"	1½"
	.430	1313	¾"	⅞"	1⅛"	¾"
	.432	1319	1⅛"	1⅜"	1⅜"	1¼"

Both the DW and the Ruger have groove diameters of .429", while the Smith goes .430". In pushing bullets through the cylinder throats by hand, it was found that the DW would accept .428 at the largest, the Ruger .430" and the Smith .432. Forty-fours are more forgiving than the .357s when it comes to bullet size, but by using the proper bullet size for each particular revolver the best results can be obtained. Sizing dies are relatively cheap; experiment and find the right size for your particular revolver.

FAVORITE CAST BULLET LOADS

BULLET	CHARGE	POWDER	CARTRIDGE	BBL LENGTH	MUZZLE VEL.
NEI 250	20.0	2400	.44 Mag	10½"	1390
NEI 295	21.5	Win-296	.44 Mag	10½"	1250
SAECO 240 SIL	20.0	2400	.44 Mag	10½"	1459
SAECO 265 SIL	22.5	H4227	.44 Mag	10½"	1423
LYMAN 215 GC	26.0	H110	.44 Mag	10½"	1605*
THREE K 295FP	20.0	Win-296	.44 Mag	10½"	1320**
SSK 310 JDJ	23.5	Win-680	.44 Mag	10½"	1466**
LYMAN 210	12.5	H110	.357 Mag	10"	1224
RCBS 35-200 FN	13.0	Win-296	.38 Special	10"	1164***
SSK210 JDJ	12.5	H110	.357 Super Mag	10"	1194
LYMAN 210	19.0	Win-296	.357 Super Mag	10½"	1526
RCBS 35-200 FN	19.0	Win-296	.357 Super Mag	10½"	1510
LYMAN 210	20.5	Win-296	.357 Super Mag	8"	1450***
RCBS 35-200 FN	20.5	Win-296	.357 Super Mag	8"	1440***
NEI 210375	17.5	2400	.375 Super Mag	8"	1385
NEI 210375	19.0	H4227	.375 Super Mag	8"	1316
NEI 210375	20.0	Win-296	.375 Super Mag	8"	1440
LYMAN 4544424	20.0	2400	.45 Colt	7½"	1250
NEI 310451	21.0	H4227	.45 Colt	7½"	1197*****
LYMAN 457191	18.5	2400	.45 Colt	7½"	1150
LYMAN 429244	17.0	2400	.44 Special	7½"	1223

*Very flat shooting load
**Ramslammers, excellent hunting loads
***Loaded in .38 cases to allow proper crimp
****Bullets are seated out farther for use in the longer cylinder of the DW
*****Cases must be trimmed to allow seating in the Ruger cylinder

The following data are the favorite loads sent to me by other cast bullet silhouette shooters. Some loads are exceedingly mild; others may be max or even over. **In short, be careful.** Watch for the usual pressure signs. Most mould types are listed, but not primers, brass or alloys. The starting loads should be safe with any normal combination as listed. Approach maximum loads with caution.

As mentioned in the beginning of this chapter, there is a great deal of satisfaction to be found in shooting good scores with your own combination of brass, powder, primers and bullets. Casting your own bullets is an added bonus, not to mention the savings in cost. Cast bullets are about one-third the cost of jacketed bullets.

To be sure, the investment in bullet casting equipment isn't cheap, but if you are shooting silhouettes on a regular basis, it will not take long to amortize the cost.

PRODUCTION GUNS

CAL.	MOULD	POWDER CHARGE
7 T/CU	145 RCBS or 071 Saeco	23-24 gr. 4895
		24-28 gr. H335
		24 gr. H322
7-R	168 RCBS	27.5 gr. 4895
	071 Saeco	27.5 gr. 748
	145 RCBS	28.5 gr. 4895
.30-30	Lyman 311041	10 gr. Unique
	165 RCBS	23 gr. 4198
	311291 Lyman or 165 RCBS	18-23 gr. 4759
	311 Saeco or 315 Saeco	22-24.5 gr. MP 5744
		25-30 gr. H335
.357 mag	180 RCBS	16.2 gr. H110
	200 RCBS	17.7 gr. 680
		12.5 gr. 296
	190 P + C	6 gr. Herco
.357 SM	200 RCBS or 180 RCBS or	17-22 gr. H4227
	356 Saeco or 180 GC NEI	17-20 gr. AA-5744
		17-19 gr. 4759
.30-H	165 RCBS	16 gr. 4227
	165 RCBS or 311291	23.5 gr. H335
	Lyman or 311 Saeco	23.5-28 gr. H335
	304 Saeco	24.5 gr. 748
.44 mag	429421 Lyman	9.5-10.5 gr. 473AA
REVOLVER		
.357 SM	200 RCBS	20 gr. 4198
		18 gr. 4759
		15 gr. 4759
	352 Saeco	
	200 RCBS or 180 RCBS or	
	356 Saeco or 180 GC NEI	18-20.5 gr. H4227
.44 mag	Any 220-250 gr. CB Keith style	22-24 gr. 296
	429421 Lyman	21 gr. 2400
		21-22 gr. 4227
		9.5-10-5 gr. 473AA
	432 Saeco	20 gr. 2400 (hot)
	310 GC NEI	21 gr. 296 (hot)

UNLIMITED GUNS

CAL.	MOULD	POWDER CHARGE
7-INT	071 Saeco	22-26 gr. 4759
		28 gr. 4895
7-BR	168 RCBS	20 gr. H322
		25.4 gr. 3031
7-R	287405 Lyman	16.5 gr. H4227
		26.5 gr. H4896

METALLIC SILHOUETTE SHOOTING

THE EXPANDED APPROACH

CHAPTER 15

Mike Dayton shoots for the three-gun aggregate title in the Indiana state championships, while his wife spots his hits and misses in .22 event with a spotting scope.

Two New Events —

.22 Silhouette And Field

Pistol Competition —

Are Being Sanctioned Now

Adele Dayton fired the first ladies' 40x40 score in the .22 unlimited category, using a custom Super 14 Contender.

THE GREAT majority of silhouetters now taking up the .22-caliber version of the game began their steel-shooting careers in Big Bore. It may appear this is a regressive path for a marksman to take, but dial the clock back to 1975, '76, '77 and '78 for a close look at the gathering hordes of silhouetters. Where did they come from?

Most were hard-boiled shooters fed up with paper punching. The traditional disciplines lacked an element of purpose: Take a bullet and punch it through a piece of paper. Okay, you've done that. What happened to all the magnum energy? What is it good for anyway?

Silhouette put *accomplishment* back into handgunning. Hitting the target was no longer good enough; you had to knock it down. Blowing that first half-inch-thick chicken off the stand at fifty meters lifted you out of the Dark Ages of Handgunning. You had given your bullet a job for which traditional target guns were useless.

Early silhouetters, as diverse a group of characters as populated a sport, were brought together by a desire to

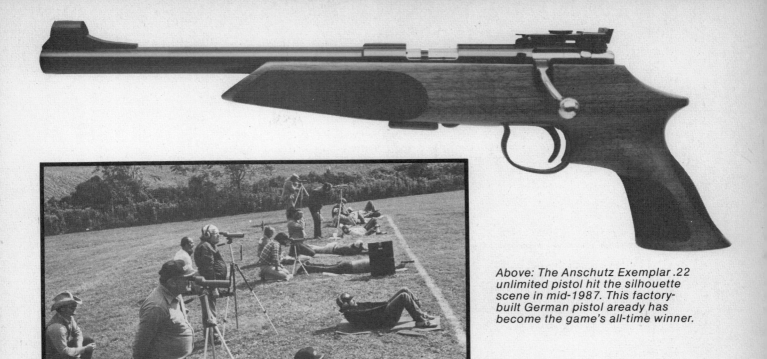

Above: The Anschutz Exemplar .22 unlimited pistol hit the silhouette scene in mid-1987. This factory-built German pistol aready has become the game's all-time winner.

This firing line scene at a .22 match conducted in New York State is typical. Note the various positions used.

explore an underdeveloped handgun wilderness. Most shared one other trait: they had learned how to shoot with the .22. Now they have come full circle

Various IHMSA clubs have held .22 silhouette matches since the late Seventies. As IHMSA did not sanction the .22 matches at that time, local clubs were free to make the targets whatever size they felt like. Competitors, however, wanted a standard course of fire, so they could travel from range to range without being put at a disadvantage by the local boys. Also, competitors wanted their accomplishments — namely records — to enjoy national status. Range tests from around the country resulted in the IHMSA adopting reduced-size silhouettes scaled to the power and accuracy of the .22 Long Rifle cartridge. Targets are cut from 3/16-inch or ¼-inch mild steel plate. Templates are available from IHMSA headquarters. The task of creating target size and rules was assigned to vice president Bert Stringfellow. The IHMSA .22 division was instituted in 1979.

One of the criteria for .22 silhouette was that clubs with limited range facilities — one hundred meters or one hundred yards — be able to accommodate the course: chickens at twenty-five meters (or yards); pigs at fifty meters (or yards); turkeys at seventy-five meters (or yards); rams at one hundred meters (or yards). If rams are at one hundred meters, then the other targets must be in meters, too. Consistency is a rule.

As the .22 game has caught on, new shooters, including youngsters, are taking advantage of the inexpensive rimfire, but make no mistake: .22 silhouette is tough. Beginners will need a sharp spotter to "get on" the diminutive animals. A pair of fried eggs would cover the ram, which, from one hundred meters, permits scant room for error in alignment of sights.

Fortunately, most children enjoy wonderful vision, their eyes being able to focus on the front sight, the rear sight and often the target simultaneously! Adults and other mere mortals would be well advised to limit their sight-seeing to *sights*. Unless it happens at the sights, it won't happen downrange.

Competition is conducted in four freestyle categories determined by the type of pistol action. Freestyle, incidentally, encompasses any safe position wherein the gun doesn't touch the ground and no part of the shooter's anatomy invades a forty-five-degree cone of space emanating from the bore/muzzle.

The categories are: production for semi-autos and single-shots; revolver, unlimited and standing. Action types are combined in the standing category, incidentally. A weight limit of four pounds applies to production guns — semi-

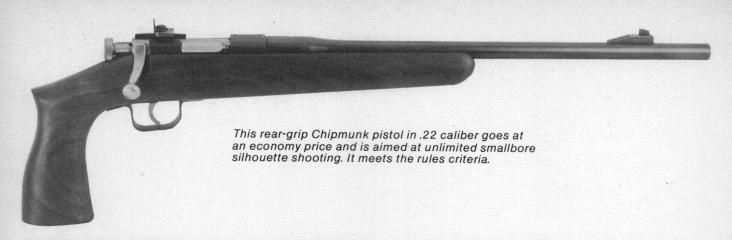

This rear-grip Chipmunk pistol in .22 caliber goes at an economy price and is aimed at unlimited smallbore silhouette shooting. It meets the rules criteria.

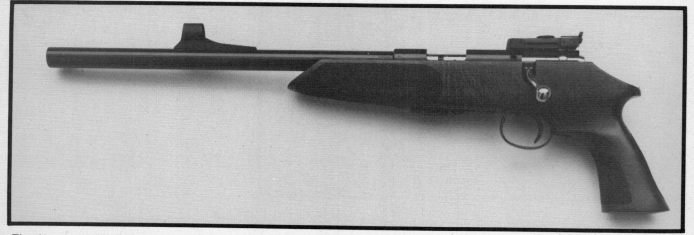

The Anschutz XIV Exemplar was added to the line in 1988. The gun boasts a 14-inch barrel for unlimited contests.

autos, revolvers and single-shots. Whereas guns in production big-bore events may have barrels of 10¾ inches in length, the maximum for .22 production competition is ten inches.

The rule for .22 unlimited category handguns is exactly the same as for big bore, with all bolt-action models classified as unlimited guns.

The low recoil and low report of the rimfire round encourage the competitor to concentrate on the fundamentals of marksmanship — a comfortable, bone-supportive position; deep breathing to sharpen the eyes and relax the grip and trigger finger — and chiseling the sights into alignment. The gentle accumulation of pressure upon the trigger is governed directly by the "bite" of the sights on the silhouette. All your preparation, all you have learned come together between your eye and the trigger.

Some of the more popular semi-autos are:

Ruger MK II Target: Adjustable sights are a must. The 5½-inch bull barrel is a good choice, but the longer sight radius and consequently, finer adjustments, give the bull ten-inch the edge. Excellent dollar value.

Smith & Wesson Model 41: It has the accuracy to do the job, but is not consistent. Cost is excessive for the quality.

High Standard: The old target models are tops. As the company has folded, service may be a problem in the future.

AMT Lightning: A rather crude copy of the Ruger auto.

Browning: The IHMSA Silhouette Model features a wood forend, silhouette sights on a ten-inch bull barrel with scope mount/rib and an adjustable trigger. Recently introduced, it already has established a reputation for top accuracy and shootability. This gun should be a big winner in .22 silhouette from now on. Cost is moderate.

Let's take a look at favored .22 revolvers:

Dan Wesson .22 VH8: Dwight David Eisenhower once said, "Russian promises are like apple pie; they're made to be broken." Dan Wesson Arms thinks the same of silhouette records. This gun has superb accuracy, a light trigger, good muzzle heft, silhouette sights and too many wins to count.

Smith & Wesson K-22: The older, the better. When they're good, they're great, but they lack the muzzle density of the DWA.

Ruger Single Six: It has generally fine accuracy. Avoid the convertible model, unless you are a trapper, as the .22 Winchester rimfire magnum barrel is oversize for the .22LR and you can't use mags in .22 silhouette.

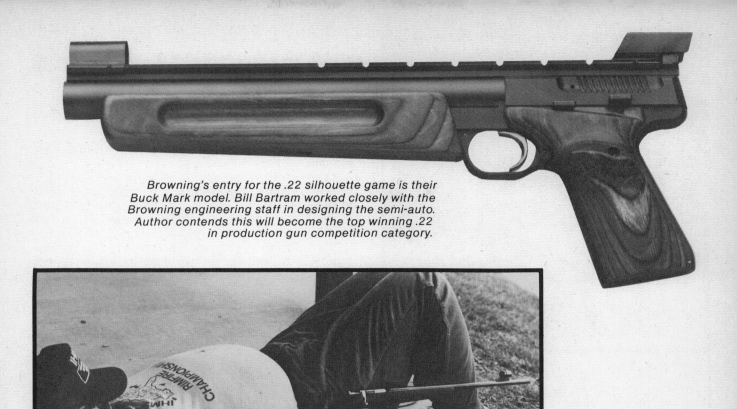

Browning's entry for the .22 silhouette game is their Buck Mark model. Bill Bartram worked closely with the Browning engineering staff in designing the semi-auto. Author contends this will become the top winning .22 in production gun competition category.

Dan Rainey, a regional director for IHMSA, tries out the Chipmunk .22 during a segment of a local contest.

There also are some real favorites that have sorted themselves out among the single-shots:

Thompson/Center Contender: Drill-hole accuracy. New T/C Ultimate sights will drive up the gun's already impressive record. A top dollar value, it has scored *beaucoup* victories. The ten-inch bull barrel is blued or has an industrial chrome Armour Alloy finish.

MOA: This lever-action falling-block has fast lock time, a heavy ten-inch bull barrel, an excellent adjustable trigger — and top accuracy.

As in the big bore silhouette events, there are some wide parameters involved in the unlimited gun category for .22 rimfires, but several guns are appearing more often:

Anschutz Exemplar: A sexy understudy to the Anschutz target rifles, this little bolt-action pistol takes a serious approach to IHMSA .22 silhouette. With its box magazine, it can outperform custom-built guns costing a bundle.

Chipmunk .22 Unlimited: An economy bolt-action single-shot, you can patiently tune, glass bed, upgrade the sights, et cetera. It needs all the help you can give it.

T/C Super 14: Here we go again — reach into your suitcase full of barrels, each with its own set of sights, and you're ready to shoot another category! An eminently satisfying pistol to shoot.

Some competitors consider .22 silhouette to be tougher than big bore. This is a purely subjective view, albeit with some basis in fact. Target ammo is subsonic, and the wind can reverse itself in the time it takes the bullet to fly the length of a football field. High velocity ammo seldom helps, for it starts supersonic, then drops transonic — and the turbulence can shake the bullet off its axis.

Sometimes a breeze will bend the competitor's mind more than it does his bullet. If the shooter jerks up to look over his gun in an effort to see the bullet strike the target,

Several ammunition manufacturers have developed .22 silhouette ammunition that is said to help scores. Federal says their round is excellent for knock-downs.

chances are he could tip the bullet just as it exits the muzzle. *Hold the gun steady all the way through the firing of the shot!* You'll hear the *clink* when it hits!

Rimfire ammunition will not shoot accurately if the mainspring has been trimmed or weakened. Light primer indentation results. Don't cut the mainspring of any gun, and check your Smith & Wesson to be sure the strain screw has not worked loose.

Silhouette .22 can teach you, train you and restore your confidence the way no other cartridge can — and without precipitating a meltdown in your piggy bank.

As though the logistics of processing thousands of tournaments annually, along with the tide of memberships and renewals, etc., weren't enough, the IHMSA in 1987 adopted Field Pistol Silhouette. Some of the impetus comes from shooters competing in NRA Hunter's Pistol events. IHMSA field pistol encompasses two categories of competition, both requiring the use of production out-of-the-box handguns.

The basic categories are: Production Open Sight; Production is defined by IHMSA rules with weight not to exceed four pounds. The gun may be drilled and tapped for a scope, but mount holes must have plug screws in place. In the production scoped category, weight limit is 4½ pounds max, with scope. Mounts and rings must be as manufactured, with no modifications.

Field pistol is shot standing. Cartridges must have straight-wall, centerfire pistol cases of standard manufacture with maximum case length of 1.29 inches as specified for that cartridge. Also allowed is the .32-20. The Dan Wesson and Seville .357 Super Mag and Ruger .357 Maximum may be used, but brass must not exceed standard .357 magnum length.

Targets are one-half big-bore size, of three-eighths-inch tempered steel. Like .22 silhouette, targets all are set in

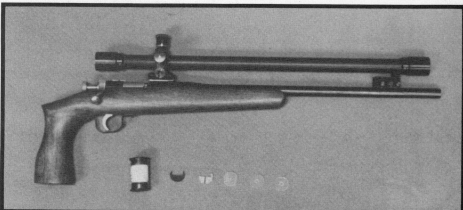

In .22 silhouette, as with the big bore game, optical sights are not allowed, but tube sights are. This rear-grip .22 Chipmunk is outfitted with a King tube sight; a variety of non-magnifying apertures are in evidence beneath the rear-grip gun.

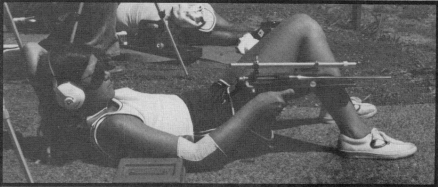

Cathy Dickerson, Fort Worth, Texas, demonstrates her Creedmoor position with an unlimited tube sighted gun.

Target setters pose behind the .22 chicken targets, with larger animal targets in the background. Targets have been painted white to contrast with green grass.

David Todd, a top shooter in .22 competition, shows his standing form for event with High Standard Citation II.

meters or all in yards, with rams at one hundred meters or yards.

While field pistol targets are one-half the height and width of their big-bore counterparts, they offer only one-fourth the surface for your bullet. The ham-fisted .44 magnum and the .357 Super Mag, rip-snortin' shells that they are, are grossly overpowered for this game. Both have the intrinsic accuracy to win, but the recoil will beat on your nerves. It's sort of like jumping out of a second story window to stomp a mouse.

Field pistol calls for finesse. Your .357 magnum, which leaves quite a few targets standing in big bore, is more than enough here. Stick with 180-grain silhouette bullets by Hornady, Sierra, Speer and Nosler for your .357. These bullets yield consistently superior performance to any lighter bullet at one hundred meters. Winchester 296 should be your choice of powder, with H110 and H4227 or IMR 4227 right behind. Start at 12.0 grains of 296 beneath a 180-grain silhouette bullet, working up in half-grain increments until accuracy is tight at twenty-five and fifty meters.

NOTE: Always stop at early signs of pressure. If accuracy

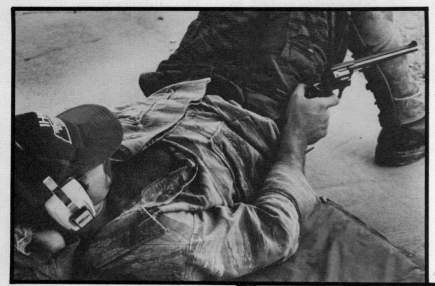

This shooter shows off his Creedmoor position for the .22 revolver with a 10-inch barrel which he has chosen.

The Dan Wesson Field Pistol Pac is available for .32 H&R magnum or in .357 magnum. Gun has the slotted Super Mag-type shroud, silhouette sights, Pachmayr grip. The extra shroud comes with a Burris scope mount and scope rings attached.

is not up to snuff, check your position, have someone of known ability group the gun/loads, or change your powder, try another bullet.

IHMSA rules for standing state that the arms shall not contact the body, nor shall the hands contact one another — or the gun — above the wrist.

Thompson/Center offers Contender barrels in .32-20, .30 M1 Carbine, 9mm Luger and .32 H&R magnum, any of which will do the job with a minimum of recoil. Bets are on the .32 H&R mag, or .32-20 which T/C smartly bored for .308 bullets. The bore runs .300 to .301 inch, with a groove diameter of .308. Twist is one turn in ten inches (1:10), obviously with silhouette in mind.

Pachmayr turned the handgun stock world on its head with the introduction of the *Gripper,* which incorporates an air pocket. This air shaft driven deep into the wide back-strap turns the grip into a shock absorber, instead of shock inflicter. All makers of powerful handguns would do well to study the T/C Gripper.

Not that a .32 H&R or .32-20 needs "air suspension."

Hardly. But you'll want it for the heftier cartridges. Once on, the Gripper will stay there.

The 100- and 110-grain flat-base .308 rifle bullets shoot flatter in the T/C ten-inch .32 H&R and .32-20 than in any .357 handgun.

T/C, Burris and Leupold offer handgun scopes with micro-click adjustments which seem favored. The T/C 1.5x actually diminishes the target somewhat, making it appear farther away than when seen with the naked eye. The T/C scopes are tough, having survived shooting at 25 below zero (that's 57 brittle degrees below freezing). You can't count clicks when it gets that cold!

Dan Wesson was poised to strike when the IHMSA adopted the field pistol event. Using the .357 magnum frame — used also for the DWA .22 — the DWA .32 H&R magnum already has staked its claim as *the* revolver for field pistol. Just how long a revolver can hold out against the single-shots remains to be seen. The better single-shot pistols have a distinct lock-time advantage over wheel guns. Add 150 feet-per-second velocity advantage to the

The venerable .45 ACP and its imitators have found a place in the IHMSA field pistol game. This shooter practices in prone position to get sighted in, but he must shoot from the standing position in sanctioned field pistol competitions.

closed breech gun firing the same load, and the mechanical limitations of the revolver begin to stack.

The field pistol scoped category gives the shooter with worn-out eyes the opportunity to be competitive once more. As it draws veterans off the bigger silhouette battles, scores will inch ever upward. Some silhouetters will specialize in the lighter-recoil stuff, as few will want to enter field pistol after spending four hours shooting the big stuff.

Light recoiling handguns provide a tempting chassis for the mounting of short eye-relief scopes. Shooters should be intelligently suspicious of such arrangements, which are emphatically frowned upon by scope manufacturers. Even light recoiling pistols come back, having no buttstock to slow the initial brunt of recoil.

The best way to get into field pistol, or .22 silhouette is to take one of your production guns and enter. Don't specialize until you've tested the water.

Firing a scoped Dan Wesson in .32 H&R magnum, John Taffin of Boise, Idaho, shot this group in tests on a javelina target at the prescribed field pistol distance.

The same scoped Dan Wesson with a 10-inch barrel and a 2x Leupold scope was used to fire the group on this paper test target. The gun shows excellent potential

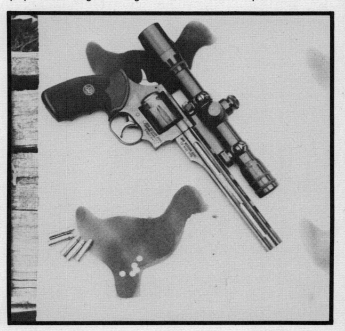

METALLIC SILHOUETTE SHOOTING

Revolver competition is among most popular categories of silhouette shooting. The shooters have learned that proper cylinder-to-barrel alignment is most important to accuracy. Several manufacturers recognize the problem.

ACCURACY & REVOLVERS

CHAPTER 16

There Are Reasons Why Cylinder Guns Can Lack Accuracy And Here's What To Do About It!

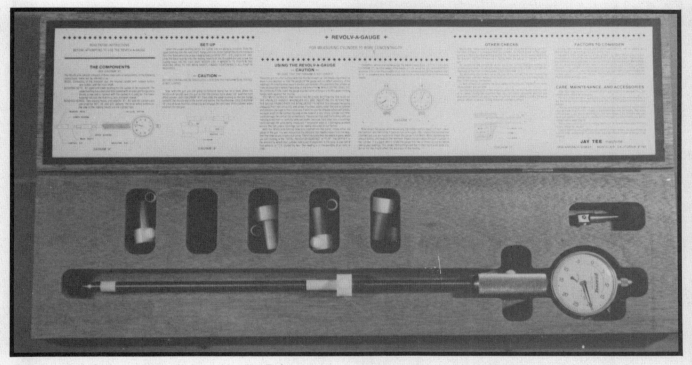

The Revolv-A-Gauge is manufactured by Jay Tee Machine. It has been found to be a precision tool that tests for chamber/cylinder runout on revolvers. It is priced at around $400; includes .357, .375, .41, .44, .45 collets.

IT IS a known fact that single-shot and/or closed-breech guns are generally more accurate than revolvers, but why?

Most experts contend that the reason for less accuracy with a revolver lies in the cylinder gap between the cylinder and the barrel. This allows a portion of the gas propellant to escape, thus reducing velocity. Depending on the possible gap variation from cylinder hole to cylinder hole caused by less than perfect machining and fitting, pressure will vary from one hole to another. Thus, no matter how carefully the power charges are weighed or metered, a thousandth or two of an inch difference from one cylinder or chamber hole to the next will change pressure and affect accuracy. This phenomenon, in itself, definitely affects ultimate accuracy and performance in all revolvers.

However, there is an even more important fault found in the cylinders of virtually all revolvers that is seldom considered or even thought of: the precision alignment of all six holes — or five, as the case may be — of the cylinder as they rotate to the firing position in front of the barrel opening. Often, the locking slots in the cylinder are machined incorrectly. They must be exact to allow precise alignment.

Nearly everyone takes it for granted that all manufacturers automatically machine and index the cylinders so that each hole does line up perfectly with the barrel opening and lock precisely in place. Unfortunately, virtually all of the them are *not* precisely aligned.

A phenomenon called "lead shaving" occurs when cylinders do not align correctly. If the cylinder is, say, ten thousandths of an inch to one side or the other when it is locked in position and the gun is fired, a sliver of lead will

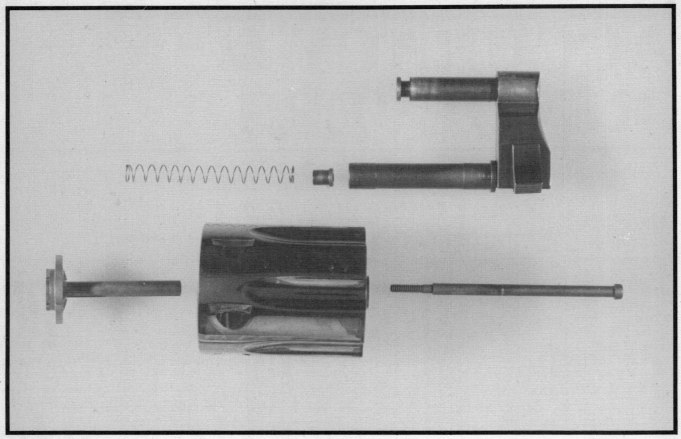

The long cylinder concept developed by Elgin Gates for his .357 and .375 Super Mag cartridge was adopted by Dan Wesson Arms and United Sporting Arms to create the more powerful revolvers for hunting, silhouette game.

be shaved off and it usually spits out to the side. Jacketed bullets will be deformed on one side. Pressure will vary. Accuracy will suffer.

Accuracy is absolutely essential in your handgun when you are trying to hit silhouette targets at distances up to two hundred meters. At best, revolvers are the most inaccurate of all handguns. With this in mind, it is important to know whether you have a revolver with a correctly aligned cylinder. Otherwise, you are wasting your time.

Revolver accuracy is the product of bringing together many individual factors. Some of the dimensional ingredients of a revolver are more important than others.

Sheldon Williams, the IHMSA 1983 production handgun champion, has designed a tool which, carefully used, will help measure some of the dimensional variables that affect revolver accuracy. It is called the Revolv-A-Gauge, and is manufactured by Sheldon Williams at Jay Tee Machine, 5650 Arrow Highway, Montclair, CA 91763.

The Revolv-A-Gauge was designed specifically to measure chamber/bore alignment. It also will measure vertical cylinder play (up and down movement of the cylinder), lockup (rotational side play) and locate any "stray" chambers.

The unit consists of three major components: the body, composed of a dial indicator, a knurled handle with release button and the main shaft; two reading heads, one for .357/.375 caliber, one for .41/.44/.45 caliber; and bushing sets for .357 .375 .41, .44 and .45.

Workmanship of the Revolv-A-Gauge is excellent throughout. To use the gauge, say on your Dan Wesson .357 Super Mag, slip the appropriate upper bushing onto the main shaft. Slip the lower bushing onto the reading head and screw the reading head to the main shaft. Lay the Revolv-A-Gauge alongside the gun barrel so that the contact ball on the reading head is one-eighth-inch to the rear of the cylinder face. Adjust the upper bushing so that its shoulder butts against the gun muzzle. The upper bushing has a set screw. Make sure the set screw is lined up with the contact ball (reading head). Finger-tighten the set screw.

Get out your notebook and prepare to record gun, caliber, bullet, groove diameter, chamber exit (average diameter), chamber runout (1,2,3,4,5,6). *Caution: Always check a firearm to see if it is loaded each and every single time you pick it up. Make sure gun is unloaded!*

Cock the revolver.

Depress the release button and slide the M shaft down the barrel. With the gun in vertical position, let go of the release button. Rotate the gauge three complete revolutions and read the indicator dial.

The amount of cylinder runout will be one half of the total indicator reading or TIR.

All of this babble may sound complex, but when you have the gauge in your hand, it's simple. Mechanical things are much better explained through illustrations and by doing.

Note: Barrel groove diameter and chamber exit hole diameter cannot be measured with the Revolv-A-Gauge.

Herman Erhart of Panama starts match with a .44 magnum that had been checked with Revolv-A-Gauge and found to have badly aligned cylinder. New cylinder increased his score. Standing competition is toughest competition category.

A precision dial caliper, preferably used in conjunction with soft metal (Cerrosafe), is needed. A dial caliper (not plastic) is a smart and versatile investment for the handloader.

The chart published in this chapter indicates some of the info compiled by using the Revolv-A-Gauge.

It will be noted that the Dan Wesson .357 SM, Dan Wesson .44, Interarms .44 and Seville .357 SM have the least misalignment of all the guns measured. This probably comes as no surprise to individuals who have used the Revolv-A-Gauge on a wide selection of guns. It should be noted also that these guns have barrel grooves and chamber exits of minimal diameters.

It makes sense that the more concentric to the bore a bullet is, between the moments of primer ignition and bullet departure, the straighter the bullet will fly. But how do we correlate all these figures to reach sound conclusions? I have long maintained that it is better to squeeze a bullet than rattle it. And, certainly, handgun silhouette shooting has proven beyond a doubt that tight guns win and loose guns lose.

Tight chamber exit holes control the heel of a bullet for the critical moment when the bullet's shoulder engages the rifling. An oversize chamber exit hole will allow the bullet to tip as it hits the rifling, killing accuracy. Can the same be said for a chamber that is out of alignment with the barrel? Or, does the passage of the bullet work to center the chamber and bore?

I do not have the tools by which to make a scientific study of alignment versus accuracy. I have heard manufacturers and quality control personnel and technical editors say that groove diameter and cylinder/barrel alignment don't affect accuracy. I used to have a hard time believing self-described authorities could say such things with a

These six bullets were recovered after firing through a .44 magnum by a major manufacturer. Bullets were fired with file marks at 12 o'clock. Note the uneven engraving and obturation. Chamber misalignment was .006-inch.

Federal .44 240-grain bullets flank a split jacket in center. These bullets were fired in a Dan Wesson Arms M-44 that shot 60x60 record. Note uniform engraving.

straight face. Now I know better. Most of these individuals have limited marksmanship capability. And most have no serious experience at shooting handguns at distances greater than twenty-five yards.

A "firm groove" will grip a bullet evenly about its whole bearing surface. A "loose groove" will tend to engrave the bullet deeply on one side of the shoulder, while similarly engraving the heel on the opposite side of the bullet. A bullet so launched may actually corkscrew through the air. I'm sure some of you have seen the results of this.

Looking at the Mossberg Abilene .44, we see that it has a respectable — and I am going to introduce an acronym — CAM (chamber average misalignment) of .0024-inch, which is quite good. Groove diameter measures .428-inch, which is excellent. But alas, chamber exits measure a clumsy .434-inch. Which is *not* good. The best thing on the Abilene is the barrel, and quite often this model has a rough forcing cone. The alignment is good, which says two things: Indexing (location of a chamber relative to the stop notch — on the opposite side of the cylinder) and chamber spacing are uniform.

So here we have an excellent barrel and good alignment compromised by a what can be a poor forcing cone and watermelon exit holes.

The Smith and Wesson Model 29, with 8¾-inch barrel, has an excellent .429-inch groove barrel. Chamber exit holes measure .432-inch. With good ammunition, this gun will shoot two-inch groups at one hundred meters with monotonous regularity. (Mine is fitted with a Leupold EER 4X scope.) CAM measures .0046-inch, which is two to three times the CAM measurement taken from the DW .357 SM, the DW .44, the Interarms Silhouette .44 and the Seville .357 SM.

Lockup — or rotational side play — on the M29 measures .003- to .004-inch, depending on the chamber; that is, with the trigger held to the rear, as in firing. With the trigger relaxed, lockup measures .012-inch.

Which raises a question: What is the proper technique for using the Revolv-A-Gauge?

Instructions call for cocking the revolver, inserting the gauge, rotating the gauge through a few revolutions and taking the reading. But what if your gun is tight? Or what if you have a Python? When the hammer is cocked it raises the hand (pawl), which rotates the cylinder. This often results in a tighter lockup, especially if the gun is tightly fitted. This tightening of lockup will then continue as the trigger is squeezed. In fact, the Colt Python is designed to index with *zero* cylinder movement when the trigger is pulled.

I would add to those instructions the desirability of measuring CAM, vertical cylinder play, lockup and looking for "stray" chambers with the gun in the fired mode — with the trigger squeezed to the rear of its travel.

By measuring the Python in both cocked and fired modes, I got lockup readings of .012-inch and .000-inch, respectively. By using these techniques and recording the results, the shooter can tell whether his or her gun is in proper alignment at the moment of fire.

Chamber/bore alignment on my Dan Wesson Super Mag measures .0015, .000, .0010, .0020, .0030 and .0015 inches of runout. That lone .003-inch chamber may act as a spoiler, but I don't worry about it.

However, if one chamber is grossly out of sync with the others, chances are it will throw shots out of the group. The only remedy for that is to return the gun to the factory, where a new cylinder should be installed, hopefully at no charge. The Revolv-A-Gauge will help to pinpoint these problems.

The more you use the Revolv-A-Gauge, the more versatile an instrument it becomes and the more skilled you become at using it. Some guns consistently index out-of-time. The Ruger Redhawk listed in the chart yields a chamber average misalignment (CAM) of .0042-inch. All six chambers center at eleven o'clock to the bore (when aiming the revolver). Two other Redhawks, checked at random, exhibit misalignment at nine o'clock. CAM of one measures .0055-inch. This particular gun shoots pretty well. CAM of the other measures .0061-inch. This gun also suffers from a .432-inch groove diameter barrel; needless to say, accuracy is a disappointment.

For years I wondered why the forcing cones of some revolvers eroded evenly, while those of others showed accelerated erosion at six o'clock or twelve o'clock or two o'clock. I have long suspected that these wear patterns were due to alignment. Thanks to the Revolv-A-Gauge, I now know.

By using the Revolv-A-Gauge on a sampling of one model of gun that spans a range of serial numbers from early production to the present, certain manufacturing patterns may emerge. Very early Redhawks, for instance, show a chamber average misalignment of .002-inch — super respectable. A number of guns in the 80XXX serial range show a CAM of .005- to .006-inch — with chambers offset to the left of the bore. Everyone expected great things of the Redhawk when it came out, that it would put the competition to sleep. It is a rugged gun. General accuracy of Redhawks varies from very good to good, with relatively few being atrocious. But I think the problem lies more with oversize groove diameters than with misalignment. The only way to prove it is to test various barrels on the same gun. If you have a straight-shooting Redhawk — keep it!

A few years ago, I tested a new Spanish-made .44 magnum revolver. I could have used the Revolv-A-Gauge

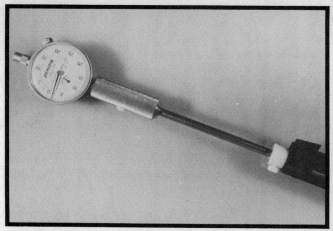

Dan Wesson .375 Super Mag tested with Revolv-A-Guage showed readings far below averages of the two largest revolver manufacturers. Tool was designed by Sheldon Williams, 1983 IHMSA production gun silhouette champion.

then. The gun had an 8½-inch barrel. The trigger had been lightened. My groups averaged twelve inches at twenty-five yards with Federal 240 JHP. That same Federal ammo, fired in my Dan Wesson VH8, dropped 7x10 turkeys and rams at 205 meters in the shootoff at the 1982 Region One Championships.

Individual chambers of the Spanish product grouped anywhere from four to ten inches at twenty-five yards. The twelve-inch average at twenty-five yards, turns into nine feet at two hundred meters.

Bushings and reading balls for the Revolv-A-Gauge are made of nylon, so that no steel comes in contact with the gun. That the reading balls will wear in time is of no consequence, since the dial indicator has no fixed zero.

One addition to the Revolv-A-Gauge that I would like to see is a reading head for detecting whether and how much the chambers tilt at an angle to the bore.

At $400, the Jay Tee Revolv-A-Gauge is too expensive for casual sales. However, every manufacturer of revolvers and all serious revolver smiths should invest in one and use it!

REVOLV-A-GAUGE MEASUREMENTS

Gun	Caliber	Barrel Length (inches)	Groove Diameter (inches)	Chamber Exit Diameter (inches)	CAM* (inches)
Colt Python	.357	6	.354	.359	.0037
DWA M40	.357 SM	8	.357	.359	.0015
Ruger SB	.44	10½	.429	.431	.0066
Ruger SB	.44	7½	.433	.431	.0050
S&W M29	.44	8⅜	.429	.432	.0046
Redhawk	.44	7½	.430	.432	.0042
S&W M629	.44	6	.429	.432	.0049
Mossberg	.44	4⅝	.428	.429	.0018
DWA M44	.44	8	.427	.429	.0022
Interarms	.44	10½	.428	.429	.0018
Seville	.357 SM	10½	.357	.358	.0014
Ruger SRM	.357 Max	10½	.357	.358	.0083

*Chamber Average Misalignment

Note: Only average chamber/barrel misalignment (runout) is listed for each gun. This is to keep the chart simple.

THE SUPER MAG STORY

...Or How A Cartridge Was Developed Over Vast Amounts Of Disinterest

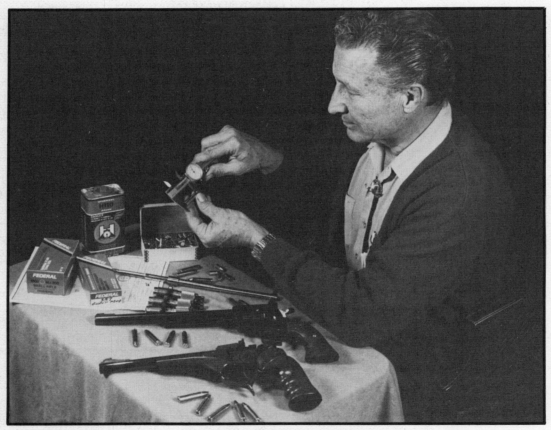

The author developed the series of Super Mag cartridges of which the .357 Super Mag has come to be the most successful revolver cartridge in the silhouette game.

ONE OF the most frustrating things in the early days of developing cartridges for the silhouette game was to get revolver makers interested. For most of the potent bottleneck designs for single-shot and unlimited bolt-action guns, it was simply a matter of rechambering barrels for the Thompson/Center Contender or rebarreling the .221 XP-100 action to the desired caliber and chambering.

Realizing that eventually silhouette competition would have a separate category for six-guns, one of my own desired goals was to come up with a revolver cartridge that would be effective and reliable against the heavy steel rams at two hundred meters.

The old .357 magnum was marginal, leaving the .44 magnum as the only effective production revolver cartridge available for the silhouette game. What we needed was a revolver cartridge with more power, better ballistics, a flatter trajectory and thus potentially better accuracy. Also needed was a better revolver to go along with it; stronger and more rugged than anything available at that time.

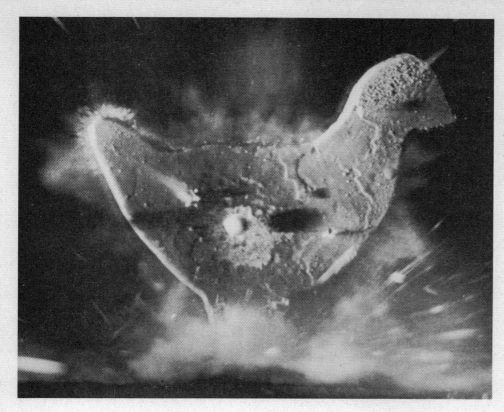

Bill Madewell of Aiken, South Carolina, photographed instant of impact by a 180-grain full patch bullet on armor-steel chicken target. Bullet was from a .357 Super Mag cartridge that was fired from Dan Wesson Model 40V8S Super Mag revolver.

The first possibility would be a revolver that could handle some of the short but potent bottleneck cartridges or a longer more powerful straight-wall cartridge.

Several attempts had been made to come up with revolvers chambered for bottleneck cartridges, but they were plagued with one problem that seemingly could not be overcome — cylinder locking.

Smith & Wesson introduced their Model 53 in 1961 to take the .22 Remington Jet which, essentially, was the .357 magnum case necked down to .22 caliber with a long, sloping shoulder. Gunwriters waxed poetic over it at first, describing its 2000 feet-per-second-plus velocities as a fantastic new ballistic breakthrough for revolvers. Ironically, this crusade for ultra-velocity out of a revolver is the thing that proved its undoing. The scramble for ever-more powerful and faster loadings expanded and stretched the brass, forcing the case back against the frame to lock the cylinder.

On the other hand, lower pressure, tapered-shoulder cartridges like the old .32-20, .38-40 and the .44-40 worked fairly well in the revolvers chambered for them. Unfortunately, these old calibers were underpowered for long-range silhouette targets.

Generally speaking, the big companies' white-smock research and development guys have steered clear of any further attempts to mate a high-power bottleneck cartridge with a revolver. In short, the "experts" say it will not work.

The second possibility was either to get more power out of existing straight-wall revolver cases or to make them longer or bigger — or possibly both. The latter is the route I took in October, 1975, when I started serious work on a series of longer and/or larger revolver cartridges. For want of a better name at the time I dubbed them Super Mags.

The first one I worked on was in .35 caliber, which I felt was the optimum for revolvers. The criteria was simple: It had to have ballistics that would at least equal the power of the .44 magnum as regarding long-range knockdown ability; hopefully a bit more. This, together with the potential flat-

Special run of .357 Super Mag prototype brass was run by Federal Cartridge Company, carries the headstamp.

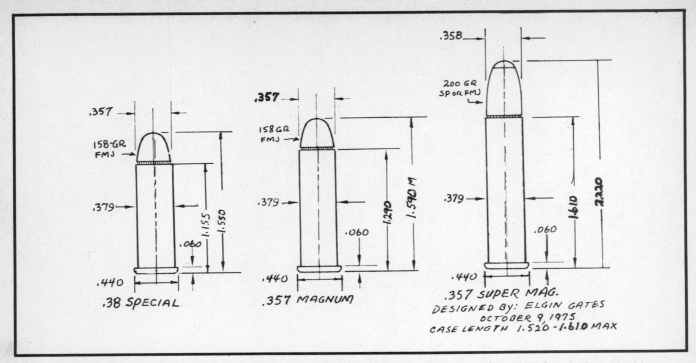

Original drawings made by the author in October, 1975, illustrate the evolution of the .357 Super Mag cartridge. The round was developed by adding .320 inch to the S&W .357 magnum case which was introduced in 1935.

ter trajectory and higher velocity of the .35 caliber bullet, should rejuvenate the old .357 magnum into a high-performance revolver cartridge.

At the time, my old long-case .357 magnum brass from my 1952 African hunting days which had been formed from .32-30 cases was in storage. I decided to lengthen standard .357 magnum brass for testing.

There being no long-cylinder revolver available at that time, original testing had to be done with rechambered Thompson/Center Contenders. By using a .44 magnum T/C barrel and a standard .357 magnum T/C barrel chambered for progressively longer cases, it was a fairly simple task to make the necessary ballistic comparisons.

And let it be stated plainly that no greater stroke of ballistic genius was required to develop the series of Super Mag cartridges than any of the other cartridges I came up with over the years. All of them used one or another of the existing brass cases as parents. Only a few have been reasonably successful for the silhouette game. None of the others amounted to much, except for the personal satisfaction of playing with them. Other cartridge innovators such as Frank Barnes and J. D. Jones have been successful with some of their individual cartridges and the series they have created and developed. It's been a lot of fun for all of us.

Lengthening the existing .357 magnum case was accomplished by the simple method of cutting off sections of one case and delicately heli-arcing them on top of another case, using a steel mandrel to hold them in line, then using an outside turner to cut the weld bead flush with the case. Sometimes these welded cases would last for four or five firings; other times, the weld would fracture the first time the case was fired. Nevertheless, they worked well enough to allow testing. Using the old Smith & Wesson-Winchester

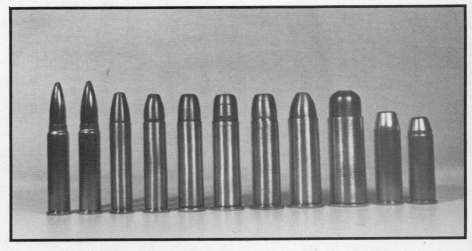

All of these Super Mag cartridges were developed by Gates utilizing case length of 1.610 inches. From left are: 7mm, .305, .357, .375, .414, .445, .455, .505 and the .610. Second from right is .45 round advertised as the world's most powerful handgun cartridge. At the extreme right is the .45 Long Colt. These last two are for comparison.

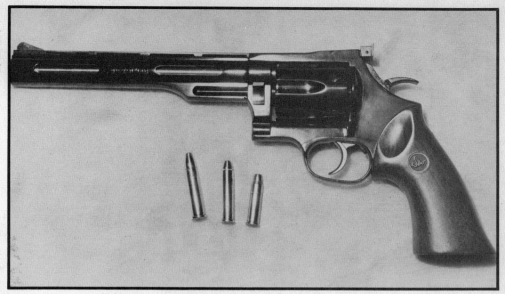

Dan Wesson Model 40V8S long-cylinder Super Mag is shown with (from left) the .375 Super Mag, .357 Super Mag and standard .357 magnum.

Silhouette competition was a reason for manufacturers to develop heavier, tougher bullets. Speer 180-grain is at left, with the 200-grain version beside it. Both are in .35 caliber.

trick of lengthening the .38 Special brass to create the .357 magnum case, I heli-arced an extra .230-inch section on the end of a regular .357 magnum case for testing. The increase in performance was excellent, but not quite the equal of the .44 magnum. The next section was .320 inch (approximately 5/16ths of an inch) and produced the desired results: performance superior to that of the .44 magnum — at least, in the T/C barrels I was using.

This case measured out to 1.610 inches in length as compared to the 1.290 .357 magnum case. As a sort of afterthought, I made up a still longer sample measuring 1.675-inch, but I did not test it.

It would be tedious to describe all the details of testing each progressively longer case in the series. I was satisfied with the performance of the 1.610 case and drew up the cartridge print accordingly.

On December 10, 1975, I sent a letter to Remington's research and development department that included the drawing and sample cases. Later, at my urging, Federal made a special run of 1.610 brass with the headstamp reading .357 Super Magnum per the drawing I sent them. This brass was used for the ongoing testing program and saved a lot of time as compared to using the heli-arced brass.

During the rest of December, 1975, and early January of 1976, I worked up a full series of Super Mag cartridges, all the same length of 1.610 inches but in different calibers. The first two were bottleneck cases which I designated as the 7mm and .305 Super Mags. Then came the .357, .375, .414, .445 .455, .505 and .610 Super Mags.

The only remaining problem in this project was to get one of the big revolver makers interested enough to build a long-cylinder gun to take the cartridges.

The cylinder length of most .357 magnum revolvers is approximately 1.600 inches; by mere coincidence, the same approximate length of the Super Mag cases without bullets.

Careful calculations from testing in the T/C Contenders brought me to the conclusion that the correct cylinder length for the new cartridge should be 2.045, in order to realize its full potential using heavy bullets in the 170-200 grain range, still leaving adequate case capacity for silhouette loadings. This measurement is nearly a half-inch longer than any existing .357 magnum revolver cylinder.

On this note, I went to the 1976 National Sporting Goods Association show with drawings and samples of the

For the sake of comparison, the .357 Super Mag (left) is shown with the standard .44 magnum cartridge. The Oehler Model 33 chronograph is used in Gates' research.

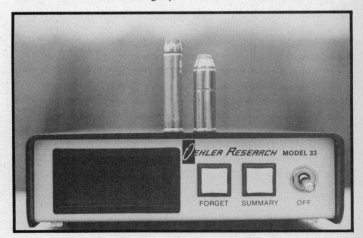

METALLIC SILHOUETTE SHOOTING

David Bradshaw draws a bead with the Ruger Maximum. Note the closeness of the bullet noses to cylinder face. This was the short-cylinder version utilizing a standard frame window. Bradshaw did much testing of the model.

Super Mag cartridges in my suitcase, optimistic that one or another — maybe even all — of the revolver makers would latch on to this new development.

I couldn't have been more wrong! It was only four months after the first handgun silhouette match ever held and none of the revolver manufacturers had a clue as to what the silhouette game was all about. Some hadn't even heard about it. Another thing I didn't count on was that the NIH (Not Invented Here) Syndrome was like a brick wall.

Nevertheless, I passed out copies of the cartridge prints and samples of dummy cartridges to representatives, officials and engineers at every revolver maker's booth and a few more besides.

Most all of them gave the prints and cartridges only a cursory glance at the time — but carefully put them in their pockets or briefcases — and proceeded to give me a polite brushoff. Basically, they were appalled at the idea of building a revolver to take a longer, more powerful cartridge.

At one booth, I got one of their engineer types aside, handed him a print of the .357 Super Mag specifications and a dummy cartridge and started explaining why we needed a more powerful cartridge to knock down fifty-pound steel rams at two hundred meters. This character could hardly conceal his impatience and contempt, and looked at me as if I were an escapee from the booby hatch. Finally, unable to stand it any longer, he fixed me with a steely glare, handed the .357 Super Mag print and sample cartridge back and exclaimed, "The 357 magnum and .44 magnum are the most powerful cartridges that can ever be used in a revolver. Clint Eastwood in the Dirty Harry film proved it to everyone's satisfaction. What you are advocating is that we use rifle ammunition in a revolver!"

He stalked away, shaking his head at the thought of having to talk to the nuts that came out of the woodwork at the trade shows. It's probably a good thing I didn't show him the prints and prototype cases of the .375, .445, .455, .505 and .610 I had in my pocket. It really would have blown his mind.

The point is, none of the wheelgun makers would touch the Super Mags with a ten-foot pole. They thought I was out of my mind.

Reluctantly, I laid the project aside temporarily to handle more pressing matters. Until someone had guts enough to produce a long-cylinder revolver, the project wasn't going anywhere, even though the single-shot makers were quick to latch onto some of the proposed cartridges.

I sent a reamer and specification print to Warren Center at Thompson/Center. In his usual courteous manner, Center paid attention to it and I soon got back two Super 14 T/C barrels chambered for the .357 Super Mag. He and others were interested, but revolver makers weren't yet.

Was the long cylinder revolver concept a lost cause? It was for at least three more years. Then, in 1979, Remington and a major revolver maker got together and developed their own version of a longer .357 magnum case, using the same old stunt of increasing its length .200-inch from 1.290 to 1.490. This was to be used in the original revolver frame by shortening the barrel extension inside of the frame without lengthening the cylinder.

Later, as testing began in 1982, using the 1.490 case, the results clearly showed that the 1.490 case was inferior to the .44 magnum, much as my own tests had revealed earlier.

To offer them the benefit of my own extended testing, I

chambered a new T/C Contender ten-inch bull barrel pistol to .357 Super Mag specs, using the 1.610 case and sent it, with a quantity of the 1.610 Federal brass, to David Bradshaw. He took it to the revolver maker's test range. The superior performance of the longer and more powerful .357 Super Mag cartridge was obvious.

Suffice to say that Remington shortly increased the length of their 1.490 case another .105 to 1.595 (still .015 short of the Super Mag) and christened it the .357 Maximum. At the same time, to accommodate this round, the revolver cylinder was increased to a length of 1.935 and the frame window made longer to accommodate it. It still wasn't enough.

In the meantime, I called Bob O'Connor, then president of Dan Wesson, who was preparing to follow the 1.935 cylinder length concept and talked him into going to a 2.075 cylinder length to handle the 1.610 Super Mag cartridge. He said he would give the revolver the same name, adding the comment that, if everything didn't work out, it would be my neck. The decision, O'Connor jokingly told

---

Remington
DUPONT

REMINGTON ARMS COMPANY, INC.

SPORTING ARMS-AMMUNITION-TARGETS-TRAPS

BRIDGEPORT, CONNECTICUT 06602

TELEX 964-201 STRATFORD,CT

TELEPHONE 203-333-1112

January 25, 1983

Mr. Elgin T. Gates, President
IHMSA, Incorporated
Box 1609
Idaho Falls, Idaho 83401

Dear Mr. Gates:

I was sorry to learn that some members of IHMSA were disturbed by a Remington representative's statement on the origin of our new 357 Remington Maximum cartridge. The statement attributes the basic idea for the cartridge to Remington and failed to acknowledge the contributions that you and others have made over the years. The record clearly shows that your design of late 1975 was the first concept of a more powerful 357 caliber cartridge for silhouette competition, and predates by several years any work done by Remington.

I can assure you and all members of IHMSA that our omission was a simple oversight and was not done intentionally. I regret any inconvenience that this may have caused you.

We at Remington are proud of our role in recognizing that the time had come to convert a good idea into a factory-produced cartridge. We also applaud the outstanding contribution made by Ruger in the development of the revolver and the input from a number of other sources, many of them within the IHMSA.

Without the IHMSA, handgun metallic competition would not have grown to the point that made development of the 357 Remington Maximum possible and practical. Let's continue to work together to promote the sport and to provide IHMSA competitors with the best possible equipment.

Sincerely,

Robert E. Fielitz

ROBERT E. FIELITZ
Director of Research

REF:jl

Robert Gates test fires the Seville .375 Super Mag. This gun was built on suggestion from silhouette clan.

me later, was easier to make with the substantial order I gave him at the time for the big-frame Dan Wessons to be chambered for the .357 Super Mag and the .375 Super Mag, with the condition that the 2.075 long cylinder be used.

The success of this revolver, since its introduction in 1983 in these two calibers, especially the .357 Super Mag, has been unequaled in the history of silhouette shooting. The Dan Wesson Model 40 V8S .357 Super Mag has won the IMHSA Internationals every year with perfect 80x80 scores beginning in 1983 and on through 1987.

Likewise, an order and a discussion with Sig Himmelman of United Sporting Arms resulted in the creation of the stainless steel single-action Seville silhouette model with a 10½-inch barrel chambered in .357 Super Mag and, shortly thereafter, the .375 Super Mag.

As a matter of personal satisfaction, one of my greatest moments was when Duane Small, national sales manager for Dan Wesson, presented me with the original .357 Dan Wesson .357 Super Mag bearing the serial number *E. Gates-1* in recognition of the help I had given them in the project.

The best part of it, as far as handgun silhouetting is concerned, was that the revolver finally had come of age. When you can launch a 180- to 200-grain .35 caliber bullet downrange at 1400 to 1500 feet per second from an eight- or ten-inch revolver, the steel rams at two hundred meters are going down. You can count on it.

What is the status of the rest of the Super Mags? Let's take them one at a time, starting with the smallest caliber of the series, the 7mm.

While much greater emphasis had been placed on the .357 and .375 Super Mags as revolver cartridges, the 7mm had not been forgotten. First mentioned in 1977, it was not offered to the firearms industry until the fall of 1987. Almost immediately, four manufacturers of single-shot pistols agreed to chamber for it and the cartridge was approved by IHMSA for production gun competition. Silhouette shooting will be the acid test for this cartridge in coming seasons.

In late 1987, I had a long discussion with Sig Himmelman, now operating as Competition Arms Company. He wanted to know what could be done to increase revolver performance even more. I gave him these ideas:

"If some genius can figure out a way to eliminate the cylinder gap gas loss," I said, "achieve perfect alignment of all cylinder holes with the barrel on regular production line guns — and come up with a revolver that will take some of the high performance bottleneck cartridges, he will be a big step ahead of the field."

"Have you got any more reamers for your 7mm Super Mag?" Sig asked.

"Yes," I answered.

Author feels the heavy-frame Dan Wesson is ideal for women shooters. The weight dampens recoil. Nanette Workman of Canada utilizes the Creedmoor position to bring her .357 Super Mag version on a distant target.

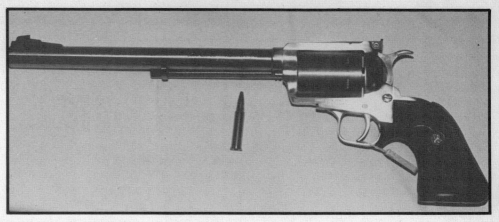

Seville silhouette revolver has the longest cylinder available. It measures 2.300 inches. The gun shown is chambered for the 7mm Super Magnum cartridge.

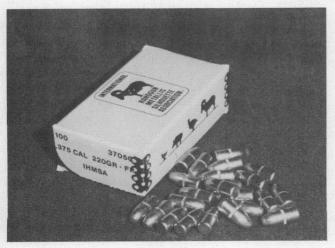

The 220-grain bullets turned out under special contract with IHMSA were manufactured for .375 Super Mag shooters.

"Send me a reamer and dies," Sig said. "And what are you using for brass?"

"The 7mm Super Mag is a regular .357 Super Mag case necked down," I explained. "Simply run a case through the 7mm seater die, then the full-length die and you have a 7mm Super Mag ready to load and shoot."

"Okay," Himmelman said, "I can handle that, and I may have a surprise for you."

He did: a brand-new stainless 10½-inch barrel revolver with an extra-long cylinder measuring 2.300 inches to take the 7mm Super Mag!

The prototype revolver is going through final heat treating as this is being written and will be tested fully as soon as possible. If the potential problem of cylinder locking encountered in the past can be overcome, this may be the first breakthrough for a series of high-performance revolvers and cartridges. The possibilities are intriguing.

The next cartridge in the series, the .305 Super Mag, is in the same position. It will follow as an extra chambering option for the manufacturers to offer to .30 caliber devotees.

The .357 Super Mag, as the first offering, already has been discussed fully. By using heavy silhouette bullets for which it was designed, the cartridge has been enormously successful in the revolver category for silhouette shooting and handgun hunting.

The downfall of one revolver that caused it to be withdrawn from production was the mania of certain people to achieve ultra velocities with light bullets. Severe top strap cutting and forcing cone erosion resulted, causing the revolver to be discontinued. Actually, to give proper credit, this revolver was quite accurate and shot well, with 180- to 200-grain silhouette bullets, using non-corrosive powders such as 4227, 4895 and others.

As for the .375 Super Mag, the two revolver makers, Dan Wesson and United Sporting Arms, have been chambering for it since 1983. In the beginning, I had a special pressure barrel made up and Hornady conducted the pressure tests in their lab. The slightly smaller base of the .375 Super Mag case (.415) — plus its C.U.P. rating of 53,000 — allowed higher pressures to be used. The big-frame Dan Wesson, for example, is rated at 43,000 C.U.P. in .44 magnum caliber. I suggested pressure testing at 45,000 C.U.P. for the .375 Super Mag. Bob Domian, chief engineer for Dan Wesson, agreed.

The pressure tests performed in Hornady's lab used a special Hornady-made IHMSA 220-grain .375 bullet that I had ordered with the cannelure moved up an extra .050 to allow secure crimping for revolver use.

While the .375 Super Mag probably never will obsolete the beloved .44 magnum with its twenty-eight-year head start, it has caught on well in the silhouette game and among handgun hunters, both in the double-action Dan Wesson and the single-action Seville. Overseas silhouette shooters and hunters are particularly intrigued with these two revolvers.

With the one major revolver maker discontinuing their long-cylinder model for the reasons mentioned, it is not clear at this time whether any of the other revolver manufacturers will jump into the long-cylinder competition in the near future.

The .445 Super Mag? Its time has come! I have just negotiated a deal with Duane Small, Vice President of Dan Wesson Arms. They will chamber for the .445 Super Mag using their big-frame, long-cylinder revolver that has been so successful with the .357 and .375 Super Mags. I've just sent a batch of special .445 Super Mag brass to Bob Talbot, Dan Wesson's new engineer, who will handle the mechanical details and design changes needed to get the gun into production.

After that, the .455 Super Mag will be next, along with the 7mm Super Mag which Dan Wesson also has agreed to chamber for.

The .505 and .610 Suger Mags? They will be waiting on the sidelines for someone to come up with a real he-man, two-fisted, super-tough revolver to handle them.

Let's see what the future brings!

Ram line at IHMSA International Championships extends over 1000 feet and contains 20 sets of steel targets. With up to 1600 entries at these championship shoots, this is the most successful handgun organization.

A MATTER OF PRICE

CHAPTER 18

Silhouette Shooters Attempt To Rule Against The Possibility Of Buying Titles With Tricked-Up Handguns

Author (center) discusses the merits of ruggedly built Rugers with their maker, Bill Ruger. The manufacturer is violently opposed to having his guns reworked and feels they qualify as is for competition. Sales to competitors has been a bonanza.

OUTSIDERS ARE constantly amazed at the phenomenal success of the handgun metallic silhouette shooting sport. The industry itself cannot fully grasp what it is that causes thousands of enthusiastic IHMSA members to participate in silhouette matches on a regular basis, although it loves the rich bonanza it is reaping in sales to IHMSA members. Even within the shooting sports no one can quite understand why IHMSA has more members than all the other handgun sports put together

The answer is quite simple, yet there is a near unanimous refusal to believe it. IHMSA is operating outside of the traditional methods used by all the shooting sports since the beginning of organized competition.

Before explaining IHMSA's success, let's briefly discuss what is called the traditional method of sport shooting competition. Even this is simple. The basic idea is to start with a standard pistol made by any one of a number of manufacturers. The next step is to perform extensive modifications to the gun. Said work may be done by the owner

Author (second from left) took part in practice for an early PPC match with police marksmen. He was firing his modified S&W Model 28. He feels this sport suffered because the custom reworked guns became the norm.

himself, but usually a professional gunsmith is hired at a price that can easily exceed the original cost of the pistol.

I call it the Goober Syndrome or the Great Equipment Race. Simply stated, it is an obsessive — but never to be admitted — desire to gain a mechanical edge over the rest of the competitors in order to win.

Once any shooting organization lets its game be prostituted with the equipment race disease — the Goober Syndrome — and they all do right from the beginning — the average man inevitably is priced out of competition and sadly bows out of the sport.

Needless to say, the afflicted shooting sport grows at a snail's pace, if at all. Many fade away to near obscurity. Take the PPC or Practical Pistol Course game for example, which started back in 1962. Originally, competition was to be with the regular "duty pistol," the kind that the cop carried on his hip while on duty.

PPC competitors, in the beginning, laughed their heads off when some cop, who had a rich wife, showed up on the range with a slab-sided big money gun — promptly got beat by those el cheapo "duty pistols." And they laughed some more when other cops bought money guns of their own and brought them to the matches. 'These characters are blowing their money for expensive guns and everybody knows our little old duty pistols are winning everything in sight.' And so they were. It was all so very funny.

Then, after another year or two, one of those big money guns finally won. But that didn't cut any ice. They still laughed and called it a fluke. A few of the better shooters didn't laugh quite so loud, though. After all, they reasoned to themselves, there just might be something to this deal where that lucky jerk with a rich wife and a big money gun won the marbles, even though everybody knows it was a fluke; an accident.

So the next year, a few of the better shooters showed up with slab-sided big money guns and the slaughter of the cheaper duty pistols began in earnest. Even so, there was still talk and laughter about things like luck, fluke, accident and

In the handgun silhouette association's unlimited class, almost anything goes so long as weight of the handgun is under 4½ pounds, barrel is no more than 15 inches. XP-100 has been rebarreled to .35 IHMSA International.

so on, but the laughter wasn't quite so loud and more and more of the better shooters quietly ordered big money guns and the stage was set for the final kill.

Suddenly, it was all over. You either had to have a big money gun to be in it or the psychological seeds had taken root in your mind to the point where you *thought* you did. Either way, you *knew* your old duty pistol wasn't good enough anymore. Shooters who couldn't afford that $1000-$2000 big money gun quietly began to drop out.

It wasn't long before all the competitors got the idea, but there was no turning back, now. Too many big money guns were out there. Besides, back in the early days, when duty pistols were winning everything, nobody thought about amending the rules to limit the competition to duty pistols for everyone. Production gun rules? That was for those who were afraid of progress. And so the rules were left wide open, which made the big money guns perfectly legal.

The finale was a bit slow in coming, at first, but it soon accelerated to an ignominious end and, instead of thousands of cops enjoying the sport with their duty pistols on an equal basis, it degenerated to a few hundred "professionals" who shot against each other with their $1000 to $2000 big money gun rigs.

Time and again this question has been asked: Why and how has IHMSA been so much more successful with its handgun silhouette game than any other handgun game ever created; more so than virtually all other shooting sports?

The answer is that IHMSA has gone in the opposite direction of virtually every shooting sport known. We believe the game is for the average guy, not a privileged few.

Let's explore this a bit: From the time the handgun was invented, it always has been thought of and used as a short-range weapon. For military use, the handgun was used as a sort of last-ditch personal defense weapon when the enemy closed in. At that, it usually was handguns for officers,

In 1987, over 60,000 entrants went through various courses of fire, with more than two million rounds being fired in metallic handgun silhouette competition. A number of foreign countries have introduced this handgun sport.

bayonets for the common soldier.

Legend has it that in the Old West, the saddle carbine was used to shoot the cattle rustlers at a distance, a six-gun to take on the bad guys at twenty paces in the middle of main street or at point-blank range in the local saloon.

You didn't need sights for this latter task, even if you had time to use them. Just blaze away or hold the trigger down and fan it. At that close distance, one slug was bound to hit home. That, at least, is the legend.

Over the years there was a great deal of competition in the handgun field, with every manufacturer trying to keep production costs down. Consequently, the idea of putting better — and more expensive — sights on handguns usually was thought of as a joke.

To be sure, when paper target competition came along for handguns, sights were improved, but shooting still was at short range. Much of the competition was with .22 rimfires and other small calibers. Little strain was put on such guns under these kind of shooting conditions.

Eventually, police departments armed their personnel with more powerful cartridges such as the .38 Special, then the .357 magnum. World Wars I and II brought on competition with the .45 ACP.

Those were larger and more powerful cartridges, true, but the ranges still were short. Practice, as well as competition, usually was with light wadcutter or "creampuff" type loads. Even the cheapest and most frail handguns could handle this.

The average guy who bought one of the big handguns like a .44 magnum seldom put a box of cartridges through it in the course of a year. The big guns weren't expected to have thousands of full-load factory rounds put through them. Nor was there any organized competition for the big magnums.

As stated in an earlier chapter, the existing handguns of the time were not given the real acid test of durability by having thousands of factory loads put through them, until the handgun silhouette game came along.

In the meantime, paper punchers had become infected with the Goober Syndrome, the essence of which is that any handgun, as it comes from the factory, is a piece of "junk" and must be modified in thirty-nine different ways before it will shoot.

With all this in mind, why should any handgun manufacturer really want to spend large sums of money in research and development to build stronger, better operating handguns

Author feels the factory-built Colt Gold Cup National Match .45 ACP model is the best precision pistol the factory can turn out. But loot shooters have spent up to $500 over original cost to buy mechanical advantage.

with better sights, et cetera, when all the buyer wanted to do was take it to a custom gunsmith to get it rebuilt — and each buyer had his own ideas about how it should be rebuilt?

This is the way it stood, basically, when IHMSA brought the handgun silhouette game to town. While we have, to be sure, the unlimited category where Goober shooters can have a field day, the backbone of our game is the production gun rule which does not allow any external or internal modifications, with the sole exception of a trigger smoothing job. In short, you shoot it the way it comes across the counter and out of the box.

The basic IHMSA philosophy is simple: If you beat me today, it is because you are a better shoooter — at least today — not because you have $500 worth of goobers in your gun. Tomorrow, I have a chance to beat you with my own out-of-the-box gun which is just as good as yours.

This is the philosophy that totally goes against the Goober Syndrome where one can buy an "edge" as a substitute for shooting skill and beat the man who has equal ability.

Goober shooters always have a cute little justification for their goobers. Almost every one of them will look you in the eye and earnestly declare: "Oh, no, none of those $500 worth of modifications make my gun shoot a bit better. It's the man that counts."

To which we've always asked this question: "That being the case, then why blow $500 for tricks and goobers?"

None of them has ever yet offered a rational or believable answer to my personal knowledge.

As the IHMSA game began to proliferate, handgun

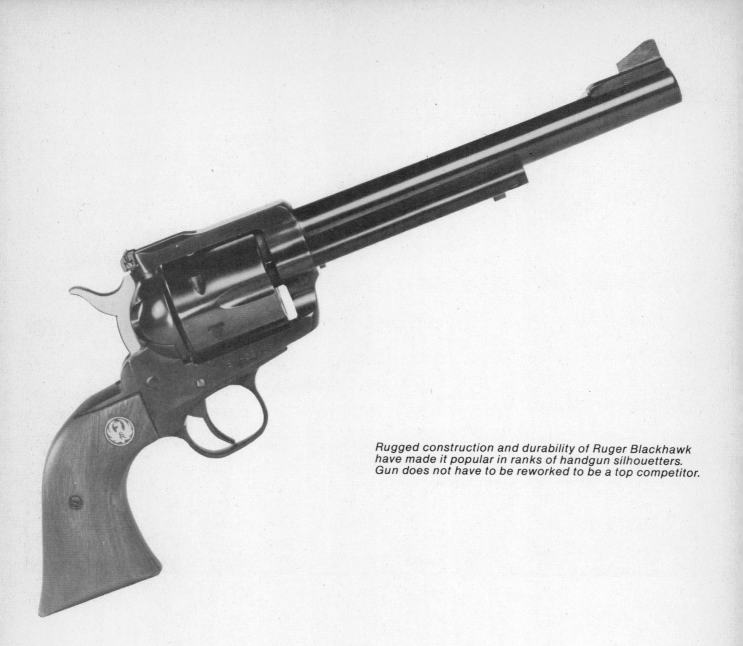

Rugged construction and durability of Ruger Blackhawk have made it popular in ranks of handgun silhouetters. Gun does not have to be reworked to be a top competitor.

manufacturers suddenly realized a new concept of competition was in existence, with honest production guns competing equally against other production guns. Some of them came to realize that, if they wanted the business, they had to create a better product, because IHMSA wasn't going to allow competitors to goober their guns.

The fact is, IHMSA is totally in favor of any manufacturer improving his own product for the simple reason that every competitor will have that same improvement and advantage at the same price and the game will continue to be a matter of the ability of one shooter against another.

It didn't take long for certain gunmakers to recognize the wisdom of improving their product, building it stronger and tougher, installing better locking systems for better safety and accuracy, better trigger mechanisms and especially, better sights.

The result is that, under IHMSA competition, the handgun has come into its own as an excellent long-range implement, a fact proved week after week on silhouette ranges across the country.

It doesn't take much imagination to understand the public relations benefits of building a handgun with the stamina and ruggedness to withstand the strain of having thousands of rounds put through it with little or no malfunction or breakage. Needless to say, this is the kind of handgun the hunter also will buy, not to mention the public as a whole.

Who doesn't want to own a more rugged, more reliable,

The IHMSA permanent range at Idaho Falls, Idaho, boasts 80 shooting positions, is 1000 yards in length. Author contends this is solid proof of the success of the philosophy connected with limitations on production guns.

more dependable, more accurate handgun than the kind of stuff that has been foisted off on the public for the past seventy years? And one that will perform as it comes over-the-counter, out-of-the-factory-box without extensive modifications?

IHMSA is proud of the part we have played with our handgun silhouette game in causing a number of the more progressive manufacturers to build better handguns.

A few makers, blind to reality, have made no visible effort to build a stronger, more rugged, more reliable product. Slowly, they are being phased out of the silhouette market. In the long run, it will be their loss.

And yes, there was a handful of loot shooters in IHMSA ranks who liked the taste of the equipment race and the big money guns that went with it. Buy that edge and win the loot. Unsatisfied with IHMSA's production gun rule, they drifted over to other organizations where the equipment race was wide open, loot shooting was in vogue and, if you had a custom built $5000 unlimited-type "production" gun, that was just tough for the peasants.

In spite of this disenchantment by a few loot shooters, IHMSA's championships drew 1436 entries the same year.

What more is there to say?

PAST, PRESENT, FUTURE

CHAPTER 19

In Its First Decade, Handgun Silhouetting Has Come Far; The Author Has Thoughts On The Next Ten Years

Permanent Western range of International Handgun Metallic Silhouette Association is backgrounded by an Idaho sunset. This photograph was taken on New Year's Day in 1985.

METALLIC SILHOUETTE shooting has made a dramatic impact on the handgun world. In the ten years since the sport was founded, it is still the fastest growing of all the shooting sports.

The International Handgun Metallic Silhouette Association, with over 40,000 members worldwide, is the sanctioning body for virtually all of the big-bore handgun silhouette matches held throughout America and in many countries around the world. Over 4000 matches were sanctioned in 1987 alone. Included in this number were IHMSA .22 caliber matches, a short range version of the big-bore competition using smaller targets at 25, 50, 75 and 100 yards or meters. Likewise, the third course of fire, called "field pistol," was added to IHMSA's operation in 1986, using half-size targets at the same distances.

Past history of the sport and the organization has been covered in Chapter 3, but some added thoughts are pertinent.

The biggest single conceptual contribution called for separating custom pistols from out-of-the-box factory guns. To this day, occasional selfish or misguided individuals

Elgin Gates, Jr., (left) and author took part in the second handgun silhouette championships held in El Paso in 1976. The gun is one of the long-barrel custom Contenders that led to unlimited category.

Joe Mott (left) in a shoot-off at 1976 championships with the author. Date was October 2; the IHMSA was founded that night in a hotel room.

dispute the wisdom of protecting the working man's gun from guns dripping with bankrolled refinements. The intention — which is to gain points for oneself or to sell a gimmick — always is masked in arm-waving proclamations of how "everyone will benefit." Those of us who have been in the trenches know better.

Shooting is expensive, though cheap compared to tearing up snow machines, skiing, racing motor bikes, or trashing ATCs. Still, shooting costs money: guns, ammunition, components, loading tools, scopes, muffs, glasses, elbow pads and entry fees for sanctioned matches. Yet, it is a *positive* activity; through silhouette, we become much better marksmen and game shots and we uphold our duty to the Bill of Rights — to know how, and be ready, to use firearms.

The United States Constitution is just a pretty piece of paper — no more, no less — until you add the Bill of Rights. The Bill of Rights is the teeth of the Constitution. It must apply to every man, woman and child in the economic strata. Otherwise, throw it out.

An individual for whom a Dan Wesson or T/C Contender represents a serious investment deserves to shoot that gun at silhouettes in competition with other guns of like kind. He works hard for that one day of relaxation. He doesn't come to the match to watch some super-star shot or to get blown away by a custom rebuilt "production" gun. Now

Since its founding as a sport, silhouette shooting has come a long way. This range in Hobart, Tasmania, has been the site of the Australian IHMSA championships. While range is relatively flat, it is not necessary.

he wants to practice his marksmanship and enjoy himself with his common, store-bought pistol.

He is the backbone of our Bill of Rights. The IHMSA believes he has the *right* to compete. By pricing him out of competition, we will have reduced his right to a *privilege*. Whenever it has been put to a vote, the vast majority of IHMSA silhouetters has firmly upheld the right of a competitor to shoot his unmodified factory handgun against other unmodified factory handguns. Out-of-the-box factory guns are required in three categories: production, revolver and standing.

"But," you say, "I've $3000 burning a hole in my pocket. I just have to spend it on a silhouette gun!"

You can build a hell of an unlimited category pistol for 3000 skins, but don't expect to use your *Creemoor Rocket* against production guns. That is not to say you must spend big to shoot unlimited. Thanks to Remington and Thompson/Center, you may enter an unlimited event at the same price you paid for your production gun. Goober it up to your heart's content. That's what unlimited is for; personalize it all you want. Just keep it within 4½ pounds, with a maximum barrel length and sight radius of fifteen inches.

In 1987, IHMSA members voted by over ninety percent to limit the retail price of production guns at $675 retail, amendable to future rises in the cost of living. I asked an IHMSA member who voted for the limit and who had — inside of one month — spent one hundred thousand dollars on motor vehicles, why he so voted.

"I just want to pick up my production guns and go shoot," he said. "I like the silhouette crowd. Plain, everyday people, with few pretentions. If I see you and others shooting thousand-dollar production guns — and winning — I'll have to get one of those guns myself. The average-income competitor won't be able to buy in, so he'll split. When he walks, we all lose."

The representative of one of our major manufacturers, prowling the firing line at the IMHSA 1987 Internationals

Handgun silhouetting got under way in Norway in 1985. Today, nearly 500 members compete in that country. The Baerum Pistol Club range near Oslo (above) has been the scene of many shoots in that nation in the North.

in Oak Ridge, Tennessee, put it another way.

"I don't know a fraction of the people here. At each Internationals, there's a crowd of new faces. At the combat matches, I see the same few faces year after year. It's a small crowd." He paused. "The IHMSA gets more people started in shooting...and we sell more bullets. I know the arguments for and against keeping production guns stock. There's no question in my mind that your production rule is where it's at. The other shooting sports should have a production category. They don't, and now they have a group of super-stars who think we owe them a living."

This much is certain: the IHMSA (the acronym is pronounced "im'sah") Production Gun Rule has inspired manufacturers to make badly needed improvements to pistols and revolvers. Whole new guns have been built to meet the performance demands of silhouetters. By way of example, the Thompson/Center Contender is a stronger, more durable, more accurate pistol then ever before. Literally millions of rounds fired through Contenders in IHMSA-sanctioned matches prove the point beyond argument.

Proponents of the unlimited-expense equipment race argue fondly that custom improvements on guns that win matches point the way for manufacturers, who will adapt the special features to the production line. There is little evidence to suggest that this has happened. On the contrary, the equipment race has been attended by an almost total absence of new guns for combat-style tournaments. The manufacturer knows that the shooter who buys a gun for combat competition will have it rebarreled, new sights installed, the action slicked up, so why bother improving the gun at the factory?

Thus, the little guy — who can't afford $1500 for a custom gat, and knows he hasn't a chance of winning without it — is frozen out.

The IHMSA Production Gun Rule has, on the other hand, inspired dozens of improvements to be built in at manufacture. Before his death, Dan Wesson was working on a .44 revolver that would literally tear up the record

Another early silhouette shooter, Bill Sparks, used a Smith & Wesson Model 29 .44 magnum with its 8⅜-inch to take Colorado mule deer at nearly a hundred yards.

Silhouette shooting also has been responsible for the further development of handgun hunting. Gary Stevens of Alaska took this trophy Dall sheep at 125 yards, with a Ruger Super Blackhawk .44 magnum with a 7½-inch barrel.

books. Direct collaboration with the IHMSA resulted in the most accurate .44 magnum revolver ever made, right out of the box. Dan Wesson Arms did not rest there. Various improvements, including silhouette sights, became production line items. Then, seizing on the recommendations, DWA built the Model 40 to chamber the .357 Super Mag. The Super Mag was attacked as a freak by many establishment gun writers, few of whom have tasted the pleasures of silhouette. Fewer still are practiced at keeping revolver bullets inside the twelve-inch, back-to-belly zone of a steel ram chiseled into lint by your front sight, because it is only 660 feet downrange of your gun muzzle.

Silhouetters were too busy winning matches with the Model 40 Super Mag to notice the bad press. Warren Center and Dan Wesson each had believed that better handgun performance should be available to everyone, right out of the box.

Ruger offered the New Model Super Blackhawk .44 with 10½-inch barrel in 1979. The introduction of the stainless Super in 1983 was accompanied by a 10½-inch bull barrel, a partridge front sight and long extractor specifically for competition in the IHMSA revolver category. These changes were made at the specific suggestion of David Bradshaw, who worked closely with Bill Ruger, Jr., on the project.

When he was put in charge of production of the Interarms Virginian Dragoon, Rod Sward sought recommendations through Bradshaw for a single-action silhouette revolver. The result was the stainless steel Silhouette Dragoon, which featured 10½-inch barrel, silhouette sights, tight cylinder lock-up and alignment, with chambers and bore held to minimal dimensions. To soften recoil, the gun was equipped with Pachmayr stocks. In either .357 or .44 mag, the Silhouette Dragoon enjoys a reputation for top accuracy.

The MOA falling-block single-shot has been refined for

Jack Mosier of Freeport, Maine, instructs his son in techniques of revolver handling during IHMSA match.

Jim Fields of Oklahoma, another who adapted silhouette style to field shooting, shot this mule deer at 150 meters. One-shot kill was accomplished with 34-grains of 4895, 162-grain Nosler solid-base bullet.

IHMSA production events and its record speaks for itself.

Other guns were created specifically for the production single-shot and production revolver categories.

The United Sporting Arms Seville, a tight-shooting stainless steel single-action chambered for the .357 Super Mag and .375 Super Mag, was built for the job of busting steel and winning.

The Wichita International pistol, designed by IHMSA vice president Bert Stringfellow, is a tip-open single-shot built for production. Stringfellow has followed up with a new single-shot of falling-block design, the BF field pistol. As its name implies, the BF is intended for shooting in the new field-pistol game.

Working with Bill Bartram, chairman of IHMSA's technical committee, Browning has introduced the Buck Mark Silhouette for competition in the .22LR production gun category. It features an adjustable trigger, walnut forend and 9⅞-inch bull barrel, with silhouette sights set atop a rib that is grooved for Weaver-type scope rings. It has been an instant winner.

The IHMSA Production Rule states, "barrel not to exceed 10¾ inches by manufacturer's specifications. Weight not to exceed four pounds, unloaded with magazine. The gun must be complete at all times in form, finish and mechanical function as manufactured, and only parts which are manufacturer's catalog items for the particular model may be used for repair or replacement. Sights must be as manufactured and furnished by the factory, including all factory catalog sights for that model. Stocks which are standard catalog items and which are finished by the maker to standard patterns may be used as replacement parts. A trigger job may be performed on a production gun and the sights may be painted to suit the competitor. No other external or internal changes may be made on a handgun which is used for competition in the production category."

New guns or improvements thereto must be submitted to

There are more ways to set targets than using pickups, motorcycles or ATVs. In Idaho Falls, Idaho, members of a local saddle club volunteered to reset targets during a tournament.

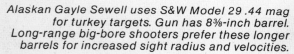

Alaskan Gayle Sewell uses S&W Model 29 .44 mag for turkey targets. Gun has 8⅜-inch barrel. Long-range big-bore shooters prefer these longer barrels for increased sight radius and velocities.

the IHMSA evaluation committee for approval.

While far from a full roll call, the guns listed above illustrate the value of a true production gun rule to the shooter whose guns are bought with blue collar dollars. If an unbridled equipment race along the firing line is the key to making better guns available to everyone, it must be a classified secret.

Manufacturers who have kept abreast of the silhouette game have reaped the reward. Other manufacturers chose to ignore the free research provided by thousands of silhouetters competing with their products. Their guns seldom appear in the winner's circle, having failed the accuracy or durability test, or both.

In 1982, I spoke separately with the representative of a major arms manufacturer and the firearms editor of a prominent outdoor magazine about the need to involve rifle hunters in disciplined marksmanship. My suggestions included utilization of existing two hundred yard/two hundred meter IHMSA ranges. The thirty-shot course of fire — ten partridge at one hundred meters, ten woodchucks at 150 meters and ten coyotes at two hundred meters — would be fired in banks of five targets each, off-hand, with factory out-of-the-box deer rifles. No bull barrels. Scopes would have a 9x magnification limit. Weight limit 8½ pounds with scope. No sling and no position in which the arms touch the body. A minimum 7mm bore would help reduce high velocity target abrasion.

Firing would be from left to right, one shot per target for five shots in thirty seconds. My tests revealed the need to separate bolt actions from all others, due to the bolt gun's generally superior trigger and rigid construction.

The factory rep liked the idea, but doubted the propriety of direct industry involvement. The gun editor said the IHMSA, with its proven organization, was the obvious vehicle for promoting field rifle silhouette as a future concept.

Three winners of the Outstanding American Handgunner Award are (from left): the late Skeeter Skelton, 1978; Bill Jordan, 1976; and Elgin Gates, 1987. Winner of the award also is inducted in the Handgunner Hall of Fame.

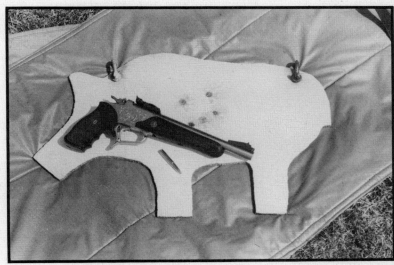

This Armour Alloy Contender silhouette gun is chambered in 7mm T/C. It is shown with a five-shot group fired at 100 meters. The Pachmayr forend and grip provide better recoil control.

IHMSA silhouette competition now includes big bore, .22 long rifle and field pistol events that require three separate sizes of targets. It would hardly be possible for the IHMSA to take on another at this time. Match directors, without whom organized silhouette wouldn't exist, experience in full measure the sweat and sacrifice of building a range, from firing line to target stands, repairing damaged targets, as well as rounding up range officers, target setters and scorekeepers. The match director soon learns the difficulty — read near impossibility — of trying to run a match and then shoot in it.

Silhouette is not a money sport. It is a family-oriented recreational sport for mom, pop and the kids. Shooters double as spotters, score keepers, safety officers and target setters. The *modus operandi* of the so-called professional, complete with acronym (arrive, shoot, split — ASS), is unbecoming to the silhouetter. Giving away guns and awarding big cash prizes has not proven to be a powerful draw. First, merchandise and cash have to come from somewhere and manufacturers have been solicited to death. Second, big-money prizes inevitably drive entry fees out of sight. Third, super-stars demand preferential treatment and refuse to shoot in the rain. Fourth, cheating destroys any semblance of a production class.

Big-money prizes and the equipment race are handmaidens. Who can resist the temptation to go inside his pistol when big bucks are at stake?

On record, it appears that the original idea of a pure production category, affirmed in referenda by over ninety percent of IHMSA silhouetters time and again, has done more to advance the handgun in ten years than had been accomplished in the previous fifty.

Considering the press given to big combat tournaments, which are attended by fewer shooters than some local IHMSA matches, one would think that the IHMSA International championships would make *The New York Times*.

David Bradshaw demonstrates correct hand position for standing event. He holds Ruger Model KS411N stainless steel .44 Super Blackhawk that was designed specifically for silhouette.

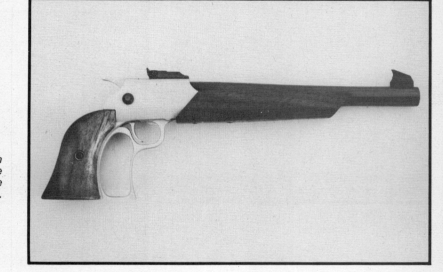

MOA falling-block pistol manufactured in Dayton, Ohio, has been successful in the production gun categories of freestyle and standing competition, author reports.

On closer examination, one sees that of the two biggest combat-style tournaments, one is named after a holster maker, the other after a gun manufacturer. Both have considerable advertising budgets and therefore carry substantial clout with magazine editors. A couple of events in one of these matches bear the names of gun magazines, not altogether coincidental.

Ironically, although the gunmaker's match was touted as a tournament for selecting the nation's best handgunner, it was scheduled to fall within the long established dates of the IHMSA Internationals. The sponsor of the match even offered a thousand-dollar bonus to anyone who won while shooting the sponsor's guns!

IHMSA Silhouette has been coming on strong in Europe and Scandinavia, with France and Norway taking hard-won trophies at the Internationals in 1986 and 1987. Gun ownership and marksmanship do not come easily to our European allies. Perhaps there is a lesson here. Freedoms, no matter how hard our forefathers fought for them, are like hayfields; they must be harvested and fertilized, lest they vanish. The IHMSA 1987 Internationals became the inaugural match of the IHMSA Eastern permanent range. Sited in Oak Ridge, Tennessee, the Eastern Permanent range was built by IHMSA volunteers Don and Myrna Rainey, Gary Bennett, Peter Rogers, Steve Arnett and a small but irrepressible core of southern silhouetters. These and others are the new champions of silhouette. Without the heroic efforts of such volunteers, silhouette shooting would not exist.

My own formal marksmanship training came through NRA small-bore and big-bore rifle programs. There was no money to be won; just prestige. I didn't mind. I learned the way of the M1 Garand from high-power masters Robert "Doc" Carroll, Hartley "High Power" Smith and the great Sam Burkehalter. Winning money never entered my mind. The knowledge I gained from their patient instruc-

The IHMSA Eastern permanent range was completed in time to hold the 1987 International competition, which drew 1142 entries. The range was constructed in the hill country near Oak Ridge, Tennessee, largely by volunteers.

tion cannot be bought and cannot be sold.

A shooter and his spotter constitute the basic unit of silhouette. There always seems to be more shooters than spotters. This is not a problem for two silhouetters who travel together; they simply alternate spotting and shooting. Finding a spotter becomes a real problem for the competitor who travels alone. Shooting alone seldom produces a top performance, nor is it as much fun. As handgun silhouette enters its second decade, the co-operative aspects of the sport must receive priority attention.

Once upon a time, America was viewed as a nation of riflemen. America never has been known as a nation of handgunners, and may never become a nation of silhouetters, but by emphasizing the fraternal aspect of organized marksmanship, we should improve our status as gunowners, while becoming better shots for our efforts.

To shooters standing behind the firing line, waiting for their relay to come up while a competitor on the line shoots alone, I would say, "Offer him or her your services as a spotter, even if it is for only one or two banks of targets. The favor will be returned someday; maybe not in the form of spotting, but perhaps as a screw to replace the one that flew out of your revolver's extractor housing."

Handgun silhouette competition has given powerful handguns a sense of direction. IHMSA members have helped open many areas to handgun hunting that would not countenance it before. Silhouette has stimulated the development of better guns, new cartridges and new bullets to meet levels of shooting performance considered impossible a few years ago. It has made the term "magnum" respectable. It has proved that women can shoot powerful handguns — and win! It has introduced youngsters to disciplined handgun marksmanship, with the crucial lesson that guns are powerful instruments that must be respected and handled carefully.

We must continue.

1988 OFFICIAL RULES

COMPETITION:
Competition will be in FOUR categories, PRODUCTION SINGLE-SHOT, PRODUCTION REVOLVER, PRODUCTION STANDING and UNLIMITED.

EQUIPMENT:

HANDGUN:

PRODUCTION: A pistol or revolver that is or was a catalog item as of January 1, 1977 or before, and was readily available to the general public. Barrel length not to exceed ten and three-quarter inches by manufacturer's specification. Weight not to exceed 4 pounds, unloaded with magazine. The gun must be complete at all times in form, finish and mechanical function as manufactured, and only parts which are manufacturer's catalog items for the particular model may be used for repair or replacement. Sights must be as manufactured and furnished by the factory, including all factory catalog sights for that model. Stocks which are standard catalog items and which are finished by that maker to standard patterns may be used as replacement parts. A trigger job may be performed on a production gun and the sights may be painted to suit the competitor. No other external or internal changes may be made on a handgun which is used for competition in the production category. The overall length of production guns may no be more than 18 inches. Measurements to be "square" or parallel to center line of bore.

No gun used in Production categories (Single-shot, Revolver, or Standing) shall cost more than $675.00 based on the factory suggested retail price of the standard (basic) model of that gun as approved by IHMSA. External factory options such as finish, sights, grips, etc. which do not affect the basic design and mechanical function of the standard model will be allowed and are NOT considered in the standard model price limit.

(Note: Factory options and changes to the IHMSA approved standard model must be submitted to and approved by IHMSA.)

The Evaluation and technical committees shall have the responsibility of determining the category in which any new model handgun will compete.

ANY guns and/or accessories manufactured after January 1, 1977 will be subject to examination by the IHMSA Evaluation Committee, composed of the Technical Committee and such other officers and directors of IHMSA as may be appointed by the President. Such guns and/or accessories will be eligible to compete only in the category if so warranted by majority vote. Otherwise, such equipment will be eligible to compete only in the Unlimited category.

Removal of the factory checkering from the stock, grip or forend of any production gun is not allowed in the process of refinishing.

Any production gun that is first fired in its own category may then be entered and fired in a higher category. The categories are ranked as Revolver, Production, and Unlimited (with Unlimited being the highest).

Standing category may be shot at any time. For competition in all production categories, revolvers must be loaded and fired as revolvers.

Any pistol used in the Unlimited category, whether it be .22 or Big Bore, may be loaded and fired single shot.

UNLIMITED:
A gun with maximum barrel length and sight radius of 15 inches and a maximum weight limit of 4½ pounds, unloaded with magazine. The sight radius to be measured from the rear edge of the front sight if an open sight is used, or from the aperture insert if a closed sight is used, to the rear surface of the blade, peep hole, post or aperture of the back sight as seen by the eye in sighting position. The overall length of all sighting apparatus, including hoods, covers, tubes, sunshades, extensions or whatever, shall not exceed 18 inches.

Barrel length is measured by inserting a rod down the barrel until it makes contact with the bolt or breech face, then a straightedge placed horizontally across the muzzle of the highest part of the crown. The distance between the bolt face or breech and the top of the crown, thus measured, is the official barrel length. The overall length of Unlimited guns may not be more than 25 inches. Measurements to be "square" or parallel to center line of bore. Shooters may not qualify in Unlimited classes with production guns.

If a muzzle brake is used it must be measured as part of the barrel length.

NOT ALLOWED:
Scopes or any optical device, artificial rests or supports, slings, padded or unnecessarily heavy clothing, or any kind of wrist or arm supports or bracelets.

Bolt action guns are not allowed in any production category.

Friction materials OR PADDING used on the shooter's clothing or on any part of the gun have been ruled as violating the Artificial Rest rule and will not be allowed.

Rubberizing the stocks and forends of unlimited guns violates the artificial rest rule and is not allowed.

A competitor placing his shoe/boot sideways on the ground may not ground the butt of his gun on the heel. This position will be allowed only if his hand or some portion thereof is between the heel and butt of his gun.

No adjustable grips will be allowed on any big bore or .22 pistol.

ALLOWED:
Flat shooting matt or ground cover of a thickness not to exceed one inch so long as it is not used as shooting aid.

Clip-on sun glasses are allowed over prescription glasses.

Athletic elbow pads or other such material used to protect shooters elbows are allowed if used as protection only, and any such pad or material may not exceed one-inch in thickness.

TRIGGERS: Any safe trigger not subject to accidental discharge will be allowed.

Shooting gloves, so long as they are not excessively padded or stiff so as to be used as a shooting aid.

Blast shields in freestyle position if used for protection only and not as a shooting aid.

Auxiliary lenses and/or loupes will be allowed so long as attached to the eye and/or eyeglass frame. Auxiliary lenses and/or loupes may not extend more than one inch beyond the eyeglass frame.

CERTIFICATION OF GUNS:

Guns must be weighed and checked before firing for score. No one may win an award with an uncertified gun.

The match director shall have the authority to appoint a three or five-man jury including himself as one member to certify guns. For complete impartiality, said jury, besides the match director, should consist of experienced silhouette competitors and/or knowledgable gunsmiths from other clubs or states who are in attendance at the match.

When a competitor's gun is checked during registration, internal inspection is not mandatory unless there is reason to believe it does not comply with the production gun rule. Then, said competitor may be asked to remove the grip, forearm and possibly the trigger assembly (from his T/C) or the stock and bolt (from his XP-221) the barrel (from his Auto Mag) the grip and sideplate (from his revolver) or similar parts from any other production gun for visual inspection by the jury.

Only the competitor or a person designated by him, shall remove or replace any parts from his gun. Upon inspection, the jury shall retire and discuss the matter. A majority vote by the jury shall be final. The jury may also request information from other knowledgeable persons to aid in making their decision.

If the gun does not comply, then the competitor's entry with that gun shall not be accepted.

Likewise, entry of a particular gun will not be allowed if any competitor refuses to remove said grip, forearm, stock or sideplate from his gun for inspection if requested.

Only one pistol per category may be certified.

GUN PROTEST:

Any gun not inspected by the jury may be protested by another competitor by posting a fee of $10 and a written protest with the match director. No competitor shall be interrupted with a protest during his course of fire. After completion of fire, the competitor will be asked to make his gun ready for inspection by the jury as previously described. If the jury determines the gun does not comply with the production gun rule, the competitor's gun shall be disqualified for that event, and the protesting party shall receive his protest fee of $10 back.

If, however, the jury determines the gun is in compliance with the rule, then the $10 protest fee shall go to the protested party.

At State, Regional or the International Championships, the match sponsor, upon request of the State, Regional or National directors, may require the trophy winners to submit their guns for inspection by the jury as previously described, and as soon after the conclusion of the match events as the various places can be determined.

POSITIONS: STANDING AND FREESTYLE:

Any standing position will be allowed with the gun being supported by one or both hands. No part of the one or both arms or hands behind the wrists shall contact any other part of the body from the shoulders out.

FREESTYLE being any SAFE position without artificial support. No part of the gun, stock or grip shall touch ground or ground cover, and the gun must be held in such a manner that the line referee and/or the Range Officer can see that the gun is visibly clear of the ground at all times when in firing position.

Nesting the barrel in the top of a shoe or boot or across the sole or notch of the heel constitutes artificial support and is not allowed.

Handicapped competitors may fire from wheelchair with one or both elbows supported, or with braced crutches or with support from chair or stool replacing leg.

IHMSA CLASSIFICATION

The first score fired in a sanctioned match by a new shooter in any category shall establish his initial class in that category. Thereafter, any two scores, including re-entry scores, fired by a competitor **during his current 12 month membership period** which exceed the break point of any class in that category will move the shooter directly to that class, effective at the next match and thereafter.

If a competitor fires a single score that exceeds the break point for a class that is two or more classes above the competitor's current class, he shall immediately be advanced to the class just under his single score class, effective in and at that match and thereafter. Example: if a Class B shooter fires a single AAA score, he is immediately reclassified into the AA class effective in and at that match and thereafter.

For classification purposes, any 60 or 80 round match fired straight through shall be averaged to arrive at the correct 40-round score basis. The 80-round is divided by two, the 60-round match multiplied by two then divided by three. Any fractional score shall be rounded to the next lower whole number.

A 60- or 80-round match is considered as only one basic 40-round match for purpose of classification.

Reclassification to a lower class will be based on eight consecutive sanctioned scores below the break-point of his current class. Demotion to a lower class is allowed only by approval of the Executive Committee. Demotions will be awarded only during the 60 days after the annual IHMSA International Championships.

KNOWN ABILITY:

Any Region Director, State Director or Match Director shall have the authority to classify or reclassify any shooter according to his known ability at any time before, during or after a match.

To determine Known Ability, any available facts and information should be taken into consideration as follows:

1. Any scores shot at sanctioned, unsanctioned or practice matches, whether said shooter is an IHMSA member or not.
2. Any and all other facts and information relating to any shooter's ability to shoot and hit silhouettes with a handgun.
3. Any IHMSA member who omits scores in order to continue competing in a lower class, is subject to suspension from IHMSA for one year.

CATEGORIES AND CLASSES
PRODUCTION SINGLE SHOT

Class	Range
INTERNATIONAL	38-40
AAA	33-37
AA	24-32
A	18-23
B	11-17
C	0-10

PRODUCTION REVOLVER

Class	Range
INTERNATIONAL	38-40
AAA	33-37
AA	24-32
A	18-23
B	11-17
C	0-10

PRODUCTION STANDING

Class	Range
INTERNATIONAL	28-40
AAA	22-27
AA	16-21
A	8-15
B	0-7

METALLIC SILHOUETTE SHOOTING

UNLIMITED

Class	Score
INTERNATIONAL	40
AAA	37-39
AA	30-36
A	25-29
B	18-24
C	0-17

ENTRY AND ELIGIBILITY

To compete in any sanctioned match, a shooter must be a member of IHMSA. To encourage new shooters, the non-member may be allowed to shoot the course of fire ONLY ONCE at the option of the match director or sponsor, but his score is not official, nor is he eligible for any IHMSA prize, trophy, or award.

COMPETITOR QUALIFICATION:

No IHMSA competitor shall solicit or accept subsidy or sponsorship from any firearm or accessory manufacturers. The IHMSA, is and shall remain, an organization for the amateur pistol competitor.

When entering any IHMSA sanctioned match, the shooter's classification card must be presented and left with the registrar. At the conclusion of the match, the registrar will enter on the card all scores shot in the match and certify them. If any such score in any category be the second score above the break point, the card shall be upgraded on the front side and so certified by the registrar or any IHMSA match director.

Any shooter of know ability who does not present his classification card shall be required to shoot in class AAA or International at the option of the sponsor.

A young shooter will remain a junior until their 16th birthday.

At all times it shall be the responsibility of the shooter that his correct scores are shown on his card.

RE-ENTRY

The first time through the course of fire-shall be for record and trophy. After any re-entry has been fired, no scores for record or trophies may be fired in any category.

Re-entry scores in any class or category shall only count toward classification of the competitor.

MATCH SPONSORS:

The match sponsor must schedule all IHMSA classes and give at least one award in each class if any properly classified shooter fires through the course.

No match will be sanctioned by IHMSA where the value of any prize, merchandise or cash award to be competed for exceeds double the entry fee. Trophy value is not included although the rule does apply to any merchandise, prize or cash which is awarded as trophies.

All donated or bonus prizes, without exception, are to be awarded in a manner whereby all competitors in the match are eligible on an equal basis.

SANCTION AND FEES:

The basic sanctioned match will be entitled HANDGUN METALLIC SILHOUETTE MATCH. To be a sanctioned match, IHMSA's rules must be adhered to.

To qualify for a sanctioned match, the hosting organization must first apply to the State Director or any Executive Director of IHMSA. Upon being awarded the match, a match package consisting of individual score cards, sign-up sheets—which is the official match report—membership applications and wall bulletin score sheets will be sent to the sponsoring organization.

UPON COMPLETION OF THE MATCH, THE SANCTION FEE OF $1.00 PER REGISTERED BIG BORE ENTRY, INCLUDING RE-ENTRIES (50 CENTS PER .22 ENTRY, $1.00 PER FIELD PISTOL ENTRY) TOGETHER WITH A COPY OF THE MATCH REPORT (SIGN-UP SHEETS) IS DUE AND PAYABLE TO IHMSA, INC., AT P.O. BOX 1609, IDAHO FALLS, IDAHO 83403.

IN ORDER TO MAINTAIN GOOD STANDING IN THE CORPORATION (IHMSA, INC.), A CLUB MUST SUBMIT ITS MATCH REPORTS AND SANCTION FEES WITHIN 30 DAYS OF THE CONCLUSION OF EACH MATCH.

CHAMPIONSHIPS:

Bids for State and Regional championships must be placed with the respective State or Regional director.

To host a State or Regional Championship, a club must have successfully held three prior sanctioned matches.

Scorekeepers must be furnished by the sponsor at all championship matches.

State or Regional titles will be awarded only to competitors who have been a resident of the state for a period of six months or more.

To participate in any state, regional or the international championships, a contestant must be a classified member of IHMSA in all categories in which he intends to compete.

With the approval of the State and Regional Director, any club holding a state championship has the option of holding a closed tournament, open only to bona-fide residents of that state. Any closed tournament must be so listed in the printed program as well as in the Silhouette Match Schedule.

CHAMPIONSHIP MATCH—COMPETITOR QUALIFICATION:

A competitor must shoot in, and complete, three separate non-championship matches within 12 months prior to entering any championship. A minimum of one entry per match is required. Big Bore Field Pistol and .22 will be considered separate.

ANNUAL INTERNATIONAL CHAMPIONSHIPS:

The International Championship match shall be under the jurisdiction of the IHMSA Executive. The IHMSA Executive shall select and furnish trophies and prizes. The IHMSA Executive shall administer the championships.

MATCH PROCEDURES:

Sighter targets of the official size and shape and set at the correct distances with the same approximate background as match targets are mandatory at all championship matches and optional by the match director at monthly matches. There is to be a minimum of one sighter target at each distance, 50, 100, 150 and 200 meters with five sighter shots allowed in two minutes. Shooter to have the option of shooting at targets of his choice.

No practice will be allowed before or during any championship match other than the five sighting shots which are only allowed prior to the competitor firing for record.

A sanctioned match (course of fire) consists of 40 rounds:
- 10 chicken targets at 50 meters
- 10 javelina targets at 100 meters
- 10 turkey targets at 150 meters
- 10 ram targets at 200 meters

Firing is in 5-round stages, 2 minutes per stage, in freestyle or standing position without artificial support.

Each competitor has a bank of 5 metal silhouettes to fire against, one shot at each, left to right in order. Hits out of sequence are misses, i.e., second shot hitting third silhouette a miss, and in this case a double miss as only the remaining 2 silhouettes may be fired on — shooter cannot fire his third shot at the untouched second silhouette. Only hits and misses are recorded and a silhouette must be knocked from its rest to score a hit. "Turning" a silhouette on stand does not count. Richochet hits count.

WHEN CALLED TO THE FIRING LINE, COMPETITORS MUST PLACE THEIR UNLOADED PISTOL IN A SAFE AND STABLE POSITION ON THE FIRING LINE WITH THE ACTION OPEN AND VISIBLE. UNTIL THE COMMAND TO "LOAD" IS GIVEN, THE PISTOL SHALL NOT BE PHYSICALLY

TOUCHED. AFTER THE LOAD COMMAND, THEY MAY NOW HANDLE THEIR PISTOL, DRY FIRE, ADJUST SIGHTS AND LOAD. THIRTY SECONDS LOADING TIME WILL BE ALLOWED BEFORE THE COMMAND TO COMMENCE FIRING. (NOTE: THIS ALLOWS THE SHOOTER TO PLACE HIS PISTOL ON A STABLE SHOOTING TABLE OR ON HIS SHOOTING BOX, CASE, ETC.)

Except when pistol failure occurs, the same pistol, barrel, grips, sights, etc. shall be used at all ranges in that particular match.

Each shooter may have one coach with him on the firing line who may have scope or binoculars and advise competitor where shots are going, keep time, or otherwise advise, but said coach may not handle shooters pistol or assist in any physical way once the command to load has been given.

AT NO TIME DURING THE COURSE OF FIRE MAY A COMPETITOR BE INTERRUPTED EXCEPT FOR A SAFETY OR RULE VIOLATION. IF A SAFETY OR RULE VIOLATION OCCURS, THE COMPETITOR SHOULD NOT BE INTERRUPTED DURING THE LOADING OR FIRING PERIOD UNLESS IT IS A SERIOUS SAFETY PROBLEM. THE MATCH DIRECTOR OR LINE OFFICER WILL GIVE THE COMPETITOR A WARNING OF THE RULE OR SAFETY VIOLATION. IF THE SAME RULE OR SAFETY VIOLATION OCCURS A SECOND TIME DURING THE SAME COURSE OF FIRE AFTER THE FIRST WARNING, THEN THE COMPETITOR SHALL BE DISQUALIFIED FOR THAT COURSE OF FIRE.

ALIBIS

The only alibi will be when a target is not available because it fell without being engaged by the competitor. TARGETS WHICH ARE STILL STANDING ON THE COMPETITOR'S BANK OR ON EITHER ADJACENT BANK MUST BE USED TO COMPLETE THE FIVE SHOT STRING OF TARGETS. IF ENOUGH TARGETS ARE NOT AVAILABLE ON THE COMPETITOR'S BANK OR ON EITHER ADJACENT BANK, THEN THE COMPETITOR'S ENTIRE BANK WILL BE RESET AND THE NUMBER OF ALIBI SHOTS WILL BE TAKEN STARTING FROM LEFT TO RIGHT REGARDLESS OF WHICH ACTUAL TARGETS FELL CAUSING THE ALIBI.

The competitor will be given 30 seconds to load and 24 seconds per alibi shot to complete his five shot string.

Pistol malfunctions and faulty ammo shall not be cause for an alibi or the allowance of extra firing time. Should a pistol fail to function during a match, another pistol of the correct category for the entry may be used to complete the match.

This rule does not imply that a competitor may use more than one pistol during a course of competition unless his primary pistol has been damaged or broken and the match director has examined said pistol and has authorized the exchange of pistols.

Under no circumstances shall a competitor's malfunction delay the progress of the competition.

SCORING

All shots are scored by marking either an "O" for a miss or an X for a hit, in the correct spaces on a score card. It is the scorekeeper's responsibility to see that the competitor observes the rules and time limits, fires no more than 5 rounds per series, and when strong winds exist, watch silhouettes closely so that he can tell when a silhouette is blown over and not knocked down by a bullet. When a silhouette is blown down before a shot, the scorekeeper will instruct the shooter to fire on remaining ones in order, then go back to the left end to fire unfired round or rounds at remaining silhouette or silhouettes. All scoring differences must be resolved immediately on completion of the series before either shooter or scorekeeper leaves the firing line or prepares for a second series at the same stand.

When there are wind conditions requiring the targets to be fastened down, one or more in each bank, then all hits shall be scored as points.

During championship matches, if one target in a bank must be secured (clamped), all targets in that bank must be clamped and hits will be counted.

If one foot or the other on any hit javelina or ram be completely off the stand, but resting on the ground or any other obstruction so as to prevent the target from falling, then the hit will be scored even if the target is still standing with the other foot still on the stand.

OTHERWISE, IN NO CASE SHALL A HIT TARGET BE AWARDED AS A SCORE POINT UNLESS IT IS KNOCKED DOWN AND/OR OFF ITS STAND.

AT ALL SANCTIONED MATCHES, THE SCORER SHALL BE ANY PERSON OTHER THAN THE SHOOTER.

TIES AND SHOOTOFFS

The match director has the option to decide how to break all ties, so long as it is listed in his program or posted at the range prior to the match.

If a tie occurs, the shooter with the greater number of rams will receive the higher position. If ties remain, the greater number of turkeys will be

used and so on to the pigs and chickens until a clear winner appears.

Shootoff targets for all sanctioned matches will be visible steel silhouette-shaped targets, chicken, javelina, turkey and ram of any size and any distance of 200 meters or less. Firing will be in five shot strings at five targets for each shooter at the distance agreed upon.

Regular loading, firing, and time procedures will be used with the same gun. The high score shall determine the winner.

SAFETY:

While in a firing position, no part of the shooter's body may be in the "Danger Zone" which is a cone-shaped area extending downrange from the muzzle at a 45 degree angle above and below and to the right and left of the center line of the bore.

ALL ACTIONS MUST BE OPEN EXCEPT ON THE FIRING LINE AFTER THE LOAD COMMAND IS GIVEN. PISTOLS MAY NOT BE HANDLED BETWEEN STAGES FOR THE SAFETY OF THE TARGET SETTERS.

Should any round be discharged before the command to load, the shooter will be disqualified for that day. Should any round be fired after the command to load, but before the command to fire it will be judged as a lost shot.

IHMSA SAFETY PROCEDURES

1) Mandatory eye and ear protection is required for all competitors, their spotters, line officers and any other personnel, spectators, etc. on the designated firing line.

2) **MUZZLE CONTROL**—At no time during the loading or firing stages shall a competitor allow the gun to point at any part of his or her anatomy, or at any other person, NOR SHALL THE COMPETITOR ALLOW THE GUN TO RECOIL PAST THE VERTICAL.

From the moment a gun is placed on the firing line, until it is removed, the muzzle shall point downrange.

3) A Match Director shall have the authority to remove from the firing line guns shaving bullet material. Competitor may substitute another gun, which must pass inspection for the appropriate category. However, the match will not be delayed.

4) **AMMUNITION**—Competitors have the responsibility of assembling ammunition that is safe to fire in the gun for which it is loaded. Since there are no commercial standards for the popular "wildcat" and "improved" cartridges, it is up to the competitor to exercise caution and common sense in working up loads. Handgun Silhouette requires higher working pressures than any other handgun usage except hunting. There is, however, no acceptable reason for exposing a gun to dangerous pressures.

ANY LOAD THAT REGULARLY REQUIRES EXTRACTION OF THE CARTRIDGE CASE BY ANY METHOD OTHER THAN THE INTERNAL EXTRACTOR OF THE PISTOL WILL BE CONSIDERED UNSAFE AND NOT ALLOWED. THE MATCH DIRECTOR HAS THE DISCRETION OF DETERMINING THE SAFETY FACTOR OF ANY RELOADED AMMUNITION AND THE AUTHORITY TO ENFORCE THIS RULE.

5) **GUNS**—Triggers that are set up too light are prone to hazardous malfunctions, and can adversely affect the timing and lockup of some guns. The alibi rule, receiving near unanimous vote at the 1979 business meeting, is designed to: 1) prevent ammunition and gun malfunction from interrupting sanctioned matches, and 2) encourages competitors to take pains to insure their guns and ammunition are safe.

6) **Note:** A misfire must be handled as a hangfire and the gun pointed safely downrange for a safe period after the trigger was pulled. It is simply not safe to open the action on a firearm immediately after it has misfired.

PROHIBITIONS:

No alcoholic beverages may be consumed or narcotic drugs used by competitors at any time during the match. Any shooter violating this provision is subject to immediate disqualification.

SPORTSMANSHIP:

Any Region, State or Match Director shall have the authority to bar any competitor from a match for unsportsmanlike conduct or acts unbecoming to the association or the sport. Should there be any question regarding this procedure or any decisions made therefrom, the matter shall be referred to the executive committee for a final decision.

RULE INTERPRETATIONS AND PROTESTS

All rule interpretations and protests will be handled by a jury appointed by the tournament director or the Match Director, and composed of any senior IHMSA officials who are present. The decisions of said JURY shall, in all instances, be final. All protests must be submitted to the Match Director in writing, accompanied with a fee of $10 within one hour of any alleged violation.

RANGE FACILITIES:

A silhouette range consists of four different target lines each having 5 silhouettes of a particular bird or animal. It will have rams at 200 meters; turkeys at 150 meters; pigs at 100 meters; and chickens at 50 meters. A 5 meter plus or minus variation in actual distance from the firing point to each individual silhouette is allowed.

The range can have a very simple set up. An existing high power range can be used. If desired, it can be put in a natural setting, such as ravine or canyon. Trees and brush need not be moved and variation in height above or below the firing point is allowed and desirable.

IHMSA will sanction matches held at ranges that have a maximum distance of 200 yards due to range construction. This is provided that all shoot announcements state that the 200-meter Rams will be shot at 200-yards.

Any club sponsoring an IHMSA sanctioned match shall have the right to bar or disqualify any gun, load and/or competitor at any time before or during a match when it comes to the attention of the club that the silhouette targets are being damaged by bullets being used by said competitor

TARGETS:

The silhouette targets are made from steel metal plate and shall be ½ inch thick for Pig and Chicken, and 3/8 inch thick for Ram and Turkey.

The "feet" upon which the silhouettes rest should be made from the same type and thickness of steel as the targets. The dimensions are: 3

inches wide and 4 inches long for the chicken, 2 inches wide and 4 inches long for the Javelina, 3 inches wide and 6 to 8 inches long for the turkey and 4 inches wide and 5 inches long for the ram.

Silhouettes are set up with five to a line. The feet of the chicken, pig and turkey targets are to be set flush with the rear of their level stands. Additional sets can be added if needed, provided the proper space is available.

The recommended distance between silhouettes is: chickens 13 inches apart; pigs 22 inches; turkeys 23 inches and rams 32 inches apart. All are placed on stands off the ground. Silhouettes should be painted with flat black paint.

At a particular club where the background prevents adequate target identification, the sponsoring club shall have the option to use other colors to permit ready target identification, BUT ONCE THE MATCH IS STARTED, TARGET COLOR MAY NOT BE CHANGED.

Tempered steel targets — at least one set — will be mandatory before any club will be allowed to sponsor a championship tournament. Or, in the event tempered steel targets are not available, the sponsoring club will waive the target damage rule which provides for a limit of 25% bullet penetration.

RAMS:

The rams shall be placed so that the center of gravity is no more than one inch in from the topple point.

As a simple explanation, the official width of the ram's feet is 4-inches. The ram should be moved carefully backward on their stands with the feet overhanging on the backside until the topple point is achieved. From that point they may be moved forward to achieve stability but, as the rule calls for, not more than one-inch forward of this topple point. IT IS SUGGESTED THAT SOME METHOD BE EMPLOYED THAT PREVENTS THE RAM FROM BEING SET FORWARD OF THE ONE INCH LIMIT BY THE TARGET SETTER.

IF THE RAM IS NOT STABLE AT THE ONE INCH FORWARD SET BECAUSE OF WIND CONDITIONS, THEN THE RAM SHOULD BE CLAMPED. AT NO TIME MAY A RAM BE SET FULL FOOT, SHIMMED, ETC., TO PREVENT IT FROM FALLING IN WIND CONDITIONS.

THIS IN NO WAY IMPLIES THAT A TARGET HIT BUT NOT KNOCKED DOWN CAN BE COUNTED (A TARGET MAY NEVER BE GIVEN UNLESS KNOCKED DOWN). THE TARGET MUST BE KNOCKED OVER TO COUNT UNLESS IT IS CLAMPED, IN WHICH CASE ALL HITS WILL COUNT.

Optional ram topple rule: A ram will be legally set if three-fourths of an inch is removed from the back side of both feet of a regulation IHMSA ram. The ram must then be set full foot on the back edge of a level steel stand.

IHMSA FIELD PISTOL
HANDGUNS

Production revolvers and pistols as defined by IHMSA rules. Weight not to exceed 4 pounds in the open sight category and 4½ pounds in the scoped category. Barrel length not to exceed 10¾ inches. Scopes, mounts and other optical devices must be as manufactured with no modifications. Per existing IHMSA rules, production guns can be drilled and tapped for scopes and still be used in the open sight category and/or big bore so long as the holes are filled with filler screws. Also, open sights can be removed to install scope mount.

Pistols and revolvers will compete together on an equal basis. Hammer extensions are allowed on scoped pistols only.

CATEGORIES

There will be two categories of competition: Production open sights and Production scoped.

POSITIONS

Standing only, as defined by IHMSA rules.

CARTRIDGES

Straight-wall, centerfire pistol cases of standard manufacture will be

METALLIC SILHOUETTE SHOOTING

allowed with a maximum case length of 1.29 inches as specified for that cartridge. Also allowed, the 32-20, length 1.32 inches.

TARGETS

Targets will be half size, of 3/8-inch or 1/2 inch tempered steel. All feet to be of the same material, 2 inches wide and 4 inches long. All targets at all distances shall be set full foot at the back edge of the level stands.

CLASSES

Production open sight and Production scope break points will be the same:

        36-40 INTERNATIONAL
        30-35 AAA
        22-29 AA
        15-21 A
        0-14 B

DISTANCES

Chickens: 25 meters (or yards), Javelinas: 50 meters (or yards), Turkeys: 75 meters (or yards), Rams: 100 meters (or yards). All targets will be set at either meters or yards at sponsor's option and posted at the match. If rams are set in meters, then all distances must be set in meters. Likewise, if rams are set in yards, then all distances must be in yards. A 2-yard/meter plus or minus variation in actual distances from firing point to targets is allowed.

SANCTIONED MATCH

Normally 40 rounds fired at 10 chickens, 10 javelinas, 10 turkeys and 10 rams at the official distances.

NOTE: Sanction fees for Field Pistol shall be $1.00 per entry.
NOTE: All other IHMSA competition rules apply.
NOTE: The IHMSA FIELD PISTOL discipline is an optional course of fire (not mandatory) for any club holding IHMSA sanctioned matches.

.22 SILHOUETTES

HANDGUNS

A pistol or revolver that is or was a catalog item on or before January 1, 1979, and was readily available to the general public. The gun must be complete at all times in form, finish and mechanical function as manufactured, and only parts which are manufacturer's catalog items for the particular model may be used for repair or replacement. A trigger job may be performed on the gun. The Technical Committee shall have the responsibility of determining the acceptability of any handgun released to the public after January 1, 1979 for competition.

ALL .22 PRODUCTION CATEGORIES AND CLASSES SHALL INCLUDE ALL .22 PISTOLS OF A STANDARD MAKE AS MANUFACTURED IN THE U.S.A., AS WELL AS THOSE PISTOLS MANUFACTURED ELSEWHERE WHICH CONFORM EITHER TO THE CRITERIA AND SPECIFICATIONS OF UIT RULES AND ALL OTHER IHMSA RULES OR THOSE .22 PISTOLS SPECIFICALLY APPROVED BY THE EUROPEAN EVALUATION COMMITTEE. ALL FREE PISTOLS ARE CLASSED UNLIMITED PROVIDING THEY COMPLY WITH IHMSA UNLIMITED .22 RULES.

.22 semi-auto pistols used in any production class or category must be loaded with five rounds and fired as such. Said pistols used in the unlimited category may be loaded and fired single-shot at the option of the competitor.

Bolt action guns are not allowed in any production category.

No adjustable grips will be allowed on any big bore or .22 pistol.

If a muzzle brake is used it must be measured as barrel length. If it is optionally removable as manufactured, and removing it allows the gun to qualify under the barrel length rule, then the gun may be used without said muzzle brake.

CLASSIFICATION

All .22 classifications will be allowed to seek their own level based on the shooters ability for each action type and are not related to big bore classifications. However, the big bore classification rules regarding initial